Legalines

Editorial Advisors:
Gloria A. Aluise
Attorney at Law
David H. Barber
Attorney at Law
Robert A. Wyler
Attorney at Law

Authors:
Gloria A. Aluise
Attorney at Law
David H. Barber
Attorney at Law
Daniel O. Bernstine
Professor of Law
D. Steven Brewster
C.P.A.
Roy L. Brooks
Professor of Law
Frank L. Bruno
Attorney at Law
Scott M. Burbank
C.P.A.
Jonathan C. Carlson
Professor of Law
Charles N. Carnes
Professor of Law
Paul S. Dempsey
Professor of Law
Jerome A. Hoffman
Professor of Law
Mark R. Lee
Professor of Law
Jonathan Neville
Attorney at Law
Laurence C. Nolan
Professor of Law
Arpiar Saunders
Professor of Law
Robert A. Wyler
Attorney at Law

SALES & SECURED TRANSACTIONS

Adaptable to Fifth Edition of Speidel Casebook

By Jonathan Neville
Attorney at Law

A COMPLETE PUBLICATIONS CATALOG IS
FEATURED AT THE BACK OF THIS BOOK.

HARCOURT BRACE LEGAL AND PROFESSIONAL PUBLICATIONS, INC.
EDITORIAL OFFICES: 111 W. Jackson Blvd., 7th Floor, Chicago, IL 60604

Legalines

REGIONAL OFFICES: Chicago, Dallas, Los Angeles, New York, Washington, D.C
Distributed by: **Harcourt Brace & Company** 6277 Sea Harbor Drive, Orlando, FL 32887 (800)787-8717

EDITOR
Astrid E. Ellis, J.D.

PRODUCTION COORDINATOR
Sanetta Hister

THIRD PRINTING—1999

Legalines™

**Features Detailed Briefs of Every Major Case,
Plus Summaries of the Black Letter Law.**

Titles Available

Administrative Law .... Keyed to Breyer	Decedents' Estates & Trusts .. Keyed to Ritchie
Administrative Law .... Keyed to Gellhorn	Domestic Relations .... Keyed to Clark
Administrative Law .... Keyed to Schwartz	Domestic Relations .... Keyed to Wadlington
Antitrust .... Keyed to Areeda	Estate & Gift Tax .... Keyed to Surrey
Antitrust .... Keyed to Handler	Evidence .... Keyed to Sutton
Civil Procedure .... Keyed to Cound	Evidence .... Keyed to Waltz
Civil Procedure .... Keyed to Field	Evidence .... Keyed to Weinstein
Civil Procedure .... Keyed to Hazard	Family Law .... Keyed to Areen
Civil Procedure .... Keyed to Rosenberg	Federal Courts .... Keyed to McCormick
Civil Procedure .... Keyed to Yeazell	Income Tax .... Keyed to Freeland
Commercial Law .... Keyed to Farnsworth	Income Tax .... Keyed to Klein
Conflict of Laws .... Keyed to Cramton	Labor Law .... Keyed to Cox
Conflict of Laws .... Keyed to Reese	Labor Law .... Keyed to Merrifield
Constitutional Law .... Keyed to Brest	Partnership & Corporate Tax .. Keyed to Surrey
Constitutional Law .... Keyed to Cohen	Property .... Keyed to Browder
Constitutional Law .... Keyed to Gunther	Property .... Keyed to Casner
Constitutional Law .... Keyed to Lockhart	Property .... Keyed to Cribbet
Constitutional Law .... Keyed to Rotunda	Property .... Keyed to Dukeminier
Constitutional Law .... Keyed to Stone	Real Property .... Keyed to Rabin
Contracts .... Keyed to Calamari	Remedies .... Keyed to Re
Contracts .... Keyed to Dawson	Remedies .... Keyed to York
Contracts .... Keyed to Farnsworth	Sales & Secured Transactions .. Keyed to Speidel
Contracts .... Keyed to Fuller	Securities Regulation .... Keyed to Jennings
Contracts .... Keyed to Kessler	Torts .... Keyed to Epstein
Contracts .... Keyed to Murphy	Torts .... Keyed to Franklin
Corporations .... Keyed to Cary	Torts .... Keyed to Henderson
Corporations .... Keyed to Choper	Torts .... Keyed to Keeton
Corporations .... Keyed to Hamilton	Torts .... Keyed to Prosser
Corporations .... Keyed to Vagts	Wills, Trusts & Estates .... Keyed to Dukeminier
Criminal Law .... Keyed to Boyce	
Criminal Law .... Keyed to Dix	
Criminal Law .... Keyed to Johnson	**Other Titles Available:**
Criminal Law .... Keyed to Kadish	Criminal Law Questions & Answers
Criminal Law .... Keyed to LaFave	Excelling on Exams/How to Study
Criminal Procedure .... Keyed to Kamisar	Torts Questions & Answers

*All Titles Available at Your Law School Bookstore,
or Call to Order: 1-800-787-8717*

Harcourt Brace Legal and Professional Publications, Inc.
111 West Jackson Boulevard, Seventh Floor
Chicago, IL 60604

SHORT SUMMARY OF CONTENTS

TABLE OF CONTENTS AND SHORT REVIEW OUTLINE

I. INTRODUCTION

A. THE UNIFORM COMMERCIAL CODE

1. **Reasons for Development.** Although the common law dealt with problems of commercial transactions, the law became difficult to apply as the various states applied their own laws to increasingly complex interstate business transactions. To clarify the rules and encourage uniformity among the states, the American Law Institute and the National Conference of Commissioners joined in sponsoring development of the Uniform Commercial Code ("UCC"). The UCC has been adopted by all the states in some form.

2. **Reliance on Case Law.** The UCC was not intended to replace all common law principles. Instead, it relies on past case law, as well as continuing judicial development, to fill out its provisions. Case law remains critical in the interpretation of the UCC and the development of commercial law in general.

3. **Organization.** The UCC is organized into nine articles which together govern the major areas of commercial law.

   a. **Article 1.** General provisions.
   b. **Article 2.** Sale of goods.
   c. **Article 2A.** Leases.
   d. **Article 3.** Commercial paper.
   e. **Article 4.** Bank deposits and collection.
   f. **Article 4A.** Funds transfers.
   g. **Article 5.** Letters of credit.
   h. **Article 6.** Bulk sales.
   i. **Article 7.** Documents of title.
   j. **Article 8.** Investment securities.
   k. **Article 9.** Secured transactions.

4. **Scope of Article 1.**

   a. **Introduction.** The common law doctrine of accord and satisfaction allows the parties to resolve a disputed debt by providing that a payment, when accepted, of a part of the whole disputed debt is good satisfaction of the entire debt. The theory is that the acceptance of the partial payment creates a new contract that replaces the original one. The pre-1990 versions of the UCC included a provision, section 1-207, that affected the common law accord and satisfaction rules, but it was unclear exactly how.

   b. **UCC supersedes common law--Horn Waterproofing Corp. v. Bushwick Iron & Steel Co.**, 497 N.Y.S.2d 310, 488 N.E.2d 56 (1985).

Horn Waterproofing Corp. v. Bushwick Iron & Steel Co.

      1) **Facts.** Bushwick Iron & Steel Co. (D) orally contracted to have Horn Waterproofing Corp. (P) repair its roof. P worked for two days before determining that D's roof needed to be replaced. P charged $1,241 for its work. When D objected, P

Sales & Secured Transactions - 1

lowered its bill to $1,080. D sent P a check for $500, with a notation on the indorsement side stating "This check is accepted in full payment, settlement, satisfaction, release and discharge of any and all claims and/or demands of whatsoever kind and nature." P printed the words "Under Protest" under D's statement, indorsed the check, and deposited it. P sued for the balance of $580. D moved for summary judgment, claiming the parties had entered a common law accord and satisfaction. The trial court denied the motion and found for P, holding that the UCC modified the common law. The appellate court reversed, holding that the agreement was not covered by the UCC because it was a contract for services. P appeals.

2) **Issue.** Is the common law doctrine of accord and satisfaction superseded by UCC section 1-207 when a debtor tenders a negotiable instrument as full payment of a disputed claim and the creditor deposits the check, reserving its right to recover the balance from the debtor?

3) **Held.** Yes. Judgment reversed.

   a) There is a conflict among the jurisdictions that have analyzed the effect of UCC section 1-207 on common law accord and satisfaction. The problem with accord and satisfaction is that the creditor is presented with a difficult situation of having to choose between partial payment and preserving a claim for the unpaid balance. But the debtor has a reasonable expectation that the offer will either be accepted or the check returned.

   b) UCC section 1-207 provides that "A party who with explicit reservation of rights performs or promises performance or assents to performance in a manner demanded or offered by the other party does not thereby prejudice the rights reserved. Such words as 'without prejudice,' 'under protest' or the like are sufficient." This language is sufficiently broad to alter the common law doctrine of accord and satisfaction so that a creditor may reserve its rights even though it accepts the debtor's check.

   c) Section 1 of the UCC is an introductory section that applies to any commercial transactions within the scope of the substantive articles. It does not matter whether the underlying transaction was covered by the UCC; the use of a check or other commercial paper is covered by Article 3, and thus by section 1-207. This approach fulfills the policy of section 1-207, which is to favor a preservation of rights despite acceptance of partial satisfaction of the underlying obligation.

County Fire
Door Corp.
v. C.F.
Wooding Co.

c. **UCC does not supersede common law--County Fire Door Corp. v. C.F. Wooding Co.**, 520 A.2d 1028 (Conn. 1987).

1) **Facts.** C.F. Wooding Co. (D) ordered doors and door frames from County Fire Door Corp. (P). Because P was late in delivering the doors, D back charged P $2,180 to reflect its increased costs. P denied the validity of the back charge. D sent P a check for $416.88, bearing a legend on its face that said "Final payment." On the back, D wrote "By its indorsement, the payee accepts this check in full satisfaction of all claims against D arising out of or relating to the [project]." Before

depositing the check, P crossed out the conditional language and wrote "This check is accepted under protest and with full reservation of rights to collect the unpaid balance for which this check is offered in settlement." P then sued for the balance. The trial court awarded P a judgment, holding that section 1-207 granted P the option of reserving its rights and that D had paid no more than it had calculated was due to P. D appeals, claiming the parties had a valid accord and satisfaction that was not prohibited by the UCC.

2) **Issue.** Is the common law doctrine of accord and satisfaction superseded by UCC section 1-207 when a debtor tenders a negotiable instrument as full payment of a disputed claim and the creditor deposits the check, reserving its right to recover the balance from the debtor?

3) **Held.** No. Judgment reversed.

   a) A common law contract of accord and satisfaction is supported by consideration when it settles a monetary claim that is unliquidated in amount. In this case, D offered in good faith to settle an unliquidated debt by tendering an amount less than P demanded in full satisfaction of the debt. At common law, P could not both cash the check and disclaim the condition on which D had tendered it. Therefore, P's suit should have been dismissed unless the UCC changed the common law.

   b) Article 3 does not support an interpretation of section 1-207 that would change common law accord and satisfaction. Section 3-112 specifically preserves the negotiability of a check that includes a statement by the debtor that the payee's cashing of the check constitutes full satisfaction of the debt. Nothing in Article 3 provides that a payee can negate such a condition. Section 3-207 provides that any alteration of an instrument either discharges the liability on the instrument of any party whose contract is thereby changed, or continues the enforceability of the instrument according to its original tenor.

   c) Under Article 3, D's check was enforceable only according to its original tenor. Section 1-207, which refers to "performance," applies to Article 2 transactions, which involve "performance." Article 3 instruments are not "performed." Furthermore, the majority of jurisdictions that have considered this issue have determined that section 1-207 does not change the common law doctrine of accord and satisfaction.

d. **1990 Official Text.** The 1990 Official Text of the UCC addresses the issue by providing in section 1-207(2) that section 1-207 does not apply to an accord and satisfaction. The 1990 version also adds section 3-311, which governs if an accord and satisfaction is attempted by tender of a negotiable instrument. Section 3-311 follows the common law rule, whereby the creditor must either return the check or accept it in full satisfaction as stated in the annotation on the check. Section 3-311(a) provides that an accord and satisfaction will arise when the check is offered in good faith, the amount is unliquidated or subject to a bona fide dispute, and the claimant obtains payment of the instrument. If those three requirements are met, the claim is discharged under section 3-311(b) if there was a conspicuous statement that the instrument was tendered in full satisfaction, unless certain exceptions set forth in section 3-311(c) apply.

B. AREAS OF SPECIAL ATTENTION

1. **Knowledge of Business Practices.** To practice commercial law effectively, a lawyer must understand how business functions. A lawyer must be able to anticipate potential problems and plan transactions so as to avoid unnecessary difficulties. When problems do arise, the lawyer must be able to effectively resolve them.

2. **Note to the Student.** Effective practice of commercial law requires a comfortable familiarity with the UCC. The student should prepare for class by carefully reading the UCC provisions involved in the various cases.

II. SECURITY INTERESTS IN PERSONALTY

A. INTRODUCTION TO SECURITY INTERESTS

1. **Definition of Security Interest.** A security interest is a credit seize the property of a debtor in the event that the debtor fails loan as agreed. It is defined in UCC section 1-201(37) as "a personal property or fixtures which secures payment or perfo obligation." The interest is typically created by a contract between creditor and the debtor; security interests are thus consensual. As the UCC applies only to personal property, a real estate mortgage is not a security interest under the UCC, although in some respects it may be similar to a security interest.

    a. **Debtor's objectives.** A debtor typically intends to repay the debt out of income, not by forfeiting property, and therefore would like to get as much needed credit as possible without tying up any more property than is absolutely necessary. The debtor may persuade the creditor to make a loan with no security other than the debtor's promise to repay. Such a creditor is "unsecured," meaning that if the debtor failed to pay, the creditor would have to go to court, win a judgment, and have the sheriff execute the judgment on the debtor's property. If the creditor refuses to provide an unsecured loan, the debtor must either obtain a surety (guarantor) to back up his or her promise, or must furnish collateral (the debtor's own property) that can be seized in the event of default.

    b. **Creditor's objectives.** In extending credit, the creditor expects repayment plus a profit. The surety and collateral are resources available to insure collection of at least some of the debt if the debtor defaults. If the debtor goes bankrupt, there may be other creditors with some claim to the surety or collateral. Each creditor competes for priority. The creditor thus seeks the greatest degree of protection available when the loan is made.

    c. **UCC.** Article 9 of the UCC focuses on the creditor's rights in the collateral. It does not regulate the creditor's recourse against the debtor's surety, which is left to the common law or other statutes.

2. **Pre-UCC Approach.** Article 9 introduced an innovative unitary security device. Prior to the adoption of the UCC, various specialized security devices were used.

    a. **Pledge.** A pledge occurred when the creditor took possession of the debtor's property (collateral) during the debt period. The pledge is still a widely used security device.

    b. **Chattel mortgage.** A chattel mortgage was a mortgage on the debtor's personal property filed in the appropriate place to give notice of the creditor's interest.

    c. **Conditional sale.** A conditional sale occurred when the seller of property retained title (but not possession) until the buyer completely paid for the goods.

d. **Trust receipt.** The trust receipt was a form of inventory financing in which a bank purchased goods from a manufacturer and then released them "in trust" to the retailer, after filing a notice that it was engaged in such financing.

e. **Factor's acts.** Factor's acts were state statutes allowing financers to perfect their interests in inventory goods which their extensions of credit had helped produce.

f. **Caveat emptor approach--McIntosh & Began v. Hill,** 1 S.W. 680 (Ark. 1886).

   1) **Facts.** Wann agreed to sell a mule for $90 to Overton, on credit, with Wann remaining as the owner. Overton agreed to return the mule to Wann and pay for its use if he was unable to pay the full price. Overton then mortgaged the mule to McIntosh & Began (Ps) for supplies, and told Ps that he had bought it on credit. Ps recorded the mortgage. Overton died, but the mule was used to raise a crop anyway. The crop satisfied all but $40 of the mortgage. Overton's successors returned the mule to Wann and paid for its use. Wann then sold it to Hill (D). The mule was then worth between $50 and $60. Ps replevied the mule from D, but the trial court found for D. Ps appeal.

   2) **Issue.** Does a seller with a security interest prevail against a bona fide purchaser for value from the vendee in possession?

   3) **Held.** Yes. Judgment affirmed.

      a) Wann retained a security interest in the mule; title was not to pass until the purchase money was paid. The fact that Overton had possession did not give him the authority to mortgage the mule.

      b) Possession alone gives no right to transfer title. A conditional vendee such as Overton was has no title and can confer none. The doctrine of caveat emptor prevails, and, while possession may constitute prima facie evidence of title, such title must yield to actual title. Ps, buyers who trusted appearances, must suffer the loss.

g. **Conditional sales contract--*In re* Craig Lumber Co.,** 269 Fed. 755 (9th Cir. 1921).

   1) **Facts.** A contractor agreed to furnish machinery, fittings and equipment, plus construct the necessary buildings, for Craig Lumber Co. (D) to operate a sawmill in Alaska. The contract provided that title to the apparatus and material would not pass until D paid the price in full, and that upon default the contractor could retake the property sold and keep the amounts paid as liquidated damages. Before D had paid the full price, it declared bankruptcy. It still owed the contractor nearly $10,000. The sawmill was built on tidelands owned by the government. The Bank of Alaska had a mortgage on the mill and the machinery, but had notice of the contract when it executed the mortgage. After a trial, the court entered judgment for the contractor for the amount due. The trustee in bankruptcy appeals.

   2) **Issue.** Does a seller under a conditional sales contract have a security interest with greater priority than a trustee in bankruptcy?

3) Held. Yes. Judgment affirmed.

  a) The appellants claim that the contractor was just an employee, but by the terms of the contract, the contractor bought the equipment with its own money and then sold it to D. Nothing in the contract indicates that the contractor was an agent for the company. By its express terms, the sale was conditional.

  b) The court awarded judgment solely for the purchase price of the machinery and apparatus. It did not award money for the construction of the buildings and the services of installing the machinery.

  c) The trustee is not in the position of an attaching creditor with rights superior to the contractor. The trustee assumes the legal position of a creditor holding a legal or equitable lien, but such a creditor would not be able to successfully attack the contractor's title.

  d) Other cases have held that a conditional seller of a chattel does not have priority over a third party without notice of the condition once the property is changed to realty by being affixed to the soil. This rule does not apply here, however. The machinery never became a fixture because the sawmill was built on government land in which there was no freehold estate.

4) Comment. The court essentially held in favor of the contractor because the debtor never received the title; his successors in interest could not have a greater interest than he. Under modern law, however, the trustee would prevail under UCC section 9-301(1)(b) and section 544(a) of the Bankruptcy Code.

3. Article 9. The original (1962) version of Article 9 is in effect in many states. Other states have adopted the Revised Article 9, or 1972 version.

  a. Organization. Article 9 contains five parts:

  1) Part 1. Short Title, Applicability, and Definitions.

  2) Part 2. Validity of Security Agreement and Rights of Parties Thereto.

  3) Part 3. Rights of Third Parties; Perfected and Unperfected Security Interests; Rules of Priority.

  4) Part 4. Filing.

  5) Part 5. Default.

  b. Basic terms.

  1) **Attachment.** Attachment is the process by which the debtor and creditor create a security interest in the debtor's property that is effective between these two parties.

2) **Perfection.** Perfection is the process by which the security interest is made effective against most of the rest of the world.

3) **Security agreement.** The security agreement is the contract signed by the debtor and creditor to create the security interest.

4) **Financing statement.** The financing statement is the document filed in the place mandated by UCC section 9-401 which notifies the world of the creditor's interest in the debtor's property.

5) **Secured party.** A secured party is the creditor who has a security interest, or the buyer in the sale of accounts or chattel paper.

6) **Debtor.** A debtor is the person owing the obligation giving rise to the security interest, or the seller in the sale of accounts or chattel paper.

7) **Lien.** A lien is a creditor interest in debtor property. It may be (i) consensual, or created by agreement, such as an Article 9 security interest; (ii) a judicial lien, or one created by judicial proceedings; or (iii) a statutory lien, which is created by statute or common law for specific unsecured creditors.

B. CREATION OF THE SECURITY INTEREST

1. **Introduction.** A security interest in a debtor's collateral is created by the debtor and the creditor. The interest becomes effective between the parties through attachment; it becomes effective against other parties through perfection.

   a. **Security agreement.** A security agreement is a contract between the debtor and the creditor that sets forth the rights and duties of the parties. It is separate from the financing statement which contains certain information about the creditor's secured interest. The security agreement is usually used to perfect the security interest by filing in the appropriate place.

   b. **Attachment.** Under UCC section 9-203, a security interest attaches when it becomes enforceable against the debtor with respect to the collateral. Attachment occurs the moment all of the three following requirements are met, regardless of the order:

      1) The debtor has rights in the collateral;

      2) The parties have an agreement that the security interest attach; and

      3) Value is given by the secured party.

   c. **Perfection.** The process of perfection is a set of actions which, when accomplished, give the secured party priority over certain other classes of the debtor's creditors in the exercise of the security interest. There are three methods of perfection.

1) **Filing a financing statement.** Filing is the most common method of perfection, and is the only means for perfecting an interest in accounts and intangibles. [UCC §9-302] The statement must be filed in the public office specified by the particular state's version of the UCC. Of all the Article 9 claims available to trustees in bankruptcy, improper filing is probably the most frequently raised.

2) **Possession.** The concept of the pledge is continued in UCC section 9-305.

3) **Automatic perfection.** Certain transactions result in perfection automatically upon attachment of the security interest.

2. **Rights in the Collateral.** The UCC does not define the term "rights in the collateral," but it refers to some ownership interest or right to obtain possession on the part of the debtor. The term "rights" does include remedies under section 1-201(36). The concept of "title" is irrelevant to secured transactions under section 9-202.

a. **When acquired.** The 1972 version of the UCC eliminates the various rules formerly contained in section 9-204(2) with respect to when rights in collateral could be acquired. The issue is left to be resolved on a case-by-case basis. For example, a buyer of goods has rights in the goods as soon as they are identified by the seller as intended for the buyer, even before the buyer takes possession.

b. **Rights created under UCC section 2-403 sufficient to permit attachment--*In re* Samuels & Co.**, 526 F.2d 1238 (5th Cir. 1976), *cert. denied*, 429 U.S. 834 (1976). *In re* Samuels & Co.

1) **Facts.** C.I.T. provided financing for Samuels & Co. (D), a meat processor, and had a perfected security interest in all of D's livestock and other inventory, both existing and after-acquired. Stowers sold cattle to D for slaughter on a "grade and yield" basis, under which the price was determined after slaughter and inspection by the USDA. D paid by check. D resold the carcasses. Within 10 days, D declared bankruptcy and its checks were dishonored. Stowers sought reclamation of the cattle it sold to D and asserted a right to the proceeds of the sale of the meat. The referee found that Stowers had priority. The case was eventually appealed to the U.S. Supreme Court, which held that state law, not federal law, was determinative. On remand, the court of appeals held that Stowers had priority. The court then granted a rehearing en banc.

2) **Issue.** Is the interest of an unpaid cash seller in goods already delivered to a buyer superior to the interest of a holder of a perfected security interest in those same goods?

3) **Held.** No. Judgment for C.I.T.

a) UCC section 2-403 provides that a person with voidable title can transfer good title to a good faith purchaser for value. D thus had the power to transfer good title even though he lacked the right to do so under section 2-507. The term "purchaser" includes a secured party. C.I.T. had a security agreement with D and gave value in the form of preexisting indebtedness. Its security interest would therefore attach to the cattle if D had rights in the cattle.

b) D paid Stowers with a check which was subsequently dishonored. Still, by virtue of the delivery, D had the power to transfer a security interest to a secured party such as C.I.T. These rights in the property, though marginal, are sufficient to allow attachment of a lien. Because the goods were after-acquired property subject to C.I.T.'s lien, the lien properly attached to the cattle. C.I.T. acted in good faith despite its knowledge of D's business operations.

c) Stowers' reclamation right under UCC section 2-507 does not concern his rights against third parties. Section 2-507 expressly precludes recovery by cash sellers as against a buyer's creditor who has a security interest in after-acquired property. In addition, Stowers failed to make a demand against D within 10 days of D's receipt.

d) Although section 2-511 makes payment by check conditional, this only affects Stowers' claim against D, not C.I.T.'s interest as a secured party.

e) Under pre-UCC law, Stowers could have reserved title after surrendering possession to D. Under section 2-402, however, any such reservation is limited to a reservation of a security interest. This applies to both cash and credit sales. Stowers' security interest was subject to Article 9 and was unperfected, so it is subordinate to C.I.T.'s perfected security interest. D's interest upon delivery was sufficient to allow attachment.

f) Stowers could have protected its interests by complying with the UCC's purchase-money provisions.

4) Comment. In this case, Article 9 applied to give the third party greater rights than the debtor himself had. Before Article 9 can be relied upon, though, the debtor's rights under law other than Article 9 must be assessed. In this case, D had sufficient rights under Article 2 to transfer good title to a good faith purchaser.

3. Scope of the Security Agreement. A security agreement must contain a description of the collateral involved. The description is sufficient if it reasonably identifies what collateral the parties intended the security interest to cover. Description problems arise in two contexts: (i) the description in the *security agreement* must cover the particular loan and collateral involved; and (ii) the description in the *financing statement* must be adequate to perfect a security interest in the particular collateral and loan involved. The first situation involves interpretation of a private contract, but the second requires that a public document be construed.

a. Precise identification not necessary. Under prior law, collateral had to be specifically identified. Under the UCC, general language such as "all equipment located at . . ." is permissible, so long as it reasonably identifies the property. The description may be made through incorporating by reference a description contained in the financing statement or another document. An error in the description does not defeat the security agreement so long as the true intent of the parties may be ascertained. A common issue is whether the security agreement covers after-acquired collateral.

b. **Security agreement limited to collateral described--Idaho Bank & Trust Co. v. Cargill, Inc.,** 665 P.2d 1093 (Idaho 1983).

1) **Facts.** Idaho Bank & Trust Co. (P) made loans to Idle, a grain dealer, receiving as security an assignment of the proceeds of certain grain contracts Idle had with Cargill, Inc. (D). P sent a copy of the written assignment to D and asked that D make P a joint payee on all future checks. D did so until P cut off Idle's line of credit and Idle entered new contracts with D and told D not to put P's name on the contracts. After these contracts were performed, D resumed performance of the contracts it had assigned to P, but directed D not to make the checks payable to P. When Idle declared bankruptcy, some of the loans had still not been paid off. P sought payment from D, claiming D was an account debtor because it paid the proceeds directly to Idle despite the notice P had sent D. D refused to pay, and P sued. The trial court held that P did not have a security interest in the contracts and found for D. P appeals.

2) **Issue.** Does a security agreement cover property not specifically included in its description of the collateral?

3) **Held.** No. Judgment affirmed.

   a) P argues that under UCC section 9-318(3), once the account debtor receives notice of an assignment, it is required to pay the assignee and not the assignor. Payment to an assignor does not relieve the account debtor of its obligation to pay the assignee without the assignee's consent.

   b) The relationship between the assignee and the account debtor does not come into existence unless the assignee has a security interest in the subject of the assignment. The agreement between P and Idle was sufficient to constitute a security agreement. It also was clear enough to apply to any grain contracts between Idle and D at the time D received notice of the assignment.

   c) However, the assignment applied only to "all monies now due or to become due under certain grain contracts held in" Idle's warehouse. Thus, it did not apply to contracts between Idle and D not then in existence. Nor did it provide security for future advances.

   d) P argues that the course of dealing and course of performance of the parties should be considered in construing the scope and meaning of the assignment. While D did provide joint payment checks over a long period of time, it was not a party to the assignment. D could properly rely on the assignment language in deciding to follow Idle's instructions. Since the assignment did not state it was intended to cover future advances, D did not have to infer that such was the intent. D was not an account debtor with respect to the proceeds in question.

4. **Value.** The value given by the creditor is usually an advance of money or a delivery of goods but may include anything that satisfies the definition of value given in section 1-201(44). This includes acquisition of rights in collateral:

   a. In return for any consideration sufficient to support a simple contract;

   b. As security for preexisting claims or in partial or total satisfaction thereof;

   c. By accepting delivery under a preexisting contract for purchase; or

   d. In return for a binding commitment to extend credit, whether or not such credit is ever used.

5. **Signed Writing Requirement.**

   a. **Basic rule.** UCC section 9-203(1)(b) requires that the security agreement be signed because (i) an evidentiary function is served by requiring a signed security agreement and (ii) a written agreement obviates any Statute of Frauds problems with the debtor-creditor relationship. The financing statement gives public notice to other creditors that a security interest is claimed in the debtor's collateral.

In re Bollinger

   b. **Documents showing intent to create security interest--*In re* Bollinger,** 614 F.2d 924 (3d Cir. 1980).

      1) **Facts.** The Bollinger Corp. (D) borrowed $150,000 and signed a security agreement giving ICC, the creditor, a security interest in certain machinery and equipment. ICC perfected its interest by filing a financing statement. After paying off $85,000 of the loan, D borrowed another $150,000, this time from Z & J. Z & J agreed to pay off the amount due to ICC in return for an assignment from ICC of the original note and security agreement. D executed a promissory note to Z & J which included a provision describing security interests held by Z & J, but no formal security agreement was ever executed between D and Z & J. When D was adjudicated bankrupt, Z & J asserted a secured claim for $150,000. The trustee conceded that the assignment to Z & J of ICC's secured claim gave Z & J a secured claim for $65,000, but refused to recognize the additional secured claim for $85,000. Z & J appealed to the district court, which reversed the bankruptcy court. The trustee appeals.

      2) **Issue.** May a creditor assert a secured claim against a debtor when no formal security agreement was ever signed, but where various documents executed in connection with the loan demonstrate an intent to create a security interest?

      3) **Held.** Yes. Judgment affirmed.

         a) Section 9-203 contains minimal formal requirements for the creation of a security agreement. Under section 9-402, a security agreement may serve as a financing statement if it is signed by both parties, but it is unclear whether the converse is true. The courts are split on that issue, some requiring language actually granting a security interest to a creditor, and others permitting the financing statement alone to stand as the security agreement.

b) The better rule permits the financing statement, when read in conjunction with other documents executed by the parties, to satisfy the requirements of section 9-203(1)(b).

c) In this case, D had executed a promissory note to Z & J, which, when read in conjunction with the financing statement and correspondence during the course of the transaction between the parties, created a valid security agreement. The correspondence clearly shows that the parties intended a security agreement. The financing statement contains a detailed list of the collateral and was signed by D.

6. **Security Interest in Proceeds.** The term "proceeds" includes anything the debtor receives upon sale, exchange or other disposition of collateral or proceeds from a prior disposition of collateral. Money, checks, and deposit accounts are cash proceeds; everything else is non-cash proceeds. Section 9-306 determines how a security interest is affected by proceeds. Insurance payments are also proceeds.

a. **Development of the rule.** Under pre-UCC law, a security interest was treated as a fraudulent transfer which could be set aside by a trustee in bankruptcy if the debtor was allowed to use or to dispose of the collateral or to retain the proceeds from disposition thereof. Section 9-205 specifically changed this rule. Consequently, the parties may agree that the debtor may use or dispose of all the collateral and the proceeds thereof.

b. **Presumption.** Under section 9-306(2), neither the security agreement nor the financing statement need expressly refer to proceeds. The secured party's rights with respect to proceeds are deemed to arise by operation of law unless the parties agree otherwise.

c. **Secured party's option.** The secured party may not be limited to recourse against the proceeds. If the security interest continues in the original collateral despite the transfer to a third person, the secured party may assert its interest in both the proceeds and the original collateral until the debt is satisfied.

d. **Attachment and perfection.** If the secured party's interest in the original collateral was perfected, the interest normally continues automatically and permanently in the identifiable proceeds received by the debtor. This rule applies even when the debtor acquired the proceeds in violation of the security agreement. However, if a security interest in the proceeds cannot be perfected by filing, such as a negotiable note (which requires perfection by possession), or the place of original filing is not the appropriate place for filing as to the proceeds, the security interest terminates 10 days after the debtor receives the proceeds, unless a new perfection is accomplished.

e. **Processed goods as proceeds of farm products--*In re* San Juan Packers,** 696 F.2d 707 (9th Cir. 1983).

1) **Facts.** San Juan Packers (D), a food processor, bought cans on credit from National Can Corp. ("NCC") and granted NCC a floating lien on all of D's inventory. D also bought vegetables from several farmers who had granted Peoples State Bank (P) a security interest in their crops and the proceeds thereof. D processed and sold part, but not all, of the vegetables before it filed for bankruptcy. Consequently, D did not pay the farmers, and they did not pay P. P sought relief in bankruptcy court against all of D's secured creditors. The parties agreed to sell the remaining vegetables to create a cash fund. The court found for P. NCC appealed to the district court, which affirmed. NCC appeals.

2) **Issue.** Do proceeds from the sale of processed goods constitute proceeds from the sale of the raw ingredients?

3) **Held.** Yes. Judgment vacated and remanded for further fact findings.

a) Under UCC section 9-306(1), proceeds includes whatever is received when collateral or proceeds is sold, exchanged, collected or otherwise disposed of. The money D received for the vegetables is proceeds because the security interest continues in collateral notwithstanding sale. The fact that D sold the goods, while the farmers were the debtors to P, does not change this result. Under section 9-105(1)(d), the term "debtor" means the owner of the collateral when the property is transferred subject to a secured debt of the transferor which the transferee does not assume. P could follow these vegetables into the hands of the ultimate consumer.

b) NCC argues that P's security interest continued only in identifiable proceeds under section 9-306(2), so that once D mixed together vegetables purchased from various farmers, P's interest was lost. However, under section 9-315(1), where collateral loses its identity by commingling or processing, the security interest continues in the product.

c) NCC also contends that under section 9-315, it was entitled to share in the cash fund because it had a security interest in the vegetables held by D that were grown by unsecured farmers. However, it is impossible to tell from this record whether any of the secured farmers' vegetables were sold before D filed a bankruptcy petition. On remand, the court must determine when deliveries from unsecured farmers were made, in which NCC would have a security interest.

f. **Payments for not planting crops--McLemore, Trustee v. Mid-South Agri-Chemical Corp.,** 41 B.R. 369 (Bankr. M.D. Tenn. 1984).

1) **Facts.** Mid-South Agri-Chemical Corp. (D) held a security interest in the debtors' corn crop and proceeds, which it perfected on June 2, 1982. The Farmers Home Administration ("FHA") held a security interest in all the debtors' crops and proceeds, which it perfected on June 23, 1982. In 1983, the debtors entered the PIK Diversion Program by which they would receive payments for nonproduction. They assigned their payments for nonproduction of wheat to D. When the debtors filed for bankruptcy, they had some PIK certificates, corn worth $25,153.24, and wheat worth $2,677.67. McLemore, trustee, (P) seeks to recover the PIK certificates.

2) **Issue.** Are payments to farmers for nonproduction of crops "proceeds" to which a creditor's security interest in crops attaches even though the crops are never planted?

3) **Held.** Yes. Judgment for P in part.

   a) D would prevail over P if PIK entitlements constituted proceeds to which D's security interest in crops attaches. Other courts have held that crop subsidy and crop entitlement payments are proceeds of the crops involved. Such payments are an integral part of the farming business.

   b) Any corn grown on the debtors' farm would have been covered by D's security interest, so the crop substitute, which was PIK benefits, should be treated the same. PIK benefits are intended to compensate producers who reduce their acreage which would otherwise have been planted. PIK is considered as production.

   c) The PIK entitlements are substitutes for specific crops on specific acreage. The close nexus between the entitlements and the original collateral indicates that participation in the PIK program was a substitute for the planting of the crop collateral.

   d) P's interpretation of the federal program would undermine the effectiveness of the subsidy programs by eliminating the interests of crop financers in crop collateral. It would allow a farmer to defeat a creditor's security by participating in the program.

   e) D has first priority in the debtors' corn crop and corn proceeds, and FHA has a continuing security interest in all of the debtors' crops and crop proceeds.

C. PERFECTION OF SECURITY INTERESTS

1. **Introduction.** Under UCC section 9-301, unperfected security interests are subordinate to perfected security interests. Perfection itself is not defined, but it consists of a series of actions that give the secured party priority over certain other classes of the debtor's creditors in the exercise of the security interest. The critical requirement is that a proper method be used in a proper time. A security interest may be perfected by (i) filing a financing agreement; (ii) possessing the collateral; or (iii) through the mere attachment of the security interest.

2. **Classifying the Collateral.**

a. **Types of collateral.** Article 9 applies to transactions intended to create a security interest in personal property or fixtures and to any sale of accounts or chattel paper. The three basic categories of collateral are (i) tangible collateral such as goods, (ii) quasi-tangible collateral, or legal rights represented by paper, and (iii) intangible collateral such as accounts receivable.

1) **Goods.** Goods are fixtures or any tangible that is movable when the security interest attaches. This includes unborn animals, growing crops, and timber, but does not include unextracted minerals. Four types of goods are specifically recognized by section 9-109:

   a) Consumer goods, which are bought for use primarily for personal, family or household purposes;

   b) Inventory, which are goods held for sale or lease to others in the ordinary course of business, including raw materials;

   c) Farm products, which are used or produced in farming operations and are in the possession of the farmer, but only before going through a manufacturing process; and

   d) Equipment, which are goods used in a business or government entity or any goods that do not fall within the other three categories.

2) **Quasi-intangible collateral.** This category includes instruments such as Article 3 checks, drafts, etc. and Article 8 securities (stocks and bonds). It also includes documents of title and chattel paper, which is a writing that contains both a promise to pay money and a security interest in or lease of chattels.

3) **Intangible collateral.** Intangible collateral consists of accounts receivable, which are rights to payment for goods or services sold or leased but not evidenced by an instrument or chattel paper, and general intangibles such as goodwill, research reports, and possibly government-allocated rights such as a liquor license.

In re K.L.
Smith Enter-
prises, Ltd.

b. **Livestock not inventory or equipment--*In re* K.L. Smith Enterprises, Ltd.,** 2 B.R. 280 (Bankr. D. Colo. 1980).

1) **Facts.** K.L. Smith Enterprises, Ltd. (D) operated a major and unique egg production facility. Once collected, the eggs were cooled and processed by washing, spraying with a light oil to seal the shell, and candling (a method used to detect defects). The eggs were then sorted and packaged in cartons. D borrowed $2.4 million from the Bank of Denver ("Bank"), and Bank in turn obtained a security interest in all of D's inventory, accounts and contract rights, plus the proceeds therefrom. Bank also took a security interest in all of D's equipment and machinery. D filed for bankruptcy the day before it both billed a major customer for an egg shipment and received a cash payment for other eggs. D subsequently delivered other shipments of eggs and sold 120,000 chickens to a soup company. Bank asserts a security interest in the eggs and chickens on the ground that they are inventory, or possibly that the chickens are equipment instead. D claims that the eggs and chickens are farm products not covered by the security interests.

2) **Issue.** May livestock or the products of livestock be considered as inventory or equipment?

3) **Held.** No. Judgment for D.

    a) Under UCC section 9-109, farm products are livestock used in farming operations or the products of livestock in their unmanufactured states, such as eggs. If goods are farm products, they are neither equipment nor inventory.

    b) Bank claims that when the sole business enterprise is the production of eggs, the eggs are not farm products but are inventory in the operation of a business. This claim simply contradicts the plain language of the statute.

    c) Farm products may become inventory once they are subjected to a manufacturing process. In this case, however, there was no manufacturing process. The eggs were merely washed, sprayed, candled, and packaged. This does not constitute manufacturing.

    d) Since Bank did not obtain a security interest in D's farm products, its claim must fail except as to any account under section 9-106 that was generated before the petition was filed.

3. **Perfection by Filing.** Filing is the most common method of perfecting a security interest, and is the only method of perfecting an interest in accounts and intangibles. This method consists of filing a proper document in the public office specified under the applicable state law.

  a. **Where to file.** UCC section 9-401 provides three different filing systems for states to choose from.

    1) Alternative 1 provides that most filings be done with the secretary of state, except that when collateral is minerals, timber to be cut, or goods that are or will be fixtures, the place to file is where a mortgage on the real estate would be filed. Few states have adopted this alternative.

    2) Alternative 2 requires that filings for consumer goods, farm equipment and farm products be in a designated county office (local filing). Fixtures, minerals, timber or growing crops must be filed in the office where the land is located, and all other filings are with the secretary of state. This is the most commonly adopted alternative.

    3) Alternative 3 adds a requirement to Alternative 2, namely that a filing with the secretary of state must also be filed in the county of the debtor's place of business or in the county of the debtor's residence.

  b. **What to file.** The parties may file a copy of the security agreement, which would give complete notice of the debt and collateral to all who read the record. The favored filing, however, is of a brief financing statement. The financing statement usually gives little specific information about the details of the underlying transaction, but it puts creditors on notice of the existence of a security agreement. [UCC §9-402(1)]

1) **Contents of a financing statement.** A financing statement must include at least the following information, although some states have additional requirements:

   a) The names of both the debtor and secured party;

   b) The address of the secured party from which information concerning the secured interest may be obtained;

   c) A mailing address of the debtor;

   d) A statement indicating the types or describing the items of collateral; and

   e) The debtor's signature.

2) **Sufficiency.** Errors in the financing statement do not render it defective so long as they are minor and are not seriously misleading.

3) **Effective date.** Filing is deemed effective when the financing statement is presented for filing and the filing fee is tendered or the filing officer accepts the statement. [UCC §9-403(1)] The filing officer's subsequent conduct does not affect the effective date, so an erroneous filing by the filing officer does not eliminate the perfection.

4) **Duration.** A financing statement is effective for five years after the date of filing. This period is extended if insolvency proceedings are initiated against the debtor until the termination of the proceedings, plus 60 days. The secured party may also file a continuation statement to add another five years to the effective date, but this must be filed within six months before expiration of the exiting filing. If a filing lapses, the security interest becomes unperfected. When the security interest expires, the secured party must provide a termination statement which the debtor can then file.

5) **Amendments.** If an amendment adds collateral to that already described in the financing statement, it is effective for the new collateral only from the filing date of the amendment under UCC section 9-402(4). Amendments to the original financing statements which merely change names, amounts or descriptions have no effect on perfection or priority of the secured interest because they are considered part of the original financing statement.

In re Lintz West Side Lumber, Inc.

c. **Listing principals instead of debtor corporation as debtor is inadequate--** *In re* **Lintz West Side Lumber, Inc.,** 655 F.2d 786 (7th Cir. 1981).

   1) **Facts.** Lintz West Side Lumber, Inc. (D) was owned by John and Mayella Lintz. D owed the Farmers & Merchants Bank ("Bank") $90,000, for which Bank received a security interest in D's inventory and accounts receivable. The financing statement was duly filed but it listed the debtor as John and Mayella Lintz. When D filed a voluntary petition in bankruptcy, the trustee claimed the financing statement did not perfect Bank's security interest because of the incorrect listing of the debtor. The trial court upheld the trustee's claim. Bank appeals, claiming that because D is

a close corporation in a small town, it provided sufficient notice of Bank's security interest to other creditors in the community.

2) Issue. Is a security interest in a close corporation perfected if the filed financing statement lists the principals, not the corporation, as the debtor?

3) Held. No. Judgment affirmed.

　a) D was a duly constituted corporation, legally separate and distinct from John and Mayella Lintz. To discover that corporate assets were encumbered, a creditor would have to search for the security interest held by others in the Lintz' personal property. However, a creditor would ordinarily assume that corporate assets would not be encumbered by a security interest filed under the names of the principals.

　b) Even though Bank acted in good faith and without intent to defraud creditors, good faith is not the only requirement for perfection.

　c) The fact that no creditor was actually misled does not change the result. The trustee in bankruptcy has the status of an ideal, imaginary creditor without notice. The trustee could thus be considered to have been prejudiced by Bank's misleading financing statement.

d. Filing under trade name--*In re* Glasco, Inc., 642 F.2d 793 (5th Cir. 1981).

In re Glasco, Inc.

1) Facts. Glasco, Inc. (D), a boat manufacturer, operated its business solely under the name "Elite Boats, Division of Glasco, Inc." The Citizens Bank ("Bank") provided marine engine financing for D, which in turn executed promissory notes and a security agreement in its business name. When Bank filed the financing statement, it listed the debtor by D's business name. The financing statement was not cross-indexed under "Glasco, Inc." D later filed for bankruptcy. The financing statement was not disclosed to the trustee, and the trustee sold the engines. Bank then sued the trustee for the proceeds of the sale. The trustee's motion for summary judgment was granted by the bankruptcy court because the financing statement did not list D by its legal name. The district court affirmed and Bank appeals.

2) Issue. May a financing statement be adequate even if it lists the debtor by the name in which it did business rather than its legal corporate name?

3) Held. Yes. Judgment reversed.

　a) The filing system is intended to give notice to creditors that a security interest exists in property of the debtor. The financing statement must provide sufficient information to put any searcher on inquiry, but perfect accuracy is not required. Substantial compliance is sufficient so long as the minor errors are not seriously misleading. [UCC §9-402(5)]

　b) The seriousness of an erroneous listing of the debtor's name depends on the particular factual circumstances of each case. D in this case held itself out to the community and to creditors under its business name; its checks, stationery and bank account all used the business name. There is no evidence that D used just "Glasco, Inc." in any of its business dealings. A reasonably prudent creditor would have searched under the business name as well as the legal name.

c) This case is different from cases in which the financing statement lists only the trade name of an individual who also uses his own name. Here, D did business only under one name, so creditors would not be misled. Listing under D's business name was not seriously misleading.

4) **Dissent.** The liberal provisions of UCC section 9-402(5) were not intended to undermine the single filing system. By protecting the Bank's rights, the majority has hindered those who must use the system to determine whether a particular debtor's property is burdened. "Glasco, Inc." is not sufficiently similar to "Elite Boats" that one searching for the former would normally find the latter. Until this decision, creditors were not required to discover trade names but could search only under the debtor's legal name. Bank could have avoided the problem by indicating both names on the financing statement, separated by the "d.b.a." notation.

In re Alexander   e. **Trade name of a rural farming business--*In re* Alexander,** 39 B.R. 110 (Bankr. D.N.D. 1984).

1) **Facts.** John Alexander and his son Larry (Ds) entered into a partnership agreement as required by the Farmers Home Administration ("FHA") for John to refinance his farming operation. However, John and Larry continued to run their separate operations with their separate machinery, seed, and expenses. FHA filed a financing statement showing both John and Larry as debtors and showing as collateral livestock, supplies, inventory, farm and other equipment and other farm products. It was indexed under the name "Alexander Farms," however. Ds petitioned for bankruptcy and the trustee seeks priority over FHA.

2) **Issue.** May a financing statement perfect a security interest if it is listed under a business name that includes the debtors' last name?

3) **Held.** Yes. Judgment for FHA.

a) Under UCC section 9-402, a financing statement is legally sufficient if it reasonably notifies a creditor of prior interests in the debtor's property.

b) Here, the financing statement was indexed under the name Alexander Farms. Any creditor interested in the property of John or Larry Alexander would examine all financing statements filed under the name Alexander. The collateral listing was not overly broad. Thus, the financing statement provided reasonable notification of FHA's security interest.

4) **Comment.** A variety of changes that arise after the filing can affect the filing. The debtor may change its name, the goods may be moved to a different state, or the collateral may change form (*i.e.,* farm products become inventory, goods become fixtures). Separate provisions cover each of these changes to some extent.

f. **Property transferred to new owner--*In re* Cohutta Mills, Inc.**, 108 B.R. 815 (N.D. Ga. 1989).

1) **Facts.** In 1977, King's Tuft, Inc. borrowed money from Cohutta Bank ("Bank") with a Small Business Administration ("SBA") guarantee. Bank filed financing statements on King's Tuft's equipment, machinery, and after-acquired property. In 1979, Bank assigned the note and security interests to the SBA. In 1980, the owners of King's Tuft transferred the company's assets to Cohutta Mills, Inc. (D). The SBA consented to the transfer on the condition that D assume the obligation as well, which D did. However, the SBA did not file new financing statements. In 1982, the SBA filed a continuation statement showing a security interest in the property of King's Tuft. D filed for bankruptcy in 1987. The bankruptcy trustee argued that the SBA did not have a perfected security interest. The bankruptcy court found that it did, and the trustee appeals.

2) **Issue.** Where property subject to a perfected security interest is transferred to a new owner, must the secured party file a financing statement that gives the name of the new debtor?

3) **Held.** Yes. Judgment reversed.

   a) Under UCC section 9-306(2), a security interest continues despite sale or exchange unless the disposition was authorized by the secured party. But section 9-402(7) provides that a filed financing statement remains effective even when the collateral is transferred. This apparent conflict is best resolved by excluding a secured party's conditional assent from section 9-306(2). In other words, a transfer of collateral is not "authorized" under section 9-306(2) if the secured party consents to the transaction on the condition that its security interest continues after the transfer.

   b) In this case, the SBA did authorize the transfer from King's Tuft to D. Because its authorization was conditioned on the continuation of its security interest, the SBA's security interest continued and D acquired the property subject to that security interest.

   c) Under UCC section 9-402(1), a financing statement must give the correct name of the debtor. Misnaming the debtor is not fatal so long as the mistake is not seriously misleading. Under section 9-402(7), if a financing statement is effective when filed but becomes seriously misleading by a subsequent change of the debtor's name or a restructuring of the debtor, the secured party is protected as to collateral covered through the time of the name change and as to property acquired by the debtor through four months thereafter.

   d) In this case, there was both a transfer of assets to D and a restructuring of the King's Tuft business. King's Tuft essentially became D when it received the assets. Thus, under section 9-402(7), the SBA's filed financing statement became seriously misleading upon the transfer of assets to D, so its interest was perfected as to D's property through four months after the transfer only. The SBA's 1982 continuation statement was seriously misleading when filed and was ineffective. As a result, the SBA's security interest in D's property was unperfected.

g. **Effectiveness period and continuation statements.** Under UCC section 9-403(2), a filed financing statement is effective for a period of five years from the date of filing. Its effectiveness lapses on the expiration of the five-year period unless a continuation statement is filed prior to the lapse. Under section 9-403(3), a continuation statement must (i) be filed within six months prior to the expiration of the original filing; (ii) contain the signature of the secured party; (iii) identify the original statement by file number; and (iv) state that the original statement is still effective. Upon timely filing of the continuation statement, the effectiveness of the original statement is continued for five years after the last date to which the filing was effective unless another continuation statement was filed prior to such lapse.

In re
Adam

1) **Filing outside the six-month window--*In re* Adam**, 96 B.R. 249 (D. N.D. 1989).

a) **Facts.** The Farmers Home Administration ("FHA") perfected a security interest in the livestock, supplies, and other farm products owned by Adam (D) by filing a UCC-1 financing statement on January 27, 1971. FHA filed continuation statements on September 8, 1975 and September 11, 1980, referring to the original financing statement. FHA filed a third continuation statement on April 18, 1985, but referred to the 1980 continuation statement instead of the original financing statement. D filed under Chapter 7 on June 19, 1986. The trustee seeks to avoid the FHA security interest in the cash proceeds from the sale of the collateral.

b) **Issue.** Is a continuation statement effective if it is filed outside the six-month window?

c) **Held.** No. Judgment for trustee.

(1) UCC section 9-402(8) provides that a financing statement that substantially complies with the statutory requirements is effective even though it contains minor errors which are not seriously misleading. Without satisfying the four basic requirements of a continuation statement under UCC section 9-403(3), there is no substantial compliance.

(2) There are two problems with FHA's 1985 continuation statement. The first is that it refers to the 1980 continuation statement instead of referring to the original financing statement file number. However, the 1980 statement does refer to the original financing statement, which provides some linkage to the original. This would put an inquiring searcher on notice, so the 1985 statement is in substantial compliance and the incorrect file number is not seriously misleading.

(3) The second problem with the 1985 filing is that it was made in April. Although this was within six months of expiration of the 1980 continuation statement, that is not the relevant time period. UCC section 9-403(3) requires that the continuation statement be

filed within six months prior to the expiration of five years from the date of filing the original financing statement, and succeeding continuations statements must be filed within six months prior to the expiration of the original financing statement as continued. This means within six months of the January date of the original filing, not within six months of the September date of the continuation statements. The April filing was premature and not in substantial compliance, so FHA's security interest lapsed on January 27, 1986.

    (4)   D filed the Chapter 7 petition in June 1986, by which time the FHA security interest was unperfected. The trustee has a first lien on D's assets.

2)   Effect of lapse--Bostwick-Braun Co. v. Owens, 634 F. Supp. 839 (E.D. Wis. 1986).

    a)   Facts. In February 1977, F & M Bank filed a financing statement covering the personal property of the Nordeens, who were partners in JoDan's Pro Hardware. F & M filed another original financing statement covering the same property in February 1982, without referring to the 1977 filing. F & M never filed a continuation statement on the 1977 filing. In November 1981, Bostwick-Braun Company (P) filed a financing statement covering the same personal property. In May 1984, JoDan's Pro Hardware filed for Chapter 7, and both P and F & M filed claims as secured creditors. Owens (D), the trustee in bankruptcy, paid the proceeds from a sale of the property into an account pending determination of the conflicting claims, each of which exceeded the proceeds. P seeks a declaratory judgment that its security interest is superior to F & M's.

    b)   Issue. Once a security interest lapses, does a subsequently-filed security interest have priority even though the second filer had actual knowledge of the prior security interest?

    c)   Held. Yes. Judgment for P.

        (1)   Under UCC section 9-403(2), a filed financing statement is effective for five years, but upon lapse, the security interest becomes unperfected. F & M failed to file a continuation statement, so its 1977 filing lapsed in 1982.

        (2)   Any notice P had as a junior secured creditor is irrelevant in this case. Court must rely on constructive or statutory notice alone, since the purpose of statutory filing requirements is to resolve notice disputes consistently and predictably.

        (3)   The courts cannot give equitable relief in situations such as this because to do so would undermine the ability of parties to rely on the statutory rules.

        (4)   Since P filed its financing statement before F & M filed its second statement, P's interest has priority over F & M's.

4. **Perfection in Fixtures.** The UCC does not define the term "fixture" so local non-UCC law must be used to determine what is and is not a fixture. Generally, a fixture is personal property permanently attached to real property. Section 9-313 deals with fixtures, but some states have not adopted this section and others have made changes in it.

   a. **Fixture filing.** A fixture financer can perfect its security interest in the fixture by filing a financing statement in the place where real property records are filed. This "fixture filing" must satisfy the normal requirements for a financing statement plus recite that it is to be filed in the real estate records and must contain a description of the real estate.

   b. **Purchase money security interests.** Most security interests in fixtures are purchase money security interests. These prevail against existing and future interests in the real estate provided the purchase money security interest is perfected by a fixture filing at the time the goods are affixed to the realty or within 10 days thereafter. The debtor must also be the owner of the real estate or someone in possession, such as a lessee.

   c. **Non-purchase money security interests.** A non-purchase money security interest, or one perfected more than 10 days after the goods became a fixture, loses to prior recorded interests in the realty even if the fixture financer perfects by a fixture filing. The fixture filing will prevail over parties who obtain rights in the realty after the fixture filing is done.

Cummings,
Inc. v.
Beardsley

   d. **Application--Cummings, Inc. v. Beardsley,** 609 S.W.2d 66 (Ark. 1980).

      1) **Facts.** Cummings, Inc. (P) contracted Erect-O-Therm to make and install two large advertising signs, and received a security interest in the signs in return. P filed the financing statement, which included an agreement that the signs were not to become part of the realty, with the Secretary of State. The signs were installed on steel poles set in a concrete foundation. Erect-O-Therm's bank foreclosed on the mortgage on the realty and took the signs, and then resold the entire property to Beardsley (Ds). P brought a foreclosure suit against Ds for the unpaid purchase price and sought possession of the signs and a deficiency judgment for any deficit remaining after resale of the signs. Ds responded that they had not bought the signs from P and had no knowledge of the indebtedness. Ds' motion for summary judgment was granted and P appeals.

      2) **Issue.** When a seller takes a security interest in personal property that would be a fixture but for an agreement between the seller and the buyer, must the seller file the financing statement where a mortgage on the real estate is filed?

      3) **Held.** Yes. Judgment affirmed.

         a) There is no question that Ds did not buy the signs from P and that Ds were not personally liable to P under the security agreement, since they were not parties to the agreement.

         b) A financing statement covering fixtures must be filed in the office where a mortgage on the real estate concerned would be filed or recorded. In this case, that would be in the county office, not with the secretary of state.

    c) Even though the signs were not fixtures as between P and Erect-O-Therm, they were clearly fixtures as between P and Ds since they were anchored deep in concrete. To protect its security interest, P should have filed with the county.

5. Perfection by Possession.

a. Introduction. UCC section 9-305 retains the pre-UCC concept of pledges by allowing perfection by possession. This method of perfection has the advantages of solving any Statute of Frauds problems and of assuring perfection. It also reduces the risk of third parties being misled. While perfection by possession is possible for all types of goods, it is the only means for perfecting a security interest in money or instruments.

b. Rights and duties of possessor. The UCC spells out certain rights and duties of the secured party in possession.

    1) Duty of reasonable care. The secured party must use reasonable care in storing and preserving the collateral.

    2) Right to reimbursement. The secured party may charge the debtor for reasonable expenses incurred during custody and may hold the collateral as security for these expenses.

    3) Right to repledge. The secured party may repledge the collateral so long as the debtor's ability to redeem is not impaired.

    4) Right to use. The secured party may operate or use the collateral only if such action is necessary to preserve the collateral or its value.

c. Possession of indispensable instruments--M.M. Landy, Inc. v. Nicholas, 221 F.2d 923 (5th Cir. 1955).

M.M. Landy, Inc. v. Nicholas

    1) Facts. M.M. Landy, Inc. (P) took an assignment of accounts receivable due from the United States government to Continental Charterers as security for a loan to Continental. P also took possession of warrants which were nonnegotiable orders on the United States Treasury. Continental went bankrupt and Nicholas (D), the trustee, attacked P's security. The referee in bankruptcy held that P's security was not perfected because the filing requirements were not met. P appeals.

    2) Issue. Is filing necessary for perfection where the creditor takes possession of a pledgeable asset?

    3) Held. No. Judgment reversed.

        a) Under UCC section 9-203(1)(a), possession of collateral by the secured party pursuant to agreement suffices to perfect the security interest if value has been given and the debtor has rights in the collateral. These requirements were met here.

b) Not all instruments are pledgeable. To be pledgeable, the instrument must embody the obligation. Such instruments are treated as if they were themselves the obligations. Examples are a savings bankbook, an insurance policy, and a stock certificate.

c) Under the Restatement of Security, only an "indispensable instrument" may be used for a pledge. Such instruments are those the possession of which is necessary for the enjoyment, transfer, or enforcement of the interest in the intangible.

d) The warrants at issue here satisfy the requirements of pledgeability.

Cooke v. Haddon

d. Duty to preserve collateral--Cooke v. Haddon, 176 Eng. Rep. 103 (1862).

1) Facts. Cooke (P) borrowed money from Haddon (D) and gave as collateral four cases of champagne and a note. P did not pay the entire debt and D obtained a judgment for the balance. After D executed the judgment and the debt was satisfied, P demanded the return of the champagne. D referred P to a third party, who told P that part of the champagne had been drunk. P brought suit for the value of the champagne, and D claimed that the execution of the judgment did not satisfy the debt because of a miscalculation.

2) Issue. Does a pledgee have a duty to preserve collateral in his possession?

3) Held. Yes. Judgment for P.

a) A pledgee may not dispose of collateral, because by so doing he forfeits his lien.

b) Here, D allowed the collateral to be used up and is therefore liable for the value of the champagne.

Capos v. Mid-America National Bank of Chicago

e. Duty to foreclose--Capos v. Mid-America National Bank of Chicago, 581 F.2d 676 (7th Cir. 1978).

1) Facts. Capos (P) bought 10,000 shares of stock in Diversified Metals Corp., using half of them as collateral. P moved the loan to Mid-America National Bank of Chicago (D) and consolidated it with other loans for a total indebtedness of $120,000, secured by 6000 shares of Diversified worth $360,000. P borrowed more money from D, including some to buy more stock. Under Federal Reserve Board Regulation U, stock used as collateral to buy more stock must be valued at considerably less than its market value. Over time, the value of the stock fell. D had the right to sell the collateral when its value reached the amount of indebtedness, but it did not do so. When the value of the stock fell to $88,000, D proposed to sell the stock even though the debt was $147,000. P started a repayment plan instead and D did not sell the stock. The stock price continued to decline until it became almost worthless. P then brought suit claiming that D violated its duty to foreclose on the collateral when its value fell to the vicinity of the amount owed. D counterclaimed for principal and interest due. The trial court found for D on both claims and P appeals.

2)   Issue. Does a creditor have a duty to foreclose on collateral when its value becomes roughly equivalent to the amount of the debt secured?

3)   Held. No. Judgment affirmed.

   a)   P could have sold the stock before its value declined, since it was his investment and he knew what its value was. Once it declined below the amount of the debt, P could have agreed when D proposed to sell it. Any negligence in not cutting the loss was at least equally P's.

   b)   A creditor has no duty to the debtor to sell collateral stock that is declining in value. The debtor makes the investment decisions. The creditor has no duty to act as an investment adviser.

   c)   UCC section 9-207(1) requires a secured party to use reasonable care in the preservation of collateral in his possession, but this only applies to physical care of the chattel. It has no reference to the loss in market value of securities.

f.   Securities--General Electric Co. v. Tracey Service Co., Inc., 729 F.2d 1446 (3d Cir. 1984).

General Electric Co. v. Tracey Service Co., Inc.

1)   Facts. General Electric Co. (P) obtained a judgment against Tracey Service Co., Inc. (D). D owned a subsidiary, but had lost the stock certificate evidencing that ownership. P obtained a court order that resulted in the subsidiary issuing a certificate of stock in D's name. P obtained the certificate and sought a court order directing the marshall to seize it for execution. Continental Bank then intervened, based on a security agreement it had with D which gave Continental a security interest in all of D's general intangibles, including instruments. Continental had also filed a financing statement that covered all general intangibles and all proceeds of such. Continental claimed that it thus had a perfected security interest in D's stock in its subsidiary that was prior in time to P's levy. The trial court found for P on the ground that the security agreement did not cover the proceeds of general intangibles. Continental's interest in the subsidiary's stock depended on the security agreement's reference to instruments, but as to these, the filing of the financing statement did not perfect Continental's security interest against third parties. Continental appeals.

2)   Issue. May a creditor with a security agreement covering general intangibles, but not the proceeds of such intangibles, obtain a security interest in the proceeds by including them in the filed financing statement?

3)   Held. No. Judgment affirmed.

   a)   UCC section 9-306(c)(1) provides that a security interest in proceeds becomes unperfected 10 days after the debtor receives the proceeds unless the filed financing statement covers the original collateral and the proceeds are collateral in which a security interest may be perfected. Continental's filed financing statement covers general intangibles, and contains a description of the proceeds as instruments. It thus would satisfy section 9-306(c)(1).

b)   However, UCC section 9-203(a)(1) provides that a security interest is not enforceable against the debtor or third parties unless the collateral is in the possession of the secured party or the debtor has signed a security agreement which contains a description of the collateral. The financing statement D signed does not cover the proceeds of general intangibles. Continental's interest in the subsidiary terminated when D's interest in it changed from the general intangible of unissued stock to issued stock, an instrument.

c)   The secured party must take possession in order to perfect a security interest in instruments. The exception is for instruments which are proceeds of secured interests which may be perfected by filing [UCC §9-304(a)] but the proceeds become unperfected 10 days after receipt by the debtor unless the security interest in them is first perfected. [UCC §9-306(c)(3)] Continental did not obtain possession of the stock certificate within 10 days.

4)   Concurrence. D's interest in the subsidiary was an instrument, not a general intangible, so Continental never had a security interest in the stock. It never had possession of the instrument. Its security agreement did not describe the instrument. The fact that the instrument was not negotiable and was lost does not change the fact that Continental did not have a security interest in the instrument.

6.   Automatic Perfection. A financing statement must be filed to perfect all security interests except for some specific security interests set forth in UCC section 9-302(1). For these security interests, perfection occurs automatically upon attachment of the security interest. Probably the most significant of these is section 9-302(1)(d)—the purchase money security interest in consumer goods.

    a.   Basic rules. A purchase money security interest arises when the secured party advances money or credit to enable the debtor to purchase the collateral. Perfection occurs without filing. This rule recognizes the impracticality of a retail merchant filing for everything sold in retail installment contract. Also, because consumer goods are rarely used as collateral apart from the purchase price, there is little likelihood that later creditors would benefit from a filing. Consumer goods are those goods used or bought primarily for personal, family or household purposes. However, motor vehicles are specifically excluded from the purchase money rules under section 9-302(1)(d).

        1)   Secured party. The purchase money secured party may be either the seller who provides credit, or any other lender who gives value or incurs an obligation to allow the debtor to acquire the collateral or rights in it, but only if such value is actually used in the transaction by the debtor.

        2)   Extent of security interest. The purchase money security interest extends only to the amount advanced by the secured party.

3) **Security agreement.** Although no filing is necessary, the secured party must have a signed security agreement for the security interest to arise.

4) **Priority rules for non-inventory.** Under UCC section 9-312(4), a purchase money security interest in collateral other than inventory has priority over conflicting security interests in the same collateral, if the interest is perfected when the debtor takes possession of the collateral or within 10 days thereafter. It does not matter that the purchase money secured party knew that security interests were already filed at the time of sale. The rationale is that the other creditors are in no worse position than if the debtor had not acquired the goods.

5) **Priority rules for inventory.** A creditor may acquire a purchase money security interest in goods that will be inventory in the debtor's hands if the purchase money security interest is perfected when the debtor receives possession of the collateral and if the secured party gives prior written notice to any other secured party who has previously filed a financing statement covering inventory of the same type of goods that will be covered by the purchase money security interest.

b. **Limited scope--*In re* Manuel,** 507 F.2d 990 (5th Cir. 1975).

In re Manuel

1) **Facts.** Manuel (D) purchased furniture and later a TV from Roberts Furniture Co. He signed a purchase money security agreement for the TV which referred to the furniture contract and provided that the goods together would secure both contracts, as well as any future liabilities D might have toward Roberts. D filed a voluntary bankruptcy petition. Roberts sought reclamation in bankruptcy, but the bankruptcy judge found that, except for the TV, Roberts did not acquire a purchase money security interest and did not perfect its security interest. The district court agreed, and would have denied reclamation for the TV as well except that there was no cross appeal on that issue. D appeals.

2) **Issue.** Does a purchase money security interest in consumer goods arise when the security interest covers property in addition to that purchased when the security interest was created?

3) **Held.** No. Judgment affirmed.

a) A purchase money security interest must be in the item purchased. It cannot exceed the price of what is purchased in the transaction that created the security interest.

b) Here, Roberts took a security interest in collateral to secure debt other than its own price, which is beyond the scope of a purchase money security interest.

7. **Transactions in More Than One State.** Multistate transactions and removal of collateral from one state to another are fairly common occurrences. UCC section 9-103 provides rules for how security interests may be perfected in such situations.

a.   **Last event test.** Perfection is determined by the law of the state where the collateral is located when the last event occurs on which is based the assertion that the security interest is perfected or unperfected. [UCC §9-103(1)(b)] Usually, filing is the last event, so the filing must be done where the collateral is located when the filing takes place.

b.   **Removal of collateral to another state.** If a debtor moves collateral to a state other than that wherein the security interest was properly perfected, the security interest must be reperfected in the new state within four months after the removal. This rule applies whether or not the secured party knew or consented to the removal. If reperfection is accomplished within the four months, the perfection relates back to the date of the original perfection. If the four months lapse before reperfection, the relation back rule does not apply and the security interest is subordinate to intervening lien creditors.

c.   **Motor vehicles.** Goods covered by a certificate of title law are not subject to the normal filing requirements. In states with a certificate of title system, a security interest can be perfected only by complying with the state system. Some states do not have a certificate of title system or do not require that liens be recorded on the certificate. In such states, a filing under the UCC is the proper way to perfect a security interest in a motor vehicle.

d.   **Interstate transfer of motor vehicles.** The different systems of perfecting security interests in motor vehicles raises potential for fraud. A person could buy a car in a non-certificate state, then take it to a certificate state and obtain a clear title because the second state does not check the filing records of the first state. The four-month rule for reperfecting applies to such cases. However, if a motor vehicle is covered by a certificate of title showing the security interest, the interest remains perfected wherever the vehicle is taken until the vehicle is registered in another state.

Konkel v.
Golden Plains
Credit Union

e.   **Filing on farm equipment--Konkel v. Golden Plains Credit Union,** 778 P.2d 660 (Colo. 1989).

1)   **Facts.** Golden Plains Credit Union (P) filed a financing statement in May 1978 on two combines it financed for Lewis. P filed in Hamilton County, Kansas, where Lewis lived. In 1979, Lewis took the combines to Baca County, Colorado, where he had purchased a farm. Lewis sold one of the combines to Konkel (D) in Colorado. D had no actual knowledge of P's security interest and did not search to find P's filing. D sold the combine to a Colorado farmer. P sued D in Colorado for conversion. D moved for summary judgment on the ground that P had failed to file a financing statement in Colorado within four months of the date Lewis moved the combine there as required by UCC section 9-103(1)(d)(i). The trial court granted the motion. The court of appeals reversed, holding that section 9-103(3) governing mobile goods was the applicable provision, so that P's interest was good until four months after a change in Lewis's location. The Colorado Supreme Court granted certiorari.

2)   **Issue.** Is a security interest in farm equipment perfected if filed in the county where it is normally used?

3)   **Held.** Yes. Judgment reversed and remanded.

a)   D claims P never perfected its security interest because it did not file with the Kansas Secretary of State. Under the Kansas UCC section 9-401(1)(a), a security interest in equipment used in farming operations may be filed in the county where the debtor lives (a "local filing"). This is an exception to the normal practice of "central filing" with the secretary of state, which would be required if the combine is classified as commercial equipment.

b)   In the absence of a statutory definition, courts have applied various tests to determine whether collateral is "equipment used in farming operations." The "normal use test" focuses on the collateral's inherent qualities and its normal uses. The "intended use test" focuses on the use the debtor intended to make of the collateral as contemplated by the parties at the time of sale. The "actual use test" focuses on the debtor's actual use of the collateral.

c)   Most courts use the latter two tests, but the Kansas legislature prefers the actual use test. On remand, the trial court must classify the combine by applying the actual use test to determine whether P's local filing was sufficient.

d)   If the trial court classifies the combine as "equipment used in farming operations" based on Lewis' actual use, it must then decide whether P's security interest remained in effect after D bought it. This requires classification of the combine as an "ordinary good" or a "mobile good." Under UCC section 9-103(1), a security interest in ordinary goods properly perfected in one state expires four months after being taken to another state. This gives secured creditors four months to relocate the goods and file a second financing statement before losing priority. Under section 9-103(3), a security interest in mobile goods properly perfected in one state expires four months after a change in the debtor's location to another jurisdiction.

e)   The combine in this case is a mobile good under UCC section 9-103(3)(a), which cites commercial harvesting machinery as an example. Thus, the date Lewis brought the combine into Colorado is irrelevant. On remand, the court must determine whether and when Lewis changed his location.

4)   **Comment.** The intended use test favors the secured creditor, who can rely on the debtor's statement, possibly included in the financing documents, about the intended use at the time the loan is made. The actual use test favors third-party creditors. In close cases, prudent creditors should file financing statements both locally and centrally to protect against adverse subsequent judicial classifications.

f.   **Certificate of title rule--*In re* Nunley**, 21 B.R. 826 (Bankr. E.D. Tenn. 1982).   *In re* Nunley

1)   **Facts.** Nunley (D), a Virginia resident, bought a tractor truck and executed a security agreement, which was assigned to Associates Commercial Corp. (P). P obtained a Virginia certificate of title reflecting its lien. D then registered the truck in Florida as requested by his employer. A year later, D registered the truck in Oklahoma. A few months later D moved to

Tennessee. More than four months later, D filed for bankruptcy. P claims it has a perfected security interest.

2) **Issue.** Does a creditor's perfected security interest in a vehicle, shown on a certificate of title, remain perfected even though the vehicle is registered in another state, and the debtor then removes the vehicle to a third state?

3) **Held.** Yes. Judgment for P.

a) Under UCC section 9-103(4), if personal property is covered by a certificate of title which requires indication on the title of any security interest in the property as a condition of perfection, then the perfection is governed by the law of the jurisdiction which issued the certificate. Thus, Virginia law applies.

b) In a comparable case decided by the sixth circuit, the court held that under the 1972 version of section 9-103(4), a security interest noted on a certificate of title is properly perfected as against a bankruptcy trustee. The only difference between that case and this one is that here, D registered the truck in two other states before removing it from Virginia to Tennessee.

c) Under the Virginia version of UCC section 9-103(2)(b), perfection is governed by Virginia law until four months after the goods are removed from the state and thereafter until the goods are registered in another jurisdiction. There was no registration of the truck in another jurisdiction after D removed it from Virginia to Tennessee. Thus, Virginia law applies and the interest remains perfected because the Virginia certificate of title is valid and unsurrendered.

Citicorp (USA) v. Davidson Lumber Co.

8. **Perfection in Proceeds--Citicorp (USA) v. Davidson Lumber Co.,** 718 F.2d 1030 (11th Cir. 1983).

a. **Facts.** Citicorp (USA) and another bank (Ps) shared a perfected security interest in various assets owned by Davidson Lumber Co. (D), including general intangibles. Before D's creditors filed an involuntary petition under Chapter 7, D received a federal tax refund of about $1.3 million. Ps knew D would receive this money, but did not know when. Unknown to Ps, D used the refund to buy a certificate of deposit ("CD"). Ps did not take possession of the CD. The bankruptcy court held that Ps' security interest was unperfected. The district court held that the CD was case proceeds and that Ps had a continuing perfected security interest in the CD under UCC section 9-306(1). The trustee appeals.

b. **Issue.** Is a certificate of deposit cash proceeds?

c. **Held.** No. Judgment reversed.

1) A perfected security interest in collateral continues in the proceeds generated by disposition of that collateral for at least 10 days, and may continue beyond the tenth day depending on how the proceeds are classified under UCC section 9-306.

2)   A perfected security interest in collateral may continue as a perfected security interest beyond 10 days after the debtor receives the proceeds if a filed financing statement covers the original collateral and the proceeds are identifiable cash proceeds. Money, checks, deposit accounts, and the like are cash proceeds; all other proceeds are non-cash proceeds.

3)   A CD is not a check or money. Under a 1979 amendment to UCC section 9-105(1)(e), the term "deposit account" means something other than an account evidenced by a certificate of deposit. Since the legislature specifically excluded CDs from the definition of deposit account, it would be illogical to interpret the term "and the like" to include CDs. The legislature clearly intended that CDs are not cash proceeds.

4)   Ps argue that this result would allow a debtor to conceal proceeds of collateral from secured creditors and secretly convert them to CDs, which require perfection by possession, thereby extinguishing the secured creditor's rights. However, creditors may contractually require debtors to permit on-premises inspections of their books or may require that payments owed to the debtor be sent directly to the creditor, including tax refunds.

9.   **Perfection in Multiple Assets Through Chattel Paper--*In re* Leasing Consultants, Inc.**, 486 F.2d 367 (2d Cir. 1973).

In re Leasing Consultants, Inc.

a.   **Facts.** Leasing Consultants, Inc., a New York corporation, leased heavy equipment to Plastimetrix Corp. The leased equipment was located in New Jersey. Leasing assigned the leases to First National City Bank (P) as security for a loan. The agreement provided that Leasing assigned "a continuing security interest in the leases and the property leased." P filed the security agreement in New York but not in New Jersey. Leasing went bankrupt in New York and two weeks later Plastimetrix went bankrupt in New Jersey. Leasing's trustee (D) and P agreed to sell the equipment and retain their respective rights in the proceeds. D petitioned the bankruptcy referee to direct P to turn over the proceeds. The referee did so on the ground that P was required to file a financing statement in New Jersey in order to perfect a security interest in the equipment. The district court agreed, and P appeals.

b.   **Issue.** Must a security interest in goods be filed where the goods are located in order to be perfected?

c.   **Held.** Yes. Judgment affirmed.

1)   If the lease was intended as a security device, Plastimetrix would become the owner at the end of the term and Leasing would hold a security interest but no reversionary right. If the lease was a true lease, however, Leasing would have a reversionary interest in the goods.

2)   Because P received a security interest, the provisions of the UCC apply. Clearly, P perfected a security interest in the chattel paper by filing in New York and by taking possession of the leases. However,

the rights in the lease and the rights in the goods are different.

3) The equipment itself is goods under the UCC. Because it was located in New Jersey, any security interest in the equipment can be perfected only be complying with New Jersey law. P failed to do so, and D as trustee has priority under section 9-301.

4) P claims that the reversionary interest was an intangible interest located in New York. However, the interest is in goods, not intangibles, so this argument fails.

5) The case must be remanded to determine whether the lease was a true lease and, if so, whether the proceeds of the sale represent the sale of the leasehold in addition to the sale of the reversionary interest.

d. **Comment**. The requirement that a security interest be filed where the goods are located reflects the practical consideration that a potential creditor who observes the heavy equipment would believe he could discover all nonpossessory interests within the state in which the goods are located.

D. PRIORITIES

1. **Introduction.** When collateral is insufficient to satisfy all security interests in the collateral, the competing interests must be sorted out to determine who recovers first; in other words, which security interest has priority. The first party to obtain a security interest is not necessarily the one who prevails. It is helpful in evaluating priority cases to remember the various types of claimants that may assert a claim.

   a. **Debtor.** The person owing payment or other performance of the secured obligation is the debtor. This is usually the owner of the collateral.

   b. **Unsecured or general creditor.** A creditor who has a personal claim against the debtor, but no security interest in collateral, is an unsecured creditor. An unsecured creditor can obtain a security interest if the debtor agrees to give him one, or if the creditor sues on the claim, prevails, and then uses the judicial process to levy on the collateral.

   c. **Judicial lien creditor.** A formerly unsecured or general creditor may acquire a lien through the judicial process, thereby becoming a judicial lien creditor. The UCC uses this term to apply to a trustee in bankruptcy as well.

   d. **Secured creditor.** A creditor who receives a security interest in specific collateral from the debtor and then takes the necessary steps for the security interest to attach is a secured creditor.

e. **Perfected and secured creditor.** A secured creditor who takes the necessary steps to perfect its security interest becomes a perfected and secured creditor.

f. **Statutory lien creditor.** Certain liens arise automatically by statute or common law. These include tax liens, mechanics liens, and liens by landlords, lawyers, artisans, and so forth.

g. **Buyers.** If the debtor sells the collateral to a good faith buyer, the buyer's interest generally prevails over the debtor's creditors.

2. **Priority Among Competing Security Interests in the Same Collateral.**

a. **Unperfected creditors.** Between unperfected creditors, the order of attachment determines priority. An unperfected creditor is subordinate to any perfected secured party and to any judicial lien creditors. [UCC §9-310]

b. **Perfected creditors.** Under section 9-312(5) of the 1972 version of the UCC, the secured party who is the first either to file or perfect its security interest has priority. This gives the party who files first top priority, even over a later creditor who perfects first, such as by taking possession after the first creditor's filing. An interest perfected by a method other than filing has priority over a competing interest filed after the perfection.

c. **Purchase money security.** As discussed previously, a purchase money security interest has priority over other perfected security interests so long as the requirements of UCC section 9-312(4) are complied with.

d. **Cattle bred from collateral--*In re* Smith,** 29 B.R. 690 (Bankr. W.D. Mo. 1983).   *In re Smith*

    1) **Facts.** In August 1976, the Bank (P) took and properly filed a security interest in "all livestock now owned and after acquired" by Smith (D). At the time, D did not own any livestock. In March 1979, D borrowed money from the Farmers Home Administration ("FHA"), giving FHA a security interest in cattle and hogs. The financing statement was filed and designated proceeds and products thereof, including livestock, as security. D used the money to buy 19 cows and 20 pigs. Between June 1981 and January 1982, D borrowed more money from P. D gave P four financial statements which did not refer to the debt to FHA. In August 1981, P filed a continuation statement of its earlier UCC filing. In March 1982, FHA foreclosed its security interest in the cattle and sold 13 cows and seven calves, applying the proceeds against the loan. D did not own any pigs at the time. D filed for bankruptcy, and P filed this petition seeking a determination of priorities.

    2) **Issue.** Are cattle bred from security for a purchase money security interest themselves purchase money security?

    3) **Held.** No. Judgment for P.

a)   FHA filed its financing statement before it loaned the money, and D used a substantial part of the money to buy the pigs and cattle within two months of the advance. FHA had a purchase money security interest which was perfected when D received the collateral. Therefore, FHA had priority in the purchased cattle over P's "after-acquired" rights.

b)   P claims that FHA's security agreement lost its purchase money character and priority as to cattle produced from those purchased. UCC sections 9-314 and 9-315 allow a security interest to follow collateral even if it is transformed, but this applies for collateral that is transformed, not collateral that expands through its own effort such as cattle do.

c)   Because the purchase money security interest priority is an exception to the general rule, it is narrowly construed. This is not a case where new calves were bought to replace cattle that had died. The calves were bred, not purchased, and are thus after-acquired. The purchase money security interest does not apply to the calves.

d)   Although FHA's security agreement covers all increases, P's security interest has priority because it was first in time. Therefore, P is entitled to the proceeds from the sale of those cattle which did not retain purchase money character at the time of foreclosure.

e.   **After-acquired property clause--John Deere Co. v. Production Credit Association of Murfreesboro,** 686 S.W.2d 904 (Ct. App. Tenn. 1984).

1)   **Facts.** The Production Credit Association of Murfreesboro (D) acquired a security interest in all farm machinery and equipment, including harvesting equipment, owned by Willis and all such property acquired in the future. Several months later, Willis's combine burned and the insurance proceeds were paid to D and applied to Willis's debt. Willis then borrowed about $18,000 from D to use as a down payment on a new combine. Willis signed a retail installment contract for the balance of the purchase price of $59,000. The financing statement and security agreement were assigned to John Deere Co. (P). Willis later defaulted on both debts and released the combine to D. He owed P over $52,000 and owed D the full amount of its loan, since Willis never made payments on D's loan. P sued seeking possession and sale of the combine. D claimed it had a purchase money security interest in the combine for the amount loaned for the down payment. The lower court held that neither had priority over the other and that their rights in the proceeds were pro rata, according to the amount each loaned to Willis. P appeals.

2)   **Issue.** Is an after-acquired property clause in a filed financing statement sufficient to create a purchase money security interest when the creditor lends additional money for the purchase of specific collateral?

3)   **Held.** Yes. Judgment reversed in part.

a)   When value given is used by the debtor to purchase collateral, the secured party has a purchase money security interest in the collateral which has priority over other security interests in the same collateral, so long as the interest is perfected by filing a financing statement within 20 days of the debtor receiving possession of the collateral.

b)   Clearly P has a perfected purchase money security interest in the combine. D also clearly gave Willis money to purchase the collateral. However, D did not file a financing statement after this loan; it is relying instead on the earlier filing which contained an after-acquired property clause.

c)   The financing statement D had on file would have notified P of the possibility that D had an interest in the collateral, if P had checked the filings. P was responsible to investigate further if it wanted to make sure it had the highest priority in the collateral. D only has a purchase money security interest to the extent of the purchase money, not for the other amounts it lent. D was not required to file a second financing statement to ensure a purchase money security interest.

d)   Since both P and D have perfected purchase money security interests in the combine, priority is determined by which filed first. D filed well before P, so its interest is superior to P's. D is entitled to its money out of the sale of the combine, and P is entitled to the balance.

3.   **Buyers of Goods.** A buyer of collateral subject to an unperfected security interest almost always takes the property free of the creditor's right to reclaim it. A buyer of goods from a dealer's inventory in the ordinary course of business takes free of perfected security interests in the inventory held by the dealer's creditors, even if the buyer knows that the inventory is covered by a security interest, so long as the buyer does not know that the sale violates the terms of the security agreement. [UCC §9-307(1)]

a.   **Prepaying buyer--Chrysler Corp. v. Adamatic, Inc.,** 208 N.W.2d 97 (Wis. 1973).

    Chrysler Corp. v. Adamatic, Inc.

1)   **Facts.** Adamatic, Inc. (D) was a machinery manufacturer financed by Lakeshore Commercial Finance Corp. ("Lakeshore"), which had taken and perfected a security interest in D's inventory and other assets. Chrysler Corp. (P) contracted with D for the purchase of a prototype six-coil stator winder, used to construct alternators. D was to build the machine to P's specifications and was to also make a cell inserter to be used with the winder. The total price for the two units was about $81,000. P agreed to make progress payments and paid 90% of the price when D delivered the machines to P. The winder failed to work satisfactorily, and P returned it to D for additional work. The parties agreed that D would convert the six-coil winder to a 12-coil winder for an additional $22,000. P retained title to the goods. P also contracted to buy three 12-coil winders at a price of nearly $84,000 per unit. P knew Lakeshore was financing D. Due to D's poor financial position, P agreed to make progress payments to help finance the production. P paid $105,000 in progress payments to D, which turned the money over to Lakeshore. D was nearly finished with only one of the 12-coil winders when construction was

slowed because D was unable to pay its suppliers. P attempted to take delivery of the first 12-coil winder, even though it was incomplete, but Lakeshore objected, asserting its rights to possession pursuant to its perfected security interest in the machines. P brought a replevin action against D, and the sheriff seized the 12-coil winders, the cell inserter, and the six-coil winder which had been stripped of usable parts. The goods were given to P, and D went into receivership. At trial, the jury found that P was a buyer in the ordinary course of business and that Lakeshore had wrongfully caused D to retain the property. It awarded P damages. The trial court entered judgment that P was entitled to the goods but had to pay Lakeshore the value of the machines less the amounts which P had already paid D. P appeals.

2) **Issue.** Does a buyer who makes progress payments under a sales contract become a buyer in ordinary course of business when it takes delivery of the goods by replevin?

3) **Held.** No. Judgment reversed.

   a) Title to the six-coil winder and the cell inserter had been transferred to P when the goods were shipped to P. It was a completed sale, and under UCC section 9-307(1), P took the machines free of Lakeshore's security interest. Although P was displeased with the performance of the winder, P never rejected it, but instead treated it as its own. P never relinquished title, even when it returned the winder to D for further work. Lakeshore's security interest could not re-attach without a rejection by P. D held these goods as bailee, so P was entitled to replevin of the six-coil winder and cell inserter.

   b) If P had not seized the 12-coil winders, they would have been part of D's inventory and upon D's default Lakeshore could have taken possession of the machines and sold them. Lakeshore's security interest follows the collateral into the hands of subsequent owners, including P, and P's possession is subject to Lakeshore's interest unless P is a buyer in ordinary course of business.

   c) P claims it became a buyer in ordinary course of business when it entered the contract to buy the 12-coil winders, thereby cutting off Lakeshore's security interest. However, a buyer in ordinary course must buy without the knowledge that the sale violates the rights of a third party. When P replevied, it knew of Lakeshore's perfected security interest.

   d) A buyer who obtains title to the goods does not lose its status as a buyer in ordinary course just because it has not taken possession. But P claims it is a buyer in ordinary course because the replevin action was part of the process by which title passed. Replevin is an unusual step. Taking possession by replevin is not in the ordinary course of business.

   e) Because P was not a buyer in ordinary course of business, it holds the machines subject to the security interest of Lakeshore. P cannot complain of the result merely because it made progress payments. It could have taken steps to protect its interests.

b. **Course of dealing may constitute consent--Lisbon Bank & Trust Co. v. Murray,** 206 N.W.2d 96 (Iowa 1973).

1) **Facts.** The Lisbon Bank & Trust Co. (P) loaned money to Meier to purchase 48 heifers and received a duly perfected security interest in the cattle. Meier sold 12 of the heifers to Murray (D), and later defaulted on his debt to P and filed bankruptcy. P sued to recover from D the money he had paid to Meier for the heifers. The trial court dismissed P's suit, finding that the sale was made free of P's lien because Meier was authorized to sell the cattle. P appeals.

2) **Issue.** May a lender's course of dealing with a debtor constitute implied consent to the sale of collateral by the debtor?

3) **Held.** Yes. Judgment affirmed.

   a) Meier had operated a farm which P financed over a period of time. Even though the security agreements did not authorize sales, the parties had a general course of dealing that permitted Meier to sell collateral and apply the proceeds either to substitutions or on the notes. P claims it did not know of the sale until after Meier declared bankruptcy, but Meier claims he told P when he deposited D's check what the payment was for. Meier also claimed he used the money to buy substitute collateral.

   b) Meier and D both testified that Meier told D about the security agreement and that Meier would take care of it. The waiver was between P and Meier; when the sale is authorized, the lien is divested and the buyer takes the property free of it.

   c) Under UCC section 1-205(3), evidence of a course of dealing may give particular meaning to and supplement or qualify terms of an agreement. Authority to sell may be implied from a prior course of dealing in the absence of a security agreement provision prohibiting sale without written consent. This authority is not impaired by the fact that Meier did not use the proceeds to pay on the debt.

4. **Priority Among Buyers of Intangibles.**

a. **Basic rules.** Certain buyers of quasi-tangible paper collateral such as instruments, documents and chattel paper, may acquire the property free of perfected security interests in the paper. [UCC §9-309] The buyer must be (i) a holder in due course of negotiable instruments; (ii) a holder to whom a negotiable document of title has been negotiated; or (iii) a bona fide purchaser of investment securities (instruments). A buyer of chattel paper who gives new value and takes possession of the collateral in the ordinary course of business takes free of any security interest it does not know about at the time of purchase if the security interest is only temporarily perfected under sections 9-304 or 9-306.

Rex Financial
Corp. v.
Great Western
Bank & Trust

b. **Inventory financer--Rex Financial Corp. v. Great Western Bank & Trust,** 532 P.2d 558 (Ct. App. Ariz. 1975).

1) **Facts.** Rex Financial Corp. (P) agreed to finance a mobile home dealer's inventory of mobile homes, and received manufacturer's certificates of origin as security, together with a security interest in the homes through a security agreement. The dealer sold four of the homes in the regular course of business to individuals on security agreement contracts. These contracts were then sold and assigned to Great Western Bank & Trust (D). The dealer did not use the proceeds to pay P, however. P brought suit to determine the parties' priorities. The trial court granted summary judgment for D and P appeals.

2) **Issue.** Does an inventory financer lose priority in proceeds when the purchaser gives chattel paper which is then sold and transferred to another financer in the ordinary course of his business?

3) **Held.** Yes. Judgment affirmed.

a) D knew of P's security interest when it bought the paper. Under UCC section 9-308, a purchaser of chattel paper who gives new value and takes possession of it in the ordinary course of his business has priority over a security interest in chattel paper which is claimed merely as proceeds of inventory subject to a security interest, even though he knows that the specific paper is subject to the security interest.

b) P argues that the manufacturer's certificates of origin were part of the chattel paper and would have to be possessed by D for D to have priority. However, the certificates do not fall within the definition of chattel paper given in UCC section 9-105(1)(b).

c) UCC section 9-308 also requires that the buyer of chattel paper act in the ordinary course of his business. D acted as it normally does to obtain this type of chattel paper. D expected the dealer to pay P. This is not the same requirement as the buyer in the ordinary course of business used elsewhere in the UCC.

d) P claims its security interest merely as proceeds of inventory subject to a security interest. P, an inventory financer, had a security in the mobile homes and the proceeds upon sale, but it did not enter any new transaction with the dealer. P could have protected itself by requiring all security agreements executed on sale of the homes to be turned over immediately to P, or if sold, that all payments for the security agreements be made to P.

Transamerica
Insurance Co.
v. Barnett
Bank of
Marion Coun-
ty, N.A.

c. **Priority among claims to accounts--Transamerica Insurance Co. v. Barnett Bank of Marion County, N.A.,** 540 So. 2d 113 (Fla. 1989).

1) **Facts.** Transamerica Insurance Company (P) contracted with Turner to provide surety bonds for Turner's construction projects. The parties had an indemnity agreement that constituted a security agreement and provided that, in the event of default, Turner's accounts receivable were assigned to P. Turner obtained loans from Barnett Bank of Marion County, N.A. (D) and gave D a security interest in its accounts receivable. D filed its security interest before P filed its security interest. Each construction contract provided for retainages for the respective owners as well as the payment and performance bonds. Turner defaulted, and P sued to recover on the accounts receivable. The trial court held that D's prior perfection gave it priority over P's claims based on equitable subrogation. The court found that P's equitable subrogation rights arose from standing in Turner's shoes, not in the shoes of the owner/obligee and labors and materialmen involved in the construction projects. The appellate court affirmed, and the Florida Supreme Court granted certiorari.

2) **Issue.** Are a surety's equitable subrogation rights limited to rights it obtains by standing in the shoes of the defaulting contractor?

3) **Held.** No. Judgment reversed.

   a) The lower courts rejected the "federal view" that sureties have priority through equitable subrogation arising from owner/obligees, laborers, and materialmen. This narrow approach is inconsistent with the purpose of a surety bond, which is to protect the obligees. A surety who pays the debt of another is entitled to all the rights of the person he paid to enforce his right to be reimbursed. Sureties such as P undertake duties that allow them to step into three sets of shoes.

   b) When the contractor defaults and the surety pays all the bills of the job and completes the job, it stands in the shoes of the contractor for receivables due; in the shoes of the laborers and materialmen who have been paid by the surety and who may have had liens; and in the shoes of the owner for whom the job was completed.

   c) The lower courts held that P's assignment from Turner was a security interest, but UCC section 9-104(6) excludes assignments to assignees who are to do the performance under the contract, so the UCC does not change the well-established rules giving priority to a surety assignment. Even if P's assignment was a security interest, it would not abrogate P's surety rights under the doctrine of equitable subrogation, which arises under the law and not by contract.

   d) Giving priority to the claims of the surety is good policy because everyone involved has an interest in prompt performance of the contract by the surety.

4) **Comment.** A judge who dissented in the lower court noted that almost all post-UCC decisions have held that (i) the surety's equitable right of subrogation is not a consensual security interest; (ii) no UCC filing is necessary to perfect the surety's interest; and (iii) the surety's interest continues after adoption of the UCC to be superior to the claim of a contract assignee, such as a bank.

5. **Priority Through Transfers of Assets--Bank of the West v. Commercial Credit Financial Services, Inc.**, 852 F.2d 1162 (9th Cir. 1988).

a. **Facts.** Bank of the West (P) loaned $4 million to Allied, a wholly owned subsidiary of BWTC, and obtained a security interest in Allied's present and future-acquired inventory, accounts, and proceeds. P perfected by filing in April 1982. In 1983, P demanded repayment of the outstanding loan balance of $1.8 million due to Allied's poor financial condition, but Allied renegotiated the loan and gave P a new security agreement. On January 13, 1984, BCI, another wholly owned subsidiary of BWTC, entered a factoring agreement with Commercial Credit Financial Services, Inc. (D), which provided that BCI would assign its accounts to D. D would then collect the accounts and remit the money to BCI, less a commission. BCI granted D a security interest in its present and after-acquired accounts and inventory and proceeds. D perfected by filing in January 1984. In August 1983, BWTC contributed its beverage business to BCI. By July 1, 1994, BCI transferred the beverage business to Allied. Thus, both P and D had perfected security interests in the inventory and accounts transferred from BCI to Allied, as well as the inventory and accounts acquired by Allied after the July 1, 1984 transfer. D factored a post-transfer account, and P sued for conversion. The trial court found for P and D appeals.

b. **Issue.** May the transferee of assets subject to a security interest acquire greater rights in the assets than the transferor had?

c. **Held.** No. Judgment reversed.

   1) The trial court applied the priority rules of UCC section 9-312(5), which gives priority to the first to file. Since P filed before D, the court held that P had priority when BCI transferred the assets to Allied, because P's after-acquired property clause in its security agreement with Allied covered the assets once transferred, and D's security interest in the same assets was filed after P's filing.

   2) The facts in this case have been regarded by commentators as a hypothetical situation in which the UCC fails to resolve a priority dispute properly. Before the transfer from BCI to Allied, D had a perfected security interest in the collateral. After the transfer, D's perfected security interest suddenly becomes subordinate to P's, even though D had taken all steps required by the UCC to announce its secured interest to potential creditors of BCI. P's security interest came into play regarding BCI's assets under the after-acquired clause only because BCI made an unauthorized disposition of the collateral. Applying UCC section 9-312(5) in this situation produces an unsatisfactory result because section 9-312(5) did not contemplate the duel debtor dilemma.

   3) The better approach is to apply a liberal and flexible construction of the UCC and its objectives. Section 9-312(5) focuses on prompt filing to protect future creditors of the debtor. It penalizes creditors who have a security interest but do not file by giving priority to a later creditor who files more promptly. This solves the problem of secret security interests. But in this case, the notice-giving function

of section 9-312(5) does not apply; P can't claim that it relied to its detriment on the absence of a filing by D.

4) The second purpose of UCC section 9-312(5) is an implied commitment to a secured creditor who has filed that, except for limited situations such as a purchase money security interest, no subsequent creditor will be able to defeat the complying creditor's security interest. This "claim staking" function should give assurance to a secured creditor who has complied that its claim will prevail against subsequently arising interests in the same property. Applying section 9-312(5) to this case produces a contrary result, because D loses its claim.

5) The best approach in this case is to apply the common sense notion that a creditor cannot convey to another more than it owns; *i.e.,* Allied cannot acquire any greater rights in the beverage business's assets than BCI had in them. Under UCC section 9-306(2), a security interest follows collateral into the hands of a transferee when there is an unauthorized disposition by the transferor. Thus, Allied as the transferee of an unauthorized disposition must take subject to the security interest of BCI's creditor, D. This fulfills the claim staking function that protects D.

6. **Priority in Fixtures--*In re* Fink,** 4 B.R. 741 (Bankr. W.D.N.Y. 1980).

a. **Facts.** Fink (D) bought a mobile home from Palmer Mobile Homes and entered a retail installment contract. Palmer assigned the security interest to Endicott the same day. Endicott filed a financing statement. D had the home delivered to property she was leasing from Wemco. D contracted to buy the real estate from Wemco and gave Wemco a purchase money mortgage for the full purchase price. The home was placed on an excavated foundation of concrete footers, concrete blocks, and steel and wooden beams. A septic tank was installed, and water and electrical lines were connected. At trial, Palmer, who installed the home, testified that he could remove and transport the home for about $500. Wemco's officer testified that the house was attached to the realty the same as any frame house. Wemco had no notice of Endicott's interest in the house. The trustee brought an action to avoid Endicott's claimed security interest and to preserve Wemco's interest.

b. **Issue.** May a mobile home become a fixture even though it may be disassembled and moved?

c. **Held.** Yes. Judgment for Wemco.

1) UCC section 9-302(1)(d) applies to chattels, including mobile homes, and requires that a financing statement must be filed to perfect a security interest. Section 9-313 requires a special filing for fixtures. The filing must be in the same place where the real estate mortgage is filed. Under UCC section 9-402(5), the financing statement must show that it covers this type of collateral, must recite that it is to be indexed in the real estate records, and must contain a description of the real estate and the name of the record owner.

2) Endicott's security interest would prevail only if the home did not become a fixture by annexation to the real property. Under UCC section 9-313, goods are fixtures when they become so related to particular real estate that an interest in them arises under real estate law. A fixture is a former chattel which becomes part of realty but does not lose its separate physical identity.

3) Three requisites for fixtures have been recognized: (i) actual annexation of the real property or something appurtenant thereto; (ii) application to the use or purpose to which that part of the realty with which it is connected is appropriated; and (iii) the intention of the party making the annexation to make a permanent accession to the freehold.

4) In this case, the home was intended to become part of the realty. D bought the home shortly before buying the realty. It was installed on a permanent foundation. It had the appearance of a normal ranch house. It could only be moved by dismantling it. Thus, it is a fixture and Wemco has priority. Endicott is an unsecured creditor.

7. **Security Interests through Labor, Accession, or Commingling.**

a. **Accessions.** Security interests in accessions (goods attached to other goods) fall within the normal UCC rules. A party whose security interest attaches before the goods are installed in or affixed to other goods takes priority over a party who has an interest in the whole of the goods. [UCC §9-314(1)]

b. **Commingled and processed goods.** UCC section 9-315 provides similar rules for commingled and processed goods. So long as the collateral is still identifiable the security interest is unaffected even if the collateral changes form. When the collateral is no longer identifiable, the perfected security interest in the goods that became part of a product or mass extends to the product or mass. When more than one secured party has an interest in a mass of processed or assembled goods, each of the conflicting interests are treated equally, so that each has an interest in the mass in the ratio that the original cost of the goods covered by each security interest bears to the cost of the total mass.

First National
Bank of Brush
v. Bostron

c. **Consumption of feed by cattle--First National Bank of Brush v. Bostron,** 564 P.2d 964 (Ct. App. Colo. 1977).

1) **Facts.** Weiss raised cattle and feed crops. He entered a joint venture with Bostron (D), agreeing to provide the labor to raise heifers if D provided the money. D bought the heifers with money borrowed from the First National Bank of Brush (P), which retained a perfected purchase money security interest in the cattle. D fed both his cattle and the joint venture cattle with feed in which the Colorado High Plains Agricultural Credit Corp. ("ACC") had a security interest. D and Weiss sold their cattle at a loss, and owed P money. None of the proceeds were paid to ACC. P sued Weiss and D, and ACC intervened claiming an interest in any recovery P had against D. Weiss was bankrupt. ACC's claim against D was based solely on the

benefit which D individually received from the joint venture cattle being fed Weiss's feed. The trial court found for P and ACC appeals.

    2)   **Issue.** Does a perfected security interest in fee survive consumption of the feed by cattle in which the secured party has no interest?

    3)   **Held.** No. Judgment affirmed.

        a)   Under UCC section 9-315, a perfected security interest in goods continues in the product or mass of which the goods become a part if the identity of the goods is lost in the product or mass or if the financing statement also covers the product into which the goods have been manufactured, processed or assembled.

        b)   Cattle are neither a product nor a mass. The feed was not manufactured, processed, assembled, or commingled; it was consumed just as gasoline is consumed by motor vehicles. The feed not only lost its identity but also it ceased to exist.

        c)   ACC claims also that the cattle are proceeds of the feed under UCC section 9-306. But ACC authorized the disposition of the feed by Weiss to the joint venture. In addition, proceeds are what is received when collateral is disposed of, but nothing was received when the feed was consumed. By ACC's reasoning, it could follow the cattle through the butcher shop into the hands of consumers.

E.   DEFAULT AND FORECLOSURE

    1.   **Introduction.** The conditions or events that constitute a default are left to the parties, who are free to establish any conditions they like within certain limits. The conditions are included in the security agreement.

        a.   **Acceleration clauses.** An acceleration clause gives the secured party the option of declaring the entire unpaid balance of the obligation immediately due upon the occurrence of some default. UCC section 1-208 specifically authorizes such clauses, but limits the secured party's right to accelerate to cases in which he in good faith believes that the prospect of payment or performance is impaired. The burden is on the debtor to show that the secured party was not acting in good faith.

        b.   **Waiver of defense.** To facilitate financing and negotiability, security agreements frequently contain provisions by which the borrower or buyer agrees to "waive," as against any assignee of the seller or lender, whatever defenses the borrower might have if the seller or lender sued directly. Where the buyer signs both a negotiable instrument and a security agreement as part of a single transaction, the UCC implies a waiver of defenses against any assignee of the paper.

c.	**Remedies in general.** UCC section 9-501(1) states that the secured party's rights and remedies are cumulative. There is no requirement that the creditor make an election of remedies. The three basic remedies are:

1)	Sale or other disposition of the collateral [UCC §9-504];

2)	Retention of the collateral [UCC §9-505]; and

3)	An action for the debt [UCC §9-501(1)].

d.	**Judgment and execution.** The secured party may allow the collateral to remain with the debtor and sue upon the debt, thereby reducing his claim to judgment. Any lien that the secured party subsequently acquires through a levy on the collateral, such as by writ of execution, dates back to the date of perfection of the original security interest. [UCC §9-501(5)]

Karner v.
Willis

2.	**Default and Acceleration--Karner v. Willis,** 710 P.2d 21 (Kan. 1985).

a.	**Facts.** The Karners (Ps) won a judgment against Willis and Lloyd (Ds) for over $58,000 in Oklahoma. Ps filed the judgment in Kansas and obtained an order of garnishment directed to Ds' banks. The garnishments were sent to the wrong banks, however. Hoosier, an officer of the Kanopolis Bank, so notified the deputy sheriff, who exchanged the correct garnishment for the erroneous one. Before the sheriff did so, however, Hoosier exercised a setoff against Ds' account. Ps claimed the setoff was wrongful, but the trial court found for the bank on the ground that it acted in good faith in accelerating the debt and in setting off the note. The court of appeals affirmed and Ps appeal.

b.	**Issue.** May a bank accelerate the maturity of a debt and exercise a right of setoff against a debtor's account because a garnishment is served on it against the debtor's account?

c.	**Held.** Yes. Judgment affirmed.

1)	Under UCC section 1-208, a contractual term permitting acceleration of payments when the party deems himself insecure shall be construed to mean that he can do so only if he in good faith believes that the prospect of payment is impaired. The trial court found that the bank acted in good faith. As this is a fact issue, the appellate courts must affirm if there is substantial competent evidence to support the trial court's findings.

2)	The only witness who testified was Hoosier. He explained that the day before the garnishment was served, D's bookkeeper had requested signature cards to change the account name and signatures. Hoosier knew of P's judgment against Ds, although he did not actually know whether Ds were insolvent or not when he made the setoff. Hoosier acted because the removal of $40,000 from Ds' account would have left them with no liquidity to operate their business. Two weeks after the setoff, the bank loaned Ds another

$50,000, but in the meantime Ds had paid $99,000 on the loan and given additional collateral.

3) If good faith required objective analysis of the facts, the bank could not have been insecure. However, the good faith test is subjective. The lower court's finding is supported by substantial competent evidence.

d. **Dissent.** The judgment itself did not make the bank insecure when Hoosier learned of it. Ds' note with the bank was not delinquent and was secured by a first mortgage on real estate. The garnishment could not have affected the bank's security; the garnishment sought payment from Ps' unmortgaged assets. The good faith requirement means honesty in fact in the conduct or transaction concerned. It should not be ignored to allow the bank in this case to use its setoff authority to defeat Ps' rights under the garnishment statute. A secured party should show compelling facts of insecurity because the secured creditor is in a less precarious position than is an unsecured creditor.

3. **Creditor's Right to Repossession.** UCC section 9-503 grants the secured party the right to take possession of the collateral upon default, provided the parties have not agreed otherwise. Repossession sets the stage for sale of the collateral in satisfaction of the debt or other available remedies.

a. **Self-help.** The UCC permits repossession without judicial process (self-help repossession), so long as it can be done without breach of the peace. The reason is that in many cases the debtor will voluntarily relinquish the collateral, and thus there is no need for judicial proceedings which run up the secured party's costs.

b. **Use of sheriff's apparent authority in self-help repossession--Stone Machinery Co. v. Kessler,** 463 P.2d 651 (Wash. Ct. App. 1970).

Stone Machinery Co. v. Kessler

1) **Facts.** Stone Machinery Co. (P) sold a Caterpillar tractor to Kessler (D) under a conditional sales contract. D made erratic payments, became current, then failed to make payments for two months. P's credit manager requested payment in full or immediate possession. D refused both alternatives, promised to resist any attempt to repossess without "proper papers," and stated that he had a job which would enable him to pay on the contract. P brought suit in Washington to repossess the tractor, but the tractor was located in Oregon. P took an Oregon sheriff to the site to take possession. The sheriff told D that they had come to take the tractor. D protested and objected, but offered no physical resistance because of the sheriff. P took the tractor and resold it for the balance due plus expenses of repossession. D counterclaimed for wrongful repossession and was awarded compensatory and punitive damages. P appeals.

2) **Issue.** Does use of a sheriff's apparent authority in repossession a chattel without judicial process constitute a breach of the peace?

3) **Held.** Yes. Judgment affirmed as modified.

a) Under UCC section 9-503, a secured party may repossess the collateral without judicial process if no breach of the peace occurs. A breach of the peace does not require violence as an essential element. Force, intimidation and oppression may suffice to constitute breach of the peace.

b) Here, the officer acted as though he had authority although his office did not give him the authority to demand that D give up possession. The officer was acting *colore officii*, and the effect was to prevent D from exercising his lawful right to resist a non-judicial takeover. On these facts, there was a breach of the peace.

c) P was not wrong in taking the officer with him in order to assure his safety, but this did not justify the officer's participation in the actual repossession. Therefore, P must pay the compensatory damages, but should not be liable for punitive damages.

c. **Breaking into debtor's business to recover property--Bloomquist v. First National Bank of Elk River,** 378 N.W.2d 81 (Ct. App. Minn. 1985).

1) **Facts.** Bloomquist (P) owned and operated a car repair service. The First National Bank of Elk River (D) provided financing under two promissory notes, taking a security interest in all of P's business tools and equipment and in a jeep with a snowplow. D sent P a demand that all note obligations be brought current. P made a partial payment, and D told P it would have to start repossession. P told D he would not give D his tools. P offered another partial payment, but D refused it as inadequate. Finally, D wrote to P demanding full payment and stating it would take possession of the secured goods unless P made payment within three days. On a Saturday when P's business was closed, D's agents removed a cracked window pane and climbed through the window to open P's garage door and take P's tools and equipment. P's tenants objected to D's actions and one called the police. P did not find out about the repossession until Monday morning. P sued for unlawful repossession and conversion. In the meantime, P redeemed his jeep and D sold off the repossessed tools and equipment. The trial court granted D summary judgment and awarded D a deficiency judgment. P appeals.

2) **Issue.** May a creditor break into the debtor's place of business to repossess secured goods after default?

3) **Held.** No. Judgment reversed.

a) UCC section 9-503 authorizes self-help repossession if there is not breach of the peace and the security agreement signed by the debtor grants the creditor the right to inspect the collateral. The agreement in this case did specifically authorize D to enter P's business to repossess collateral.

b) Although Minnesota has not set forth a test to determine whether a breach of the peace has occurred, other states have created a test that depends on (i) whether there was entry by the creditor upon the debtor's premises and (ii) whether the debtor or one acting in his behalf consented to the entry and repossession.

c)   When the debtor has not consented to repossession, the creditor must pursue a judicial remedy. Self-help repossession denies to the objecting debtor an opportunity to assert a defense to the repossession such as whether the parties' course of conduct has varied the agreement.

d)   D claims there is no breach of the peace when the repossession takes place without violence or threat of violence. However, any violation of any law enacted to preserve peace and good order is a breach of the peace. No violence or threat of violence is necessary. D clearly breached the peace by breaking and entering P's business.

e)   D's sale of the unlawfully repossessed tools and equipment constitutes a conversion. On remand, there should be a trial on the issue of P's damages. The normal measure for conversion is the fair market value of the repossessed goods at the time of the conversion, plus interest from that date. P may also be entitled to lost profits, and punitive damages.

4.   **Strict Foreclosure—The Creditor's Right to Retain Collateral.** Under UCC section 9-505, the creditor who repossesses goods may elect to keep them and forget the rest of the debt. This remedy is called "strict foreclosure," and is typically used where the collateral is appreciating in value or where the cost of further action is prohibitive.

a.   **Consumer goods.** Where the repossessed collateral is consumer goods and the debtor has already paid at least 60% of the cash price or loaned amount, the creditor must resell within 90 days of repossession and return any excess to the consumer/debtor.

b.   **Notice.** In all other situations, the creditor must give the debtor and other secured parties notice of the intent to keep the collateral.

c.   **Intention implied from creditor's conduct--Schmode's Inc. v. Wilkinson,** 361 N.W.2d 557 (Neb. 1985).

Schmode's Inc. v. Wilkinson

1)   **Facts.** Schmode's Inc. (P) sold a tractor truck and trailer to Harco. Harco in turn leased the equipment to Wilkinson (D). P guaranteed Harco that if D defaulted, it would repurchase the collateral from Harco. D defaulted and delivered the collateral to P. P restored the truck and trailer and tried unsuccessfully to sell it. P then used it by leasing it to others for a total of 204,000 miles. Then, almost three years after the restoration was complete, P sold it at a public sale. P sought to recover the deficiency from D. The trial court found that the sale was not commercially reasonable and gave D a setoff for damages they suffered. D appeals, claiming that by keeping and leasing the collateral, P elected to retain it in satisfaction of the obligation and cannot have a deficiency judgment.

2) **Issue.** May acts by a secured party other than the sending of notice result in a UCC section 9-505(2) election?

3) **Held.** Yes. Judgment reversed.

    a) Under UCC section 9-505(2), a secured party in possession may propose to retain the collateral in satisfaction of the obligation by sending written notice to the debtor. In some circumstances, other acts by the secured party may also result in an election under section 9-505(2).

    b) There are three basic approaches: (i) the only possible election is by written notice; (ii) an election may be implied from an unreasonably long retention of the collateral without sale; and (iii) the secured party may make an election by acts other than an undue delay in disposition that manifest an intent to accept the collateral in satisfaction of the debt.

    c) The strict notice only approach is ill-advised because the secured party should not be allowed to penalize a debtor by asserting its own failure to give statutory notice. The other two approaches have merit, but it is unnecessary in this case to choose between them. P's three-year retention and significant use was a clear manifestation of intent to retain the collateral in satisfaction of D's obligation. The cause should be dismissed upon remand.

5. **Disposition by Sale.** Under UCC section 9-504, the secured party may dispose of the collateral by sale, lease, or other means of disposal. Disposition by sale is the most common method of realizing upon the collateral, particularly because both public and private sales are permitted and because the secured party may go after the debtor for any remaining deficiency.

    a. **Commercial reasonableness standard.** The only real limitation on the power to sell is that the secured party must act in good faith and in a commercially reasonable manner. Every aspect of the disposition, including the method, manner, time, place and terms of sale must be commercially reasonable. Generally, a sale is commercially reasonable if the party acts in good faith, avoids loss, makes an effective realization, and sells either: (i) in the usual manner in a recognized market, (ii) at the current price in a recognized market, (iii) in conformity with reasonable commercial practices among dealers in the type of property. For example, in *United States v. Willis*, 593 F.2d 247 (6th Cir. 1979), the court held that a public sale was commercially unreasonable, even though it was properly conducted. The debtor had received two private offers to sell its assets for about $200,000. The SBA, which had guaranteed the loan, insisted on a public sale, where the assets were sold for only $40,000. The SBA was barred from collecting the deficiency.

Canadian Community Bank v. Ascher Findley Co.

    b. **Effect of failure to comply--Canadian Community Bank v. Ascher Findley Co.**, 280 Cal. Rptr. 521 (1991).

    1) **Facts.** Canadian Community Bank (P) provided $4 million in financing to Ascher Findley Company, the general partner in a limited partnership, to purchase a rig. When D defaulted, P sold the rig

without giving notice of the disposition to the general and limited partners. The rig was insured for $900,000 and P sold it for $175,000. The limited partners (Ds) had assumed a $1.7 million guarantee to P. P sued to recover on the guarantee. Ds claimed that the disposition of the rig was not commercially reasonable and that therefore they were not liable to P for the deficiency. The jury found for P. The court set aside the verdict and entered a different judgment against Ds. All parties appeal.

2) **Issue.** Does a creditor's failure to comply with the notice and commercial reasonableness requirements of UCC section 9-504 necessarily bar a deficiency judgment against a limited guarantor of a note?

3) **Held.** Yes. Judgment reversed.

   a) Under section 9-504, a secured party after default may sell, lease, or otherwise dispose of the collateral and the debtor is liable for any deficiency. The creditor must notify the debtor of the disposition and conduct the disposition in a commercially reasonable manner. Failure to comply with either the notice or commercial reasonableness requirements acts as an absolute bar to a deficiency judgment.

   b) The jury found that P neither gave Ds notice of the disposition nor conducted the disposition in a commercially reasonable manner. But the jury also found that P was not required to credit the rig disposition proceeds first against that part of the liability assumed by Ds. The trial court instructed the jury that noncompliance with section 9-504 may only be asserted by a party who suffers a loss due to the noncompliance; because the proceeds were not to be applied first to the assumed portion of the liability, the amount of Ds' liability would not be affected by the amount of the proceeds.

   c) P claims that Ds, as guarantors, are not "debtors" under section 9-504. There is a split of authority on this issue, but the better rule treats a guarantor as a debtor because the guarantor, like the principal obligor, has an interest in preventing collusive or commercially unreasonable sales of collateral and also has a need for notice to be able to bid at the sale.

   d) P claims that because the unassumed portion of the liability, to which the proceeds were to be applied first, was $2.3 million, there was no way that the proceeds of the rig could have exceeded this amount to apply to Ds' assumed liability of $1.7 million. While that may be true in this particular case, in other cases a limited guarantor may be liable for a higher percentage of the total debt and thus more likely to be affected by a noncomplying disposition.

   e) There are no grounds for protecting some limited guarantors and not others. The purpose of the UCC is to create predictability and stability through clear rules that apply prospectively. The only effective approach is to enforce section 9-504 in all limited guarantee situations. Because P failed to comply with section 9-504, Ds are not liable, regardless of whether they had an actual "loss" due to P's noncompliance.

   f) There was substantial evidence to support the findings that P failed to comply with section 9-504, because P did not notify Ds that it had leased the rig with an option to buy, and because there was evidence that the sale price of $175,000 was substantially below market value.

c. **Notice must be sent--Leasing Associates Inc. v. Slaughter & Son, Inc.,** 450 F.2d 174 (8th Cir. 1971).

1) **Facts.** Slaughter & Son, Inc. (D) leased a truck from Leasing Associates, Inc. (P). D complained that the truck was not fit for its intended use, and discontinued making lease payments. D returned the truck, and P sold it to another party after so notifying D. P then brought suit for the deficiency after giving credit for the sale proceeds. D had also leased a log loader and defaulted in payments, and P resold the log loader to a third party. P later amended its complaint to seek damages from the log loader transaction. The jury found for P and D appeals. As to the judgment for the log loader, D claims that there was insufficient proof that P sent a notice.

2) **Issue.** Must a party prove that it actually sent notice to the defaulting party in order to recover a deficiency on the resale of collateral?

3) **Held.** Yes. Judgment reversed on this issue.

a) Under the UCC, there is a rebuttable presumption that the value of any collateral sold without notice is equal to the debt. Before a secured party may recover for a deficiency, it must prove either the actual value of the collateral at the time of the resale or prove that reasonable notice was sent.

b) Here, P did not prove that the proceeds of the resale of the log loader represented the fair market value of the equipment. P can recover for the deficiency only it if gave reasonable notice to D of the sale.

c) Whether notice in the form of a letter sent by regular United States mail is reasonable notice is a jury question, and proof that a letter was sent supports a verdict that the notice was reasonable.

d) P did not prove that anyone in particular actually sent the letter in question. P offered evidence that the letter went out in the normal course of business, but it did not describe the office practice. The jury was unable to determine whether the letter was handled in the normal office manner because it did not know what the office practice was. Therefore, the evidence was insufficient to support the verdict. This portion of the judgment is reversed and remanded for a new trial.

d. **Notice required despite reasonable sale--Mallicoat v. Volunteer Finance & Loan Corp.,** 415 S.W.2d 347 (Tenn. Ct. App. 1966).

1) **Facts.** Volunteer Finance & Loan Corp. (D) repossessed collateral from Mallicoat (P) and sold it without notifying P, even though P lived in the same city where D operated and where it sold the property. D knew that P was not notified. P brought suit for damages.

2) **Issue.** May a creditor sell repossessed collateral without first providing notice to the debtor if it does so in a commercially reasonable manner?

3) Held. No.

    a)   The notice requirement is as important as the commercially reasonable manner requirement. Notice allows the debtor to protect his interest in the property by paying the debt, finding a buyer, or being present at the sale to bid on the property so that it is not sold for less than its true value.

    b)   D had no excuse for not notifying P. This case differs from those in which the creditor tried unsuccessfully, but in good faith, to notify the debtor before the sale. For this reason D did not properly dispose of the collateral.

e.   Public disposition--Savage Construction, Inc. v. Challenge-Cook Bros., Inc., 714 P.2d 573 (Nev. 1986).

Savage Construction, Inc. v. Challenge-Cook Bros., Inc.

    1)   Facts. Savage Construction Inc. (D) bought four cement mixers from Challenge-Cook Bros., Inc. (P). When D fell behind in the payments, P repossessed the mixers. After providing published notice of a public sale to be held in California, P, the only bidder, purchased the mixers for $39,500 each. Within two weeks, P resold the mixers for an average price of about $48,000. One of the buyers had been negotiating a purchase with P before the auction, but P did not notify that party of the auction. P then sued for a deficiency judgment. The trial court found D liable but credited D with the price received by P at the resale. D appealed to set aside the deficiency judgment, and P cross-appealed.

    2)   Issue. If known potential buyers are not notified of an impending public auction, is the secured party's public sale commercially reasonable?

    3)   Held. No. Judgment reversed.

        a)   Under California law [UCC §9-504(3)], notice of a public sale must be given at least five days before the date of sale by publication once in a newspaper of general circulation published in the county in which the sale is to be held. While P's publications were timely, it used a Nevada newspaper and two California newspapers, the circulation of which was unknown. Since P was the only bidder at the auction, P's notice was ineffective.

        b)   The method of sale need not bring the highest possible price, but the conditions of the sale must be reasonably calculated to facilitate a sale at fair market value. The price received by P upon resale two weeks later indicates the true fair market value of the equipment, which was well below the auction sale's price.

        c)   The purpose of advertising is to induce bidders to attend the auction. Lack of attendance and purchase by the secured party does not necessarily indicate improper notice, but it may show a lack of good faith or inadequate publication by the secured party.

        d)   The most significant failure by P was not notifying the known potential buyer that an auction was going to be held. This constitutes a breach of duty by P. Because P's sale was not commercially reasonable, the court should have entered judgment for D.

Atlas Construction Co. v. Dravo-Doyle Co.

f.   Private sale--Atlas Construction Co. v. Dravo-Doyle Co., 3 U.C.C. Rep. Serv. 124 (Pa. C.P. 1965).

1)   **Facts.** Dravo-Doyle Co. (D) sold a truck crane to Atlas Construction Co. (P). When P fell behind a second time in its payments, D repossessed the crane and stored it at the property of Campbell. D sent a notice to P and P's usual address regarding a private sale of the crane. P never received the letter. D sold the crane for $19,500 to a competitor of P's in which Campbell was a principal. P sued to recover nearly $12,000 for wrongful repossession and resale. D counterclaimed for $3,750 for the deficiency due after applying the proceeds of the resale to the unpaid balance on the contract. P introduced evidence that other buyers were willing to pay between $25,000 and $28,000 for the crane. The unpaid balance on the contract of $16,000 subtracted from the possible $28,000 gives the amount of damages P sought. The jury found for both parties on their respective claims. D moves for judgment n.o.v. or for a new trial, and P moves to mold the verdict to allow interest.

2)   **Issue.** Is the reasonableness of a private sale determined with reference to what the seller could have received for the property by contacting other purchasers?

3)   **Held.** Yes. D's motions denied and P's motion granted.

a)   The evidence that another buyer would have paid more than D's buyer is supported by a trade book which lists average prices for new and used equipment (the Green Guide Handbook). This indicates that the sale was not commercially reasonable.

b)   Under UCC section 9-507(2), price is not the only consideration. Here, however, there was also evidence that D made no effort to contact another buyer. This fact combined with the inadequate price is sufficient to support a jury verdict that the sale was not commercially reasonable because D did not take adequate steps to ensure that a fair price was received.

c)   D seeks a new trial because testimony of one of its witnesses that the sale was reasonable was excluded. This exclusion was proper. An expert witness may testify as to relevant trade usage or practices, but he may not state his conclusion as to the ultimate issue involved. Here, the ultimate issue was the reasonableness of the notice given to P and testimony that the notice was reasonable would be improper.

d)   The verdict should be amended to allow addition of interest, because the jury was instructed that they did not need to compute interest.

Contrail Leasing Partners Ltd. v. Consolidated Airways

g.   Valuation of collateral after commercially unreasonable disposition--Contrail Leasing Partners Ltd. v. Consolidated Airways, 742 F.2d 1095 (7th Cir. 1984).

1)   **Facts.** Consolidated Airways (D) sold a commercial airplane to Contrail Leasing Partners LTD. (P) for $575,000 and took back a chattel mortgage

on the plane. P defaulted and D repossessed the plane. D made a deal to sell it to another airline for $675,000, but P told the airline that it objected to the sale, so the airline backed out. Later D spent $26,000 to have the plane maintained to meet FAA requirements. D earned $38,000 from short term leases of the plane. D then told P that it planned to sell the plane at a public auction. P brought suit and unsuccessfully tried to stop the sale by a preliminary injunction. Then P filed a notice of lis pendens with the FAA. D was the only bidder at the auction and bought the plane for $515,000, which was less than the unpaid balance of the mortgage plus D's expenses. Fifteen months after the trial on D's claim, the judge issued his opinion. He found that the sale had been commercially unreasonable, that the plane was worth $625,000 on the day of sale, plus the $38,000. He ordered D to pay P $133,000, the difference between the $663,000 total and the amount D owed to P on the mortgage plus D's sale expenses. Both parties appeal.

2) **Issue.** In determining the value of collateral that was not sold in a commercially reasonable way, must a court specify whether the value is based on resale or wholesale prices?

3) **Held.** Yes. Judgment reversed in part and remanded.

   a) The sale was commercially unreasonable. However, the judge failed to consider all the relevant factors in coming up with the value of the plane on the day of the auction, and he did not allow D to deduct all the expenses it was entitled to.

   b) D was not allowed to deduct the interest that had accrued on the note between the date of default and the date of sale. D was able to lease the plane only because it possessed the plane. One of the costs of possessing the plane was going without the $403,000 P owed it. The opportunity cost D incurred is represented by the interest on the note. D should also be allowed to recover the expense of required maintenance. Recomputing with these expenses, it is clear that the proceeds were less than the amount D was entitled to.

   c) Since the sale was unreasonable, and P is entitled to the fair market value of the plane on the date of sale less what D was entitled to, the fair market value must be carefully determined. The $625,000 may be a rough average, but it must be further explained.

   d) The judge did not account for the effect of the lis pendens P had filed, which normally would decrease the market value of the plane. He also did not explain why he did not consider two $750,000 offers D received shortly before the auction. He made no allowance for brokerage expenses.

   e) Finally, a secured creditor is not required to sell at retail, but may sell at wholesale, as long as the sale is in a recognized market and the product is sold in a commercially reasonable manner. Retail prices may be higher, but this is because it costs more to sell at retail. The court must specify which type of market is being used in order to correctly match expenses of sale with estimated value.

F. SCOPE OF ARTICLE 9

1. **Introduction.** Article 9 applies to a wide variety of transactions, but there are limits. The grey areas include distinguishing between leases from security agreements, real estate transactions and security agreements, and bailments and security interests. The application of Article 9 to banks in setoff actions and to the United States government when it acts as a creditor presents other problems.

2. **Leases.**

    a. **Basic rules.** UCC section 1-201(37) provides that in some circumstances a lease may be intended as security and should be treated as such. The facts of each case are determinative. The types of facts that may be relevant include (i) the total amount of rent the lessee must pay under the lease, (ii) whether the lessee acquires any equity in the leased property, (iii) the useful life of the leased good, (iv) the payment of taxes, insurance and other expenses normally incurred by an owner, and (v) the existence of a buyout provision for a nominal sum.

    b. **Leasing and security interests--***In re* **Marhoefer Packing Co., Inc.,** 674 F.2d 1139 (7th Cir. 1982).

In re Marhoefer Packing Co., Inc.

    1) **Facts.** Marhoefer Packing Co., Inc. (D) acquired two sausage stuffers from Reiser (P). D bought one under a conditional sales contract, giving P a security interest in the machine which P perfected by filing. The parties agreed to a "lease agreement" covering the second machine. D was to make monthly payments for 48 months, after making a prepayment equal to the last nine payments. P was given the right to remove the machine from D's premises if D violated any of the lease conditions or defaulted in the payments. D was also given two options in addition to the return of the machine to P at the end of the lease: (i) it could purchase the stuffer at the end of the lease for $9,968, or (ii) it could renew the lease for an additional four years at $2,990 per year and pay P $1 for the machine at the end of the second term. One year after D received the machine, it ceased payments and filed a bankruptcy petition. Thereafter the trustee sought leave to sell the machine free and clear, asserting that the lease agreement was actually security under Article 9 which P had failed to perfect. The bankruptcy court found the agreement to be a true lease and ordered the trustee to return the machine to P. The district court reversed, and P appeals.

    2) **Issue.** Is a lease necessarily intended as security if it contains an option to purchase for a nominal sum?

    3) **Held.** No. Judgment reversed.

        a) A lease may be intended as security if it is in effect a conditional sale in which the lessor retains an interest in the leased goods as security for the purchase price. The district court held that the presence of an option to purchase the machine for $1 gave rise to a conclusive presumption under UCC section 1-201(37)(b) that the lease was intended as security.

b) Clause (b) properly applies to leases structured so that the lessee must pay rent over a set period of time at the conclusion of which he automatically or for only nominal consideration becomes the owner of the leased goods, because such a lease is in substance a conditional sale and should be treated as such. In this case, however, D was not obligated to pay rent until the opportunity to buy the machine for $1 arose. To reach that point, D would first have had to exercise its option to extend the lease for four further years of significant annual payments.

c) The conclusive presumption under clause (b) arises only when the option to purchase for nominal consideration necessarily arises upon compliance with the lease. Here, however, D had the right to terminate the agreement. When the lessee has the right to terminate the transaction, it is not a conditional sale. Once D defaulted, he could not have redeemed the collateral by tendering full payment of the obligation, which is a basic aspect of a secured transaction under UCC section 9-506.

d) The trustee asserts that the option price of $9,968 is also nominal under the circumstances, so clause (b) should apply. An option price may be nominal even if it is more than a few dollars. A buyout price may be considered nominal if it is actually a substantial amount but is insubstantial compared with the fair market value of the leased goods when the option arises. The parties differ as to what the fair market value of the machine after the first four years would have been, giving a range of $9,968 up to $20,000. But even if it were worth the higher value, an option price of almost 50% of the fair market value is not nominal.

e) Under the lease, D was to pay less in payments than the original purchase price would have been. The machine had a useful life longer than the lease, so P was to receive a valuable machine at the end of the lease. Also, D was not to acquire any equity interest in the machine. Even though D was to pay for applicable taxes and repairs, the transaction was clearly a lease.

3. **Bailments.** An owner may consign goods to another for resale to third parties. A consignment may thus be used as a means to finance the retailer's business or to get the retailer to sell the consignor's goods by minimizing the retailer's risk. A consignor's interest may resemble a purchase money seller's security interest and is treated similarly under UCC sections 2-326 and 9-114. A bailment arrangement may also be used to finance a debtor's operation, as when the bailor provides goods to be used by the bailee in its business. A bailor normally has the right to recover the bailed goods. A buyer may also leave the goods in the seller's possession, a situation falling under UCC section 2-502.

Simmons
First National
Bank v. Wells

a. **Bailment coexisting with consignment--Simmons First National Bank v. Wells,** 650 S.W.2d 236 (Ark. 1983).

    1) **Facts.** Wells (P), a rice grower, had a long-term arrangement with Western Rice Mills by which Wells would sell his rice to Western, who would then mill and sell it. The Simmons First National Bank (D) loaned $520,000 to Western and received in return a security interest in all of Western's real and personal property, including inventory and after acquired property. Western later was unable to buy P's rice outright and the parties agreed that Western would mill P's rice, sell it, and give the proceeds, less the milling fee, to P. Western subsequently defaulted on its debt to D. P claimed ownership in some of the rice and proceeds from the sale of rice. The trial court found for P on the ground that his arrangement with Western was a bailment, so that UCC section 2-326 did not apply and D's inventory lien did not cover the assets claimed by P. D appeals.

    2) **Issue.** May a bailee also be a consignee of the same goods?

    3) **Held.** Yes. Judgment reversed.

        a) It does not matter whether P's agreement with Western was a bailment or a sale. UCC section 2-326 applies to any transaction in which (i) the goods are delivered for sale; (ii) the "consignment buyer" maintains a place of business at which he deals in goods of the kind so delivered; and (iii) the business name of the "consignment seller" is different than the business name of the consignment buyer. These requirements are all satisfied in this case, so the transaction must be deemed a consignment.

        b) The policy of the UCC is to resolve all reasonable doubts as to the nature of the transaction in favor of the general creditors of the buyer. UCC section 2-326 gives disclosed claims to property priority over secret claims. Whenever a transaction is deemed to constitute a consignment sale, the consignment seller must comply with the notice requirements of UCC section 2-326(3) to obtain priority over the consignment buyer's creditors. P failed to do this, so D's interest prevails.

        c) In this case, P delivered the rice to Western for sale. Western maintained a place of business at which it dealt in goods of the kind delivered. And Western's business name was different than P's. This satisfies the requirements of UCC section 2-326. P could only have priority over Western's creditors by complying with the notice requirements of section 2-326(3). P did not do so.

First State
Bank of
Wiggins v.
Simmons

b. **The "financing buyer"--First State Bank of Wiggins v. Simmons,** 13 P.2d 259 (Colo. 1932).

    1) **Facts.** Miller contracted with the Associated Seed Growers to grow a seed crop of beans. Miller was to receive compensation for his services but had no interest in the seed or the crop. Miller obtained a loan from First State Bank of Wiggins (D) and gave a chattel mortgage based on the crop. Simmons (P) brought suit against Miller for a separate debt and served a writ of garnishment on the seed company. The seed company acknowledged that it owed Miller a specified sum, and D intervened to claim the money based on the chattel mortgage. The lower court found for P and D appeals.

2) **Issue.** May a bailee surrender a security interest in the bailed property without authorization by the owner?

3) **Held.** No. Judgment affirmed.

    a) The contract between Miller and the seed company was clearly a bailment. Therefore, Miller had no property rights in the crop.

    b) An owner is not affected by an unauthorized pledge of his goods by a bailee, and one who deals with a bailee concerning the bailed property does so at his own risk and with constructive notice of its real ownership. Since Miller had no power to give a chattel mortgage, D's claim must fail.

4. **Reclaiming Seller--United States v. Westside Bank,** 732 F.2d 1258 (5th Cir. 1984).

United States v. Westside Bank

  a. **Facts.** Texas Electronics Mart, Inc. ("TEMI") borrowed money from Westside Bank (D) and gave D a security agreement and promissory note secured by the Small Business Administration, an agency of the United States (P). The security interest, which D duly perfected, covered all of TEMI's "machinery, equipment, fixtures, inventory and accounts receivable now owned, to be purchased with loan proceeds and hereafter acquired." TEMI later executed a second promissory note to D for $16,000. When TEMI defaulted on the original note, D assigned its rights to P, which in turn paid off the note to D. O'Sullivan sold goods on credit to TEMI and delivered them just before D conducted a foreclosure sale of TEMI's assets. O'Sullivan unsuccessfully sought to reclaim the goods. At the foreclosure sale, O'Sullivan repurchased most of the goods it had sold to TEMI. P deposited the proceeds for distribution to TEMI's creditors, bringing an interpleader action to determine the proper distribution. O'Sullivan asserted its priority status in the proceeds for the full sales price, or alternatively for the proceeds traceable to the goods O'Sullivan sought to reclaim. D was awarded its claim on the second note, but did not award O'Sullivan a priority right of reclamation. O'Sullivan appeals.

  b. **Issue.** Does a seller of goods that has complied with UCC section 2-701 retain a priority status to the extent of traceable proceeds from the foreclosure sale of the goods?

  c. **Held.** Yes. Judgment reversed in part.

    1) UCC section 2-702 specifically creates a right of reclamation in favor of a credit seller when three conditions are met: (i) the buyer must have received the goods on credit; (ii) the buyer must receive the goods while insolvent; and (iii) the seller must learn of the buyer's insolvency and make demand for return of the goods within 10 days from the date of delivery. Each of these conditions were met in this case.

2) O'Sullivan's interest arises from Article 2. UCC section 9-504 makes the power of foreclosure subject to Article 2, thereby creating a duty in the foreclosing creditor to recognize and protect any Article 2 interest of which the creditor is aware.

3) The seller's right of reclamation extends to traceable proceeds from the sale of goods when all prior interests in those goods have been fully satisfied. If a foreclosure terminated a reclaiming seller's rights to any remaining proceeds, the remedy would be worthless because usually a debtor has given a security interest in after-acquired property which will be foreclosed, yet the right of reclamation does not arise until the buyer is insolvent. The reclamation remedy gives priority against the buyer's unsecured creditors.

4) Under UCC section 2-702, the seller's right is subject to the rights of a buyer in the ordinary course or other good faith purchaser or lien creditor under UCC section 2-403. The buyer's general unsecured creditors are not given priority. P, in foreclosing, had a duty to apply the proceeds of the sale to the satisfaction of any junior security interests for which it received written demand.

5) Even under the Bankruptcy Act, which does not apply in this case but is useful for comparison, the trustee's status as a hypothetical lien creditor is subordinate to the seller's right of reclamation. This includes a claim against the proceeds from the sale of the goods when the goods themselves are not returned.

5. **Personal Property Security Interests in Real Estate.**

    a. **Distinction between personal property security interests and the underlying real estate.** Under UCC section 9-104(j), Article 9 does not apply to the creation or transfer of an interest in or lien on real estate, including a lease or rents thereunder. However, UCC section 9-102(3) provides that the application of Article 9 to a security interest in a secured obligation is not affected by the fact that the obligation is itself secured by a transaction or interest to which Article 9 does not apply. These provisions may be approached by distinguishing between (i) the possessory interest of a mortgagor and lessee, which if used as security must follow the rules pertaining to security in real estate, and (ii) the mortgagee's and lessor's interest, which is basically an interest in personal property consisting of promised future payments. If used as security, the personal property interest would be subject to Article 9.

In re Kennedy Mortgage Co.

    b. **Proceeds of mortgage notes--*In re* Kennedy Mortgage Co.,** 17 B.R. 957 (Bankr. D.N.J. 1982).

      1) **Facts.** Kennedy Mortgage Co. (D) processed applications for mortgages on real estate and loaned money necessary for completion of settlement. D arranged lines of credit with various banks, including the First National Bank of Boston ("FNBB"). FNBB extended D a line of credit for $10 million, receiving in return a security interest in the mortgage notes and proceeds thereof. FNBB would then warehouse the instruments for a while, and then sell them to mortgage investors or put them in a mortgage pools such as GNMA. D deliv-

ered five notes to FNBB executed by five mortgagors. D also assigned the mortgages to FNBB, although the original mortgages were recorded. The assignments of the mortgages were not recorded. D filed bankruptcy. The trustee told FNBB that the notes were to be sold and become part of the GNMA pool. The notes were sold and FNBB claimed a lien in the proceeds, which were placed in an escrow account. FNBB seeks a summary judgment determination that its lien was valid and that it was entitled to payment of the proceeds of the sale of the notes.

2) **Issue.** When the mortgagee files bankruptcy, is the mortgage financing bank entitled to the proceeds of mortgage notes in which it has an unrecorded security interest?

3) **Held.** Yes. Judgment for FNBB.

   a) Under the UCC, a creditor that does not record its lien would not have rights superior to other creditors, including the trustee of the debtor estate. The mortgage instrument is actually personal property as to the mortgagee, even though it represents a lien on real estate. In order to be effective in favor of the mortgagee as against other creditors of the mortgagor, the instrument must be recorded in the proper office where the real estate is located. The rights of the mortgagor's creditors are inferior to the rights of the mortgagee.

   b) The prevalent business practices preclude recording of security interests in mortgage instruments since these mortgages are placed throughout the United States. Mortgages are sold in blocks of millions of dollars. Requiring title searches and recordings would delay and complicate transfers, reducing the availability of funds in the mortgage market. These considerations alone are not controlling, however.

   c) When statutory language is susceptible of two reasonable meanings, the court should choose the interpretation that is consistent with current universal business practices. The UCC does not apply to an interest in real estate. [UCC §9-104] Under section 9-302(1)(a), a security interest in collateral in possession of the secured party need not be filed to be perfected; it can be perfected only by the secured party taking possession under section 9-304.

   d) As to the note executed by the mortgagor to D, FNBB has a possessory lien which is perfected by possession. As to the unrecorded assignment of the mortgage, the mortgage debt is an interest in land. Assignments of mortgages may be recorded, but this does not affect the validity of an unrecorded assignment.

   e) The purpose of recording is to give notice to possible later purchasers, grantees, creditors and assignees of the status of title or prior interest of any entity in the property involved. There was a valid recorded mortgage in this case, supported by a note showing an indebtedness by the mortgagor to D. Anyone who wanted to buy the property or obtain an assignment of the mortgage was thus on notice of the mortgage to D and would have to inquire of D as to the amount due. If the assignment is not recorded, then payment to D in satisfaction of the mortgage by anyone without knowledge of the assignment would be effective against the holder of the unrecorded assigned mortgage. But the purposes of the recording statute is being served.

f) Since FNBB was the owner of the note, secured by the mortgage, anyone who wanted an interest in the mortgage would have to obtain an interest in the debt. The trustee could not realize upon the mortgage if he did not own the obligation represented by the note. The mortgage without the debt is of no effect. FNBB has a perfected security interest in the notes and the trustee has no interest in the mortgages given to secure the notes.

In re Mary-
ville Savings
& Loan Corp.

c. **Deeds of trust--*In re* Maryville Savings & Loan Corp.**, 743 F.2d 413 (6th Cir. 1984).

1) **Facts.** The Maryville Savings & Loan Corp. (D) executed a promissory note to Peoples Bank (P) for $75,000, and assigned to P as collateral all D's rights in promissory notes and deeds of trust encumbering certain real estate. P recorded the assignment in the proper manner for recording an interest in real estate. D paid off all but $55,000 of the principal, and then borrowed another $20,000, assigning rights in additional notes and deeds of trust on real property which P recorded. When D filed a bankruptcy petition, it owed P $75,000 plus interest. P sought a ruling that its security interest was perfected. The trustee claimed that since P did not take actual possession of the notes and deeds of trust, its security interest was not perfected under UCC section 9-304(1). The district court found for P and the trustee appeals.

2) **Issue.** Does Article 9 apply to deeds of trust assigned to secure payment of a note?

3) **Held.** No. Judgment affirmed in part and reversed in part.

a) When a promissory note and a mortgage together become the subject of a security interest, only that portion of the package unrelated to the real property is governed by Article 9.

b) Under UCC section 9-102(3), the application of Article 9 to a security interest in a secured obligation is not affected by the fact that the obligation is itself secured by a transaction or interest to which Article 9 does not apply. The character of a note as personalty is not transformed into a real estate interest merely because it is secured by a mortgage or deed of trust, or assigned as security together with a mortgage or deed of trust. P did not perfect its interest in the notes because it did not take possession of them.

c) The UCC does not supersede state law governing liens upon real estate. Article 9 does not apply to P's security interest in the deeds of trust. The trustee did not claim at trial that P's security interest in the deeds of trust was not perfected even if Article 9 did not apply, so that interest must be deemed perfected.

6. Right of Set-Off.

a. **Introduction.** A person's balance in a bank account constitutes a debt owed by the bank to the depositor. If the depositor also borrows money from the bank, there may be a right of set-off that allows the bank to cancel out the mutual obligations. UCC section 9-104(i) states that Article 9 does not apply to any right of set-off. However, in certain cases a bank account may constitute proceeds and thus fall within Article 9. In addition, a bank account evidenced by a certificate of deposit is not a "deposit account" as defined by UCC section 9-105(1)(e).

b. **Bank account containing proceeds--Brown & Williamson Tobacco Corp. v. First National Bank of Blue Island,** 504 F.2d 998 (7th Cir. 1974).

Brown & Williamson Tobacco Corp. v. First National Bank of Blue Island

1) **Facts.** Koenecke, Inc. bought tobacco products from RJR and from Brown & Williamson Tobacco Corp. (P) which took a security interest in all of Koenecke's current and future inventory of P's products, accounts receivable arising from the sale of such products, and all products and proceeds of the foregoing. Koenecke agreed not to sell, assign or create any other security interest in P's collateral. First National Bank of Blue Island (D) made loans to Koenecke, and Koenecke had a checking account with D. D made an unsecured loan to Koenecke of $250,000, which was deposited in the checking account. D stopped paying checks drawn on the account when Koenecke began having financial problems, even though there were hundreds of thousands of dollars worth of checks outstanding, including several to P and RJR. RJR went to D demanding payment of checks. Koenecke had a balance of over $700,000, including over $100,000 from sales of P's products. D also demanded of Koenecke that it pay the note, and Koenecke directed that the money be paid from the checking account. The next day, with a balance of nearly $500,000 in the account, D refused to pay P's representatives who had presented several checks. D withdrew its $250,000, and after paying other checks, left a balance of only $3,000 in the account. Within a month Koenecke petitioned for bankruptcy. P refused to participate in the bankruptcy, relying on its security interest. P sued, and the district court awarded P judgment. D appeals.

2) **Issue.** Does a secured party seller lose its security interest by permitting the proceeds from the sale of its products to be commingled with other funds in the buyer's corporate account?

3) **Held.** No. Judgment affirmed.

a) Under UCC section 9-205, a security interest is not invalid by reason of the debtor's liberty to commingle all or part of the collateral of proceeds. Under UCC section 9-306(2), the security continues in any identifiable proceeds including collections received by the debtor. So long as P can trace the proceeds, the proceeds are identifiable and subject to the security interest.

b) D claims that P did not trace the collateral into D's hands, but D stipulated that $70,000 of proceeds in which P had a security interest was included in Koenecke's checking account. D claims that the $70,000 was not identified as part of the money it transferred to itself, however. Payments out of Koenecke's checking account are free of P's claim only if made in the operation of Koenecke's business. D's transfer to itself of the $250,000 was not in the ordinary course of business. Because D received the transfer of funds from the bank account outside the ordinary course of business, it had constructive notice of P's security interest in the funds.

7. **Federal Law.**

a. **The federal government as a creditor.** The United States may be a creditor under several federal statutes. UCC section 9-104(a) states that Article 9 does not apply to a security interest subject to any statute of the United States, to the extent that such statute governs the rights of parties to and third parties affected by transactions in particular types of property. However, many such federal statutes are not comprehensive, and courts apply Article 9 when necessary to enforce rights and assess liabilities. In *United States v. Kimbell Foods, Inc.*, 440 U.S. 715 (1979), the Supreme Court held that the UCC, including Article 9, is the federal common law. This rule applies if:

1) There is no congressional directive to the contrary;

2) The federal program in question need not be uniform in character nationwide;

3) The application of state law would not frustrate specific objectives of the program; and

4) The application of a federal rule would disrupt commercial relationships predicated on state law.

In re American Pouch Foods, Inc.

b. **Defense procurement--*In re* American Pouch Foods, Inc.,** 769 F.2d 1190 (7th Cir. 1985), *cert. denied*, 475 U.S. 1082 (1986).

1) **Facts.** American Pouch Foods, Inc. (D) contracted with the United States Defense Logistics Agency (P) to provide ready-to-eat combat rations. D was entitled to progress payments up to 90% of its costs. The contract contained a title vesting clause whereby title to all parts, materials, inventories, work in process and so forth vested immediately in P upon payment of the progress payments. P was also allowed to terminate for default or for the convenience of the government. P made about $13 million in progress payments, then terminated the contract for default. After the termination, D petitioned for reorganization under Chapter 11 of the Bankruptcy Code. P filed an adversary complaint to obtain possession of the property covered by the progress payments. D answered that P's title was a security interest not properly perfected and thus subordinate to the rights of D and its creditors. The trial court held that P had absolute title to the property. D appeals.

2) **Issue.** Does a government agency acquire title, and right of possession, when it makes partial payments under a procurement contract containing a title-vesting clause?

3) **Held.** Yes. Judgment affirmed.

    a)   As a debtor in possession, D has the rights and powers of a creditor with a judicial lien. D claims priority over P's interest because P had not perfected it under the Illinois UCC.

    b)   In many situations, title vesting clauses are interpreted to create only a security interest. Here, however, the language of the clause should be literally interpreted because the contract involves procurement of materials for national defense. Thus, title in P was vested when it made the progress payments. Upon termination, P becomes entitled to possession of the property to which it has title.

    c)   This same result would apply even if P's interest were only a lien. The Court of Claims has interpreted the title vesting clause as merely creating security for repayment of the progress payments, on the grounds that the payments were loans, not partial payments. [Marine Midland Bank v. United States, 687 F.2d 395 (Ct. C. 1982)] In that case, the court did not apply the state UCC, but instead held that the government's security interest under its title vesting procedures is paramount to the liens of general creditors. Still, this position has not been followed.

4) **Dissent.** The majority holds that the first element of the *Kimbell* test was not satisfied here because when Congress expressly authorized progress payments, it incorporated the past practices whereby the United States took absolute title instead of a security interest. Yet Congress did not specifically adopt that practice; it merely permitted payment of money before contract performance was finished. The proper approach in deciding whether to create federal common law instead of incorporating state law is to determine whether there is a significant conflict between a federal policy and the use of state law. Since Congress did not explicitly exercise its power to govern these commercial transactions, no federal common law should be adopted. The majority also asserts that even if P's interest were a security interest, Congress provided that such liens should be paramount and so P would prevail. This provision is a rule of priority, but it is only one rule that must be applied in the context of a complete commercial code. Thus the UCC should apply to determine the creation, validity and perfection of government liens. Since P failed to file a financing statement, P had only an unperfected security interest and its rights were subordinate to D's.

c. **Federal tax liens.** Under 26 U.S.C. section 6321, the government obtains a tax lien on all property belonging to a taxpayer for every federal tax which is not paid on demand. The lien extends to after-acquired property. It is effective from the date of assessment of the tax and, with certain exceptions, does not require public notice.

    1) **Choateness rule.** The tax lien has priority over nonfederal liens that are not "choate" before the tax lien becomes effective. To be "choate" requires that three things be established beyond any possibility of change or dispute: (i) the identity of the lienor; (ii) the property subject to the lien; and (iii) the amount of the lien.

2) **Section 6323(c) safe harbor.** The Federal Tax Lien Act of 1966 created certain limitations on the validity and priority of federal tax liens. Section 6323(c) provides that a lien is not valid with respect to a security interest which comes into existence after the tax lien is filed but which is in qualified property covered by the terms of a written agreement entered into before the tax lien filing which constitutes a commercial financing agreement and is protected under local law against a judgment lien arising out of an unsecured obligation. Qualified property is commercial financing security acquired by the taxpayer before the forty-sixth day after the date of tax lien filing.

Rice Invest-
ment Co. v.
United States

d. **Subsequently filed tax lien's priority--Rice Investment Co. v. United States,** 625 F.2d 565 (5th Cir. 1980).

1) **Facts.** The Rice Investment Company (P) loaned over $67,000 to Handy Stop, Inc. ("Debtor") which in turn gave P a security interest in all of its existing and after-acquired inventory. P filed a financing statement in October 1973. The IRS assessed taxes against the debtor in March 1974, and filed a tax lien for over $8,500 in April 1974. The IRS then levied upon Debtor's inventory in August 1974, selling the inventory for a total of $4,250. P sued to recover from the United States (D) the proceeds of the sale. P claimed that D's tax lien was junior to P's lien. However, P acknowledged that it did not know the exact date on which Debtor acquired the actual inventory seized by the IRS. It also admitted that none of the actual inventory on hand in October 1973 was part of the inventory sold by the IRS. The trial court granted summary judgment for P and D appeals.

2) **Issue.** Does a federal tax lien filed subsequent to an ordinary perfected security interest have priority in collateral acquired by the debtor after the security interest was perfected?

3) **Held.** Yes. Judgment reversed.

a) To fall within the section 6323(c) safe harbor, P would have to prove that the inventory seized by the IRS in August 1974 was qualified property, defined as property acquired by the debtor before the forty-sixth day after the filing of the tax lien, which in this case is June 11, 1974. P is unable to prove this, because it does not know and cannot find out when this inventory was acquired. Thus, the safe harbor does not apply.

b) P argues that inventory which replaces inventory held by the debtor when the tax lien is filed also falls within the safe harbor, but such a construction would ignore the clear language of the statute. It would also create an infinite priority over the tax lien. A secured lender must regularly monitor the federal tax lien status of its debtors because the lender must take prompt action when a tax lien arises.

c) The choateness doctrine does not help P either. P's security interest in inventory not yet acquired at the time of the filing of the tax lien is not choate. It does not matter that P did all it could do under state law to perfect its security interest in the debtor's after-acquired inventory because choateness depends on federal case law, not on state commercial law.

G. BANKRUPTCY

1. **Introduction.** The federal Bankruptcy Code, contained in Title 11 of the United States Code has an often complicated impact on Article 9. Bankruptcy is a federal procedure that is initiated when a petition is filed by or against a debtor in federal district court. The proceedings are held before a bankruptcy judge; appeals go to the federal district court.

   a. **Petition.** The petition filed must request that the debtor be adjudicated a bankrupt and that its debts be discharged. The debtor also files schedules of its assets, liabilities, and creditors. The creditors are notified by the court of the need to file a proof of claim. Control of the bankrupt's estate passes to the bankruptcy court when the petition is filed.

   b. **Chapters.** Certain chapters of the Bankruptcy Code describe the forms of bankruptcy available. Chapter 7 provides for liquidation (of either a business's or an individual's assets). Chapter 11 governs reorganization of a business debtor. Chapter 13 provides for wage-earner plans.

   c. **Trustee.** A trustee is always appointed under Chapters 7 and 13. Under Chapter 11, the debtor becomes the "debtor in possession" and acts as the trustee. Once the trustee is qualified, title to all of the bankrupt's property is vested in the trustee as of the filing of the petition. The trustee is responsible for marshalling the bankrupt's property, conducting an inventory, and investigating the validity of claims asserted by the bankrupt or any third party for release of the property.

   d. **Distribution of assets.** The trustee must release any assets exempt from creditor process under section 522 of the Act. Other assets are disposed of as follows.

      1) **Property subject to security interests.** Collateral subject to any kind of lien or security interest, including mortgages, judicial or statutory liens, and Article 9 interests, is generally released by the trustee to the creditor if the trustee determines the security interest was valid as of the moment of the filing of the bankruptcy petition. No deduction for the expenses of the bankruptcy proceeding is taken. However, the secured creditor must seek permission of the court or the trustee to enforce its rights, and this is where much litigation arises.

      2) **Remaining property.** Non-exempt property that is free from valid creditor liens or interests is sold and the proceeds are distributed first to any special or priority creditors as defined by section 507, including wages and retirement benefits owed to the bankrupt's employees, certain tax debts, costs of the bankruptcy

proceeding. Any remaining proceeds are distributed pro rata among the general unsecured creditors.

e.   **Discharge.** As a result of the bankruptcy proceeding, the bankrupt is granted a discharge of further personal liability for most debts.

2.   **Trustee's Avoidance Powers.** The trustee not only acquires all of the debtor's rights and interests under UCC section 541, but also receives special statutory powers to invalidate security interests that would be completely secure but for the bankruptcy proceeding.

a.   **Strong arm clause.** Under UCC section 544(a), the trustee has the powers that could have been exercised by a creditor with a writ of execution returned unsatisfied, or a creditor with a lien on all property of the bankrupt at the moment the petition for bankruptcy was filed. He also has the rights of a bona fide purchaser of real property. This provision, called the strong arm clause, means the trustee has the powers of real or hypothetical creditors. With the power of a judicial lien creditor, the trustee prevails over any claims, liens or interests not fully perfected at the time the petition was filed.

b.   **Power to set aside fraudulent interests.** Under UCC section 544(b), the trustee can assert the invalidity of any security interest that is fraudulent as against any existing creditor, or that is otherwise voidable by any creditor under any federal or state law. A security interest subject to attack under this section is rendered invalid as against all creditors, even those as to whom the transaction was not fraudulent. Transfers of property, including creation of security interests, made by an insolvent for less than fair consideration are presumed fraudulent under UCC section 548(a)(2).

In re
Plonta

c.   **Voidable interest--*In re* Plonta,** 311 F.2d 44 (6th Cir. 1962).

1)   **Facts.** Plonta bought a boat in kit form from Sears, giving a chattel mortgage for the balance of the purchase price. The security interest was filed in Muskegon County, where Plonta lived, but the boat was stored in Ottawa County. Plonta defaulted and Sears repossessed the boat. Plonta then filed for bankruptcy. Sears sold the boat for $2,300. The trustee filed a petition to require Sears to turn the $2,300 over to the estate. The referee found that the mortgage should have been filed in Ottawa County and ordered Sears to turn over the money. The trial court adopted this action. Later, the Michigan Supreme Court held that repossession by a creditor prior to filing in bankruptcy was equivalent to filing in the county of location. Sears moved for reconsideration and the trustee moved for receipt of additional testimony. At the hearing, the trustee showed that before Sears repossessed the boat, a third party extended credit to Plonta for $10. The trustee argued that under the Bankruptcy Act, the interim creditor invalidated the mortgage. The referee agreed and ordered Sears to turn over the $2,300. The trial court affirmed the order and Sears appeals.

2)   **Issue.** Does an extension of credit to a debtor while an outstanding mortgage is invalid defeat the secured interest as to the trustee in bankruptcy?

3) **Held.** Yes. Judgment affirmed.

  a) The mortgage was invalid until Sears repossessed the boat. When the third party became a secured party, therefore, the mortgage was ineffective as to him. Since the mortgage was ineffective as to the third party, it was ineffective as against the trustee.

  b) The fact that the credit extended was insignificant does not affect the legal result.

3. Preferences Under Section 547.

a. **Definition.** A preference is a transfer of any of the property of the debtor, including the perfection of an unperfected security interest, to or for the benefit of a creditor on account of an antecedent debt, made by the debtor while insolvent and within 90 days before the filing of a bankruptcy petition, the effect of which transfer is to allow the creditor to obtain a greater percentage of his debt than the creditor would otherwise have received in the bankruptcy proceeding.

  1) **Effect.** If a challenged transaction meets all of these qualifications, it is voidable by the trustee. If this happens, the preferred creditor must repay the money to the trustee. If perfection of a security interest is held preferential, the security interest is simply invalid and the creditor becomes a general, or unsecured, creditor.

  2) **Non-preferential payments.** Payments for value, and payments made to a fully secured creditor, are not voidable as preferences even if made on the eve of bankruptcy.

  3) **Excused preferences.** The trustee may not avoid certain preferences that fall within section 547(c).

  a) **Substantially contemporaneous exchange.** No preference occurs if the parties intended a contemporaneous exchange or the transfer was in fact substantially contemporaneous with the exchange.

  b) **Routine payments.** Payments made in the ordinary course of the debtor's financial affairs to pay ordinary debts within 45 days of their creation are not preferential.

b. **Trustee's valuation of collateral--*In re* Lackow Brothers, Inc.,** 752 F.2d 1529 (11th Cir. 1985).

  In re Lackow Brothers, Inc.

  1) **Facts.** In September 1980, Heller loaned money to Lackow Brothers, Inc. (D) and received a security interest in D's inventory, goods, merchandise, accounts receivable, general intangibles, and contract rights. In April 1981, D filed a petition under Chapter 11, and the case was converted to a Chapter 7 proceeding in August 1981, when the trustees (Ps) were appointed. In February 1982, Ps filed a complaint alleging that D had made preferential payments of $365,000 to Heller within 90 days of the Chapter 11 petition. Heller

claimed that the payments were excluded from Ps' avoidance power under section 547(c)(5) because its financial position did not improve within the 90 days prior to bankruptcy. The only valuation of the pledged collateral as of January 1981 was D's computer accounting records. Ps claimed the proper valuation was the liquidation value. The bankruptcy and district courts found for Heller and Ps appeal.

2) **Issue.** Must bankruptcy trustees use the standard of valuation that is applicable for both relevant dates in determining whether a creditor's position improved?

3) **Held.** Yes. Judgment affirmed.

   a) The bankruptcy court determined that the value of the pledged collateral in April 1981 was $922,000, but that D owed Heller about $1.6 million at that time. Ps thus claim that Heller was undersecured when the petition was filed, so that the payments made within 90 days of bankruptcy must apply first to the unsecured component of Heller's debt.

   b) Heller produced uncontradicted evidence based on routine computer generated accounting reports to show that in January, the pledged collateral was worth about $4.7 million while the debt was $1.9 million, while in April, the collateral was worth $3.9 million and the debt was about $1.6 million, so that it was fully secured, and his position did not improve within the 90 days before bankruptcy.

   c) The bankruptcy court decided that the proper valuation standard was the ongoing concern value of the collateral represented by the accounting reports. Ps claim that the liquidation value of the collateral, $1.2 million, is the proper value to use. Heller did not have an improvement in position under the ongoing concern valuation, but it should have had an improvement if the liquidation value is used.

   d) Generally, liquidation value should be used in a liquidation case under Chapter 7, and ongoing concern value should be used in other cases. Here, however, the only valuation available for January 1981 is the accounting report valuation. Since the January value must be compared with the April value to assess any improvement to Heller's position, only the ongoing concern valuation may be used here.

In re Gibson Products of Arizona

c. **Floating lienor's risk of losing security in proceeds--*In re* Gibson Products of Arizona,** 543 F.2d 652 (9th Cir. 1976), *cert. denied*, 430 U.S. 946 (1977).

   1) **Facts.** Gibson Products, the debtor, purchased appliances from Arizona Wholesale Supply Co., the creditor, which had a perfected security interest in the appliances. Gibson went bankrupt. During the 10-day period before instituting bankruptcy proceedings, Gibson deposited $19,505 in its bank account, including $10 from the sale of a hair dryer in which Wholesale had a perfected security interest. Wholesale made a claim for the entire $19,505 under UCC section 9-306(4), and the bankruptcy judge awarded this amount to Wholesale. The district court affirmed the award and the trustee appeals.

2) Issue. May a trustee in bankruptcy set aside as a preference the security interest which a secured party claims in nonproceeds commingled with proceeds deposited in the debtor's bank account within 10 days before filing for bankruptcy?

3) Held. Yes. Judgment reversed.

a) Under UCC section 9-306(4)(d), a creditor's security interest is extended to commingled funds without specifically tracing the creditor's proceeds into the fund when the debtor becomes insolvent. The creditor's security interest extends to the entire deposit even where only a portion of the deposit can be identified as the proceeds from the sale of the creditor's collateral. The security interest arises when the debtor institutes insolvency proceedings and when some proceeds are commingled with the debtor's deposits.

b) UCC section 9-306 was not intended to grant more rights to the creditor because the debtor goes bankrupt. Instead, it was intended to eliminate the expense of tracing proceeds through commingled funds on the assumption that the amount received by the debtor in the last 10 days would be less than the creditor could claim if it could trace proceeds deposited over an unlimited time. This assumption does not apply here.

c) UCC section 9-306(4)(d) deals with nonidentifiable cash proceeds, granting a security interest to the creditor who can show that some of his proceeds were among those in the commingled fund. If the proceeds are identifiable (not commingled), the security interest is recognized by section 9-306(4)(b). Thus, under the UCC, Wholesale would have a security interest in the entire fund deposited by Gibson.

d) However, the Bankruptcy Act allows the trustee to set aside specified security interests as preferences. The deposit of commingled funds by Gibson here falls within the definition of a transfer, and the security interest in the amount in excess of Wholesale's proceeds may be set aside as a preference.

e) Therefore, Wholesale's security interest in the fund is prima facie valid under UCC section 9-306(4) except as to the trustee. The creditor can defeat the trustee's claim of preference by identifying his own proceeds. If the creditor wants to avoid the limitations of section 9-306(4)(d) he can prevent commingling of his proceeds.

4. Limitations Other Than Avoidance. The UCC provides certain limitations upon secured creditors that may appear less intrusive than avoidance, but can have a significant impact.

a. **Automatic stay.** Section 362 provides that while the bankruptcy action is pending, the creditor may not improve its position or cause payment to be made. This prevents self-help and creditor law suits against both the property of the estate and the debtor. In other words, secured creditors are stuck in the position they are in at the time the petition is filed. In some cases, a creditor may request that the stay be lifted because he is not adequately protected. Typically, a stay is sought when collateral is declining in value.

b. **Cram down.** In some circumstances, the bankruptcy plan may modify the rights of the secured creditor over the creditor's objections. This so-called "cram-down" right exists under Chapter 11, sections 1123 and 1129, and under Chapter 13, section 1322(b)(2).

III. INTRODUCTION TO SALES

A. THE SCOPE OF ARTICLE 2

1. **Development of the Law of Sales.** Article 2 of the UCC applies to transactions in goods. It was not written in a vacuum, however; much of Article 2 reflects earlier attempts to establish reliable principles of contract law.

   a. **Common law.** The law of sales developed gradually from the law merchant in England. Local merchant courts were established and merchants themselves stated the law, acted as judges, and sat as juries. The common law courts eventually absorbed the work of the merchant courts, and by the end of the nineteenth century, the common law principles were codified as the Sale of Goods Act.

   b. **The Uniform Sales Act.** The Uniform Sales Act was promulgated in the United States, patterned after the English statute. The Act essentially codified the common law of sales developed in the nineteenth century. These principles proved inapplicable to many of the problems posed by the mass distribution of goods to consumers that began taking place in the twentieth century.

   c. **Article 2.** When the UCC was adopted, the provisions updating the Sales Act were included as Article 2.

2. **Stages of a Sale.** The term "sale" used in Article 2 means the passing of title from the seller to the buyer for a price. The typical transaction or sale consists of a progression of steps, each presenting distinct possibilities for legal disputes: agreement, preshipment, delivery, receipt and inspection, and payment.

   a. **Agreement.** Before any sale can take place, the buyer and seller must agree to a deal. Article 2 provides various rules intended to assure that the intention of the parties is realized without excessive attention to formalities. Included among these are the so-called "gap-filling" provisions which supply terms omitted by the parties in the written contract. It is important to distinguish between the Restatement (Second) of Contracts concept of a contract as "a promise or set of promises for the breach of which the law provides a remedy," and the concept of agreement under Article 2, which means a bargain including both the language of the parties and any related circumstances. [*Compare* UCC §1-201(3) *with* §1-201(11)]

   b. **Preshipment.** Often there is a delay between the agreement and the actual shipment of goods. Because either party might breach during this delay, Article 2 provides rules governing conduct during this stage.

   c. **Delivery.** Delivery of the goods or of documents of title is a critical aspect of any transaction. Under Article 2, delivery also affects rights and duties pertaining to risk of loss or destruction of the goods.

d. Receipt and inspection. Once the buyer receives the goods, he is entitled to inspect them and reject or later revoke acceptance. As this is the most common time for defects or discrepancies to become apparent, this stage has been the subject of frequent litigation.

e. Payment. While covered by Article 2, payment often implicates Article 3, which deals with commercial paper.

3. **Scope of Article 2.** As mentioned above, Article 2 applies to "transactions" in "goods." The scope of Article 2 depends on the meaning given to these terms.

Barco Auto
Leasing Corp.
v. PSI Cos-
metics, Inc.

a. **Vehicle lease as a transaction--Barco Auto Leasing Corp. v. PSI Cosmetics, Inc.**, 478 N.Y.S.2d 505 (1984).

1) **Facts.** PSI Cosmetics, Inc. (D) leased a new car from Barco Auto Leasing Corp. (P). The lease agreement was printed on P's form and provided that P retained title and a security interest in the car. D waived any and all defenses based on unsatisfactory performance of the car, and assumed responsibility for repair and replacement of parts. P disclaimed all warranties, including the implied warranties of merchantability and of fitness for a particular use. Two months after the lease began, the car's engine burned up. Repairs took over three months to complete. D continued making the lease payments. Three days after the repairs were finished, D's employee was driving the car and the engine burned again, causing the employee to miss an important meeting, which in turn cost D a $40,000 contract. D then quit making the payments. P sued for breach of the lease. D brought a counterclaim for loss of business. P moves for summary judgment.

2) **Issue.** Is a vehicle lease covered by the sales provisions of the UCC?

3) **Held.** Yes. Motion denied for lack of evidence.

a) Courts have adopted a variety of approaches in applying Article 2 to leases. These include (i) the exclusionary approach that excludes leases from coverage on the ground that Article 2 only applies to clear sales; (ii) the analogy approach that applies Article 2 to any transaction that closely resembles a sale; (iii) the policy approach that applies selective provisions of Article 2 to particular transactions to effectuate the policies behind the specific provisions; and (iv) the inclusive approach that applies Article 2 to any transaction in goods as described in 2-102.

b) The inclusive approach has not been accepted in New York, despite its attractiveness. The analogy approach must be applied to this case.

c) A lease may be treated as a security interest under UCC section 1-201(37) if the parties agree that the lessee may become the owner of the property upon full compliance with the lease terms with no significant additional consideration. The same principle applies to the question of whether Article 2 governs a particular lease. Here, D did not have an option to purchase but other factors suggest the lease was analogous to a sale.

d) D bore the full risks of ownership. There was no significant economic difference between full ownership and D's position as lessee. For that reason, Article 2 does apply to this lease.

e) The disclaimer of warranties complies with UCC section 2-316(2), but a hearing is necessary to determine whether the disclaimer was unconscionable. D's counterclaim is not cognizable, however, and must be dismissed.

b. **Goods.** The term "goods" includes all tangible chattels, or anything which is movable at the time it is identified to the contract of sale. The goods must actually exist; goods to be created become subject to Article 2 only when created or manufactured. Although real estate and any interest therein is not subject to Article 2, the following types of property are "goods" if they are severed and sold apart from the land: (i) growing crops; (ii) minerals, ice or water, or any structure on the land, if it is severed by the seller; and (iii) anything else attached to the land that can be removed without material harm thereto (fixtures).

c. **Mixed goods and services--Coakley & Williams, Inc. v. Shatterproof Glass Corp.,** 706 F.2d 456 (4th Cir. 1983).

1) **Facts.** Coakley & Williams, Inc. (P), a general contractor, was constructing a building and hired Washington Plate Glass Co. to furnish and install aluminum and glass curtain wall and store front work on the building. Washington bought the necessary glass from Shatterproof Glass Corp. (D). The glass discolored after installation, and Washington replaced it, obtaining reimbursement from D. When the glass discolored again, D refused to replace it. P sued alleging breach of implied warranties of merchantability and fitness for a particular purpose. D sought dismissal under Federal Rule of Civil Procedure 12(b)(6) for failure to state a claim upon which relief can be granted. The district court held that the UCC was not applicable to the contract so the implied warranties did not exist. P appeals from the dismissal of its suit.

2) **Issue.** May the UCC apply to a contract involving mixed goods and services?

3) **Held.** Yes. Judgment reversed for a trial.

a) The implied warranties of merchantability [UCC §2-314] and fitness for a particular purpose [UCC §2-315] apply to the sale of goods. There must be a buyer of goods for the warranties to apply.

b) Three factors should be considered in evaluating mixed services and goods contracts: (i) the contractual language; (ii) the nature of the supplier's business; and (iii) the intrinsic worth of the materials involved.

c) In this case, the contract between P and Washington involved furnishing and installing a wall and performing storefront work. Washington had to bring the materials to the work site. These materials qualify as goods under 2-105. The evidence indicates that the installation may have been fairly simple, and not as significant as supplying the glass. In that case, it could be a contract for the sale of goods.

d) The second factor is not dispositive in this case. Washington was not a dealer or a manufacturer, but it was itself clearly a buyer of goods. The issue to be determined at trial is whether these materials, or the services also provided by Washington, predominated in its contract with P.

e) The record does not disclose the value of the various parts of the contract, so this factor must be considered at trial with the others to determine whether the contract between Washington and P involved primarily goods or services.

d. **Computer software--Advent Systems Ltd. v. Unisys Corp.**, 925 F.2d 670 (3d Cir. 1991).

1) **Facts.** Advent Systems Ltd. (P) produced computer software. P entered a two-year contract with Unisys Corp. (D), a computer hardware manufacturer, to provide D with software and hardware for a document system D was to sell in the United States. The contract required P to provide marketing personnel and sales and support training for D's staff and customers. P was to invoice D for each product purchased and separately bill D for maintenance fees. Within a few months, however, D decided to develop its own document system and told P their arrangement had ended. P sued for breach of contract and fraud. The court made a pretrial ruling that the UCC did not apply because the services aspect of the contract predominated. After a trial, the jury awarded P $4,550,000 for breach of contract. D appeals.

2) **Issue.** Is computer software a "good" under the UCC?

3) **Held.** Yes. Judgment reversed.

a) The UCC applies to "transactions in goods"; "goods" include all things "which are moveable at the time of the identification for sale." Intellectual property, by itself, is not a good. The UCC does not specifically mention software.

b) Computer software is clearly the product of an intellectual process, but once incorporated into a medium such as a floppy disk or magnetic tape, it can be widely distributed. It is similar to a music recording on a compact disc; while the music itself is not a "good," the disc is. Thus, computer software is a "good" under the UCC.

c) This holding reflects the UCC policy of flexibility and adaptation to commercial and technological developments. Software is important to the commercial world, and applying the uniform and predictable UCC provisions to software is beneficial.

d) Whenever a contract includes both goods and services, the applicability of the UCC depends on which predominates. In this case, P was required to provide hardware, software, and services. Once both hardware and software are considered goods, the purpose of the contract is to transfer "products," and the UCC should apply. The services P was to provide were a comparatively small part of the contract.

    4)   **Comment.** P had also sued for tortious interference with contractual relations on the ground that D had interfered with P's ongoing contract negotiations with D's British subsidiary. However, the court held that a parent corporation is privileged in disrupting prospective contractual negotiations of its subsidiary with another party.

B. ·BASIC CONCEPTS

1.   **Basic UCC Principles.** Certain fundamental principles apply under all sections of the UCC, but they are frequently determinative of disputes under Article 2.

    a.   **Good faith.** Every contract or duty within the scope of the UCC imposes an obligation of good faith in its performance or enforcement. This obligation cannot be waived by the parties. [UCC §1-203]

    b.   **Unconscionability.** Article 2 includes the equitable concept of the unconscionable contract, although the term "unconscionable" is not defined. The definition used by the courts is a contract that is so unfair that it shocks the conscience of the court. [UCC §2-302] However, the doctrine is rarely applied in commercial cases where the buyer and seller have equal bargaining power.

    c.   **Merchants.** Article 2 distinguishes between merchants and nonmerchants and often imposes a higher standard on the former. For example, a merchant seller is held to certain implied warranties for the goods he sells, a liability not shared by nonmerchants.

    d.   **Reasonableness.** Throughout Article 2, standards of conduct are phrased in terms of "reasonableness." This term is also subject to judicial interpretation.

2.   **Definition of "Merchant"--Loeb & Co., Inc. v. Schreiner,** 321 So. 2d 199 (Ala. 1975).

    Loeb & Co., Inc. v. Schreiner

    a.   **Facts.** Schreiner (D), a cotton farmer, learned that Loeb & Co., Inc. (P) had bought cotton from D's neighbor. D called P to see if P would buy D's cotton as well, and P agreed to do so. P later claimed that D agreed to sell P 150 bales of cotton, but D denied that the conversation was anything more than an incomplete negotiation. P sent a confirming statement to D which D failed to sign, return, or otherwise acknowledge until four months later, when P called asking for it. In the meantime, the price of cotton more than doubled and D refused to sign or return the confirming statement. P sued, but the trial court found that the oral contract was not enforceable under the UCC because D was not a merchant. P appeals.

b. **Issue.** Is a farmer who sells only his own production a merchant under the UCC?

c. **Held.** No. Judgment affirmed.

1) UCC section 2-201, which is the Statute of Frauds in the UCC, requires a writing before a contract to sell goods for $500 or more may be enforced. An exception applies to merchants when a confirming statement is sent and the recipient fails to object within 10 days of receipt. Thus, if D is a merchant, he is bound; if he is not a merchant, he is not bound.

2) The term "merchant" is defined in 2-104(1) and means a person who (i) deals in goods of the kind; (ii) by his occupation holds himself out as having knowledge or skill peculiar to the practices or goods involved in the transaction; or (iii) employs an agent who by his occupation holds himself out as having such knowledge or skill.

3) In this case, D did not employ an agent. Nor did he, merely by being a farmer, hold himself out as a professional cotton merchant.

4) While D may have had a good deal of knowledge about cotton, he never sold anyone's cotton other than his own. He never became a professional seller. Since he did not fall within any of the definitions of a merchant, D is not bound by the oral contract.

Zapatha v.
Dairy Mart,
Inc.

3. **Unconscionability Among Businessmen--Zapatha v. Dairy Mart, Inc.**, 408 N.E.2d 1370 (Mass. 1980).

a. **Facts.** Zapatha (P) was discharged from his job of over 20 years and began looking to start a business of his own. He met with an agent of Dairy Mart, Inc. (D), who gave him a brochure describing D's franchise program. P agreed to operate a store under D's name. P was required to buy a starting inventory and completely run the business, paying D a franchise fee. Either party could terminate the contract without cause on 90 days' written notice. If D terminated without cause, it had to repurchase P's inventory. P had operated under the agreement for four years when D presented a new agreement for execution. The new agreement was less favorable to P, and P told D he would not sign it. Shortly thereafter, D gave P written notice of termination, although it offered to negotiate about a new agreement. P sought an injunction against termination of the agreement. The trial court, ruling that the termination provision was unconscionable, that D did not act in good faith, and that D's termination without cause was an unfair and deceptive act, granted judgment for P. D appeals.

b. **Issue.** May a franchise agreement provide for termination without cause by either party upon prior written notice?

c. **Held.** Yes. Judgment reversed.

1) The franchise agreement is not directly covered by Article 2 of the UCC because it is primarily involved with subjects other than the sale

of goods. However, the UCC policy concerning good faith and unconscionability applies to the agreement by analogy.

2) P claims the termination clause was unconscionable. The basic test for unconscionability is whether the clause is so one-sided that it could result in unfair surprise or oppression to the disadvantaged party, but it does not involve the allocation of risks. The UCC assumes that a termination without cause provision is not per se unconscionable.

3) In light of P's business experience, the termination clause should not have surprised him, and, if it did, it was not because of unfairness. Nor was the provision oppressive, because there was no potential for forfeiture or loss of investment. P did not have to invest in anything but the inventory; D was required to repurchase P's inventory upon termination.

4) The UCC defines good faith as honesty in fact and the observance of reasonable commercial standards of fair dealing in the trade. There was no evidence of the latter standards. Nor was there any evidence that D was dishonest. Even if the original brochure misstated a franchisee's status as the owner of a business, it was not dishonest about the termination clause. D did not fail to act in good faith.

5) In addition to the UCC provisions applicable by analogy to this case, there are general principles of law that protect against conduct that produces an unfair and burdensome result. A termination permitted by the contract may not be enforced if it is contrary to the spirit of the bargain, *e.g.,* where an employee is terminated in order to deprive him of commissions earned but not yet payable. The legislature has limited the right of certain franchisors to terminate agreements without cause, but these laws do not apply to all franchise agreements. Considering all of the circumstances of the case, including P's failure to accept D's offer to negotiate, there was no showing that D engaged in any unfair, deceptive, or bad faith conduct.

IV. COMING TO AGREEMENT

A. FORMATION OF THE CONTRACT

1. **Offer and Acceptance.** The requirements of offer and acceptance applicable to ordinary contract also apply to sales contracts. No specific form is required to have a sales contract. Under the UCC, a contract need not even be an oral or written agreement, because an agreement may be demonstrated by the conduct by both parties that recognizes the existence of an agreement. [UCC §2-204(1)] The exact moment of contract formation is not critical, either; a binding obligation may exist even though the exact time of agreement cannot be determined.

   a. **Firm offers.** At common law, an irrevocable offer (a firm offer or option) could be kept open only if supported by consideration. UCC section 2-205 changes this by providing that "firm" offers are irrevocable, even without consideration, if they meet certain requirements.

      1) **Requirements.** The firm offer must (i) be made in connection with a contract to sell goods; (ii) be made by a merchant; and (iii) be in a signed writing stating that it will be held open.

      2) **Duration.** If the requirements are met, the offer is irrevocable, despite absence of consideration, for the period specified in the offer or, if no period is specified, for a reasonable time, but in no event longer than three months.

   b. **Expiration--Mid-South Packers v. Shoney's, Inc.,** 761 F.2d 1117 (5th Cir. 1985).

   Mid-South Packers v. Shoney's Inc.

      1) **Facts.** Mid-South Packers (P) had a business meeting with Shoney's, Inc. (D) at which the parties discussed the sale of pork products. P gave D a written proposal containing prices and terms for the supply of the products, including a 45-day prior notice of price increases. D did not make a commitment, but did estimate its needs at 80,000 pounds per week. Over three months later, D ordered products from P, both over the telephone and by written purchase orders. A few weeks later, P informed D that the price for future orders would be increased. The next time D ordered, P told D it would fill the order only at the higher price. D agreed and continued making orders for almost two months. In D's payment for its final order, it held back over $26,000, representing an offset for the difference between the original price and the price increase for which P did not provide 45 days' notice. P sued to recover the amount offset. The district court granted summary judgment for P, and D appeals.

      2) **Issue.** Does a firm offer expire after three months if not accepted, even if the offeree thereafter makes orders that the offeror accepts?

      3) **Held.** Yes. Judgment affirmed.

a)	D claims that its orders to P constituted acceptance of P's proposal, forming a binding contract. D claims this was a requirements contract and that P was bound by the notice provision. P claims that the proposal was a firm offer that, under UCC section 2-205, expired after three months.

b)	A requirements contract includes the buyer's promise to buy exclusively from the seller either the buyer's entire requirements or up to a specified amount. Yet D's agent stated that D had the right to buy goods from other suppliers and bought from P only because it was satisfied with P's service and goods. For that reason, there was no requirements contract.

c)	The proposal was not accepted within three months and therefore expired. The only contracts in this case were the separate purchase orders. The proposal remained an offer to sell at the listed prices so as to allow D to believe its orders would close the bargain, but each purchase order was a new contract. P could properly revoke its offer and replace it by an offer to sell at a higher price. D's purchase orders made with the knowledge of this higher price were acceptances of the new offer.

d)	D's agent also admitted that D ordered the goods at the increased price to make sure that P kept shipping, with the secret intent to offset the price increase. This intent was not manifested and so was not part of the bargain. D could have reserved its rights by so stating in its purchase orders, or it could have bought from another supplier, but it could not induce performance and then demand compliance with a prior, withdrawn offer.

2.	**Battle of the Forms.** Modern business transactions are often conducted primarily through forms. Typically, the buyer sends a purchase order to the seller. The purchase order form contains the basic terms of the sale, such as price, quantity, and a description of the goods, but it also contains printed terms drafted by the buyer's attorney in favor of the buyer. After receiving the order, the seller sends a written acceptance or confirmation to the buyer. The acceptance contains the basic terms of the sale but also a series of printed terms drafted by the seller's attorney in favor of the seller. These terms may conflict with the terms printed on the purchase order.

a.	**Common law.** Standard contract law principles require that the offeree's acceptance be in the precise terms of the offer (the mirror image rule) and that any variance therefrom, material or not, constitutes a rejection of the original offer. It becomes a counteroffer.

b.	**UCC.** On the premise that both parties recognize a contract despite their clashing forms, the UCC establishes a general rule that a contract can be formed under such circumstances, unless the responding offeree (the seller) specifically states that there shall be no contract unless his set of terms is accepted by the original offeror, in which case the offeree's response is treated merely as a counteroffer. [UCC §2-207] In the absence of such a specific limitation, the existence of a contract and its terms is determined by UCC rules.

1) Proposed additional terms. If the offeree's response contains terms additional to those contained in the original offer, a contract exists consisting of the terms on which the offer and acceptance agree. The additional terms are deemed a proposal for additions to the contract. Where the parties are merchants, the proposals become part of the contract unless:

    a) The offeror's original offer expressly limited acceptance to the offered terms (take it or leave it); or

    b) The additional terms are a material alteration of the contract.

2) Proposed inconsistent terms. If the offeree's response contains terms which are actually inconsistent with those contained in the original offer, the courts look at the parties' conduct to determine whether they acted as though a contract had been formed. If so, the contract consists of those terms on which the writings agree; the conflicting terms cancel each other out and necessary terms are provided by the UCC or by custom.

Roto-Lith Ltd. v. F.P. Bartlett & Co.

c. Warranty disclaimer on seller's acknowledgment form--Roto-Lith Ltd. v. F.P. Bartlett & Co., 297 F.2d 497 (1st Cir. 1962).

1) Facts. Roto-Lith, Ltd. (P) manufactured cellophane vegetable packing bags. P ordered adhesive emulsion from F.P. Bartlett & Co. (D), stating that it was for "wet pack" bags. D returned an acknowledgment and invoice, each of which contained a conspicuous disclaimer of all warranties, including the statement that "If these terms are not acceptable, Buyer must so notify Seller at once." P accepted the emulsion without comment on the disclaimer. When the emulsion proved unsatisfactory, P sued for damages. The trial court directed a verdict for D and P appeals.

2) Issue. Is a response that includes a material alteration to the sole disadvantage of the offeror an acceptance expressly conditional on assent to the additional terms under UCC section 2-207?

3) Held. Yes. Judgment affirmed.

    a) P claims the disclaimer was merely a proposal which did not become part of the contract because P never accepted it. P also claims that D's acknowledgment did not make acceptance expressly conditional on P's assent. However, this view of the statute would render it meaningless, because no offeror will subsequently assent to adverse conditions in the offeree's acknowledgment.

    b) The statute was meant to modify the mirror-image rule so that additional terms in an acceptance are only proposals, not counteroffers. But where such terms solely disadvantage the offeror, the acceptance must be treated as expressly conditional on the offeror's consent. Otherwise they would never become part of the contract.

4) Comment. The court was applying a version of the UCC that did not include subsection (3) of UCC section 2-207.

d. **Requirement to expressly communicate conditional acceptance--Dorton v. Collins & Aikman Corp.,** 453 F.2d 1161 (6th Cir. 1972).

1) **Facts.** Dorton (P), a partner in The Carpet Mart, bought carpet from Collins & Aikman Corp. (D) in a series of transactions. P or one of D's salesmen would telephone D's order department and order carpet listed in D's catalogue. D would then type the information on its preprinted acknowledgment forms, which contained a provision that all claims arising out of the contract would be submitted to arbitration. P never objected to the forms. P subsequently learned that some of the carpets were made of a cheaper and inferior fiber than that contracted for. P sued for damages due to D's fraud, deceit, and misrepresentation. D moved for a stay pending arbitration. Finding that the arbitration agreement was not binding, the court denied the stay. D appeals.

2) **Issue.** Does a form that states that acceptance is subject to all the terms printed on the form satisfy the "expressly made conditional" requirement of UCC section 2-207(1)?

3) **Held.** No. Judgment reversed and remanded for decision under UCC section 2-207(2).

   a) The district court relied on UCC section 2-207(3) to find that the arbitration clause was ineffective. Since the parties' conduct showed that a contract existed, but the writings of the parties did not agree, the court determined that the UCC would supply any needed additional terms. But the UCC does not impose an arbitration clause.

   b) The court should first have determined whether the forms were acceptances or confirmations under UCC section 2-207. The evidence on this issue is conflicting, and the question must be resolved on remand.

   c) If the forms are acceptances under UCC section 2-207(1), the question becomes whether the arbitration provision was additional to or different from P's oral offers, and, if so, whether D's acceptances were expressly made conditional on assent to the additional terms under UCC section 2-207(1).

   d) The form did include a statement that the acceptances were subject to all the terms, including arbitration. This alone was insufficient to make the acceptance expressly conditional on P's assent to the terms. To reach that level, it must have been clear that D was unwilling to proceed with the transaction unless it was assured that P assented to the additional or different terms. Yet the acceptances by their own terms provided that P could be bound by simply retaining the form for 10 days without objection.

   e) Since P's assent to D's terms was not necessary, the additional terms must be treated as proposals under UCC section 2-207(2). The court must determine whether the arbitration provision materially altered the oral offer.

f)   If the court finds that the acknowledgment forms were confirmations of the prior oral agreements, the court would have to determine whether the arbitration clause was additional to or different from the oral agreement, and if so, whether it should treat the clause as a proposal under UCC section 2-207(2).

g)   If the court finds that the arbitration clause is a term of the contracts, D's motion for a stay pending arbitration should be granted.

Daitom, Inc. v. Pennwalt Corp.

e.   **Mutual knockout of conflicting terms--Daitom, Inc. v. Pennwalt Corp.,** 741 F.2d 1569 (10th Cir. 1984).

1)   **Facts.** Daitom, Inc. (P) planned to build and operate a plant to manufacture vitamin B-5. P arranged to purchase automated drying equipment from Pennwalt Corp. (D). D sent P a written proposal that described the equipment, the price, and the terms of shipment. It also contained various terms and conditions including a limitation of warranties and a one-year limit from the date of delivery in which P could bring any action for breach of warranty. P accepted the proposal by sending a purchase order that itself contained additional warranties, including those available at law, and a statement that the seller's acceptance of the purchase order would constitute acceptance of all its terms. D delivered the dryers, but they were left in their crate for over a year while P's plant was being constructed. Two days after the dryers were finally used, P discovered they were defective and so notified D. P sued for breach of warranties, but the district court granted D's motion for summary judgment on the ground that the one-year limitations period in D's proposal barred P's action. P appeals.

2)   **Issue.** When the seller's proposal contains a material provision that conflicts with a provision on the same subject in the buyer's confirmation, do the provisions cancel each other out?

3)   **Held.** Yes. Judgment reversed.

a)   The trial court correctly found that the UCC applies to this transaction and that the parties entered a binding contract under UCC section 2-207(1). Even though P's purchase order contains language to the effect that D's acceptance would be expressly limited to the terms and conditions of the purchase order, it does manifest agreement on the essential terms of equipment specifications, price, and terms of shipment and payment. The approach taken in *Dorton v. Collins & Aikman Corp.* (*supra*) is the best view; P did not explicitly communicate its unwillingness to proceed with the transaction unless the additional or different terms in its response were accepted by D.

b)   Since there was a contract under UCC section 2-207(1), it is necessary to evaluate the effect of the additional or different terms under 2-207(2). The trial court held that because P's acceptance was silent about the limitations period, that period controlled. However, P reserved its legal rights and remedies in its purchase order, and by implication reserved the statutory limitations period of four years. [UCC §2-725(1)] This conflict in terms must be resolved by the court.

c) Under UCC section 2-207(2), additional terms become part of the contract unless one of the three limitations applies. That section does not mention different terms, and it is not clear how different terms are to be treated. There are three basic approaches; (i) treatment as additional terms that materially alter the contract (meaning the offeror's terms) and thus never become part of the contract; (ii) treatment as irrelevant because only additional terms may become part of the contract, so that the offeree's terms control; and (iii) treatment as mutual objections by each party resulting in mutual knockout of the conflicting terms.

d) The third approach is best. It produces a contract that includes all the nonconflicting terms plus any terms supplied by the UCC. This prevents the offeror from taking advantage, as D did in this case, solely because he or she sent the first form. While the offeree could simply object to the terms, the purpose of UCC section 2-207 is to preserve a contract where there would not be one under the common law mirror-image rule. Section 2-207 reflects the commercial reality that merchants do not, and probably cannot, scrutinize each form they receive.

e) Since the provisions regarding period of limitations and warranties cancel one another, the UCC must provide the missing terms. In this case, the UCC would supply a four-year period of limitations, an express warranty, and implied warranties of merchantability and fitness for a particular purpose.

4) **Dissent.** The knockout rule should not be reached in this case because P's purchase order did not contain any terms in conflict with the express one-year limitation contained in D's proposal. Since P's claim is thus time-barred, the conflict in warranty provisions is irrelevant.

3. **The Statute of Frauds.** The Statute of Frauds generally makes sales contracts unenforceable unless there is either a writing sufficient to indicate that a contract has been formed or some other act deemed sufficient to prove the existence of a contract. The rule is intended to prevent fraud but, in fact, results in fraud itself by permitting the avoidance of contracts that both parties knew existed. The UCC responded to these policies by retaining the Statute, but it made changes to minimize the technical formalities.

a. **Basic provisions.**

1) **Scope.** UCC section 2-201, the Statute of Frauds, applies only to contracts to sell or sales of goods having a price of $500 or more. The dollar figure represents price, not value.

2) **Effect.** A sales contract which violates UCC section 2-201 is unenforceable, but not void. In other words, if the parties choose to perform, enforceable rights may be created. Only the parties to the contract may assert the lack of a writing.

3) **Writing.** Under the UCC, if the writing indicates that a sales contract has been made and specifies the quantity term, it is sufficient. The writing must also be signed by the party against whom the contract is being asserted.

4) **Exceptions.** Despite failure to comply with the statute, a contract may be enforceable if it falls within certain exceptions.

   a) **Partial acceptance.** At common law, acceptance of any part of the goods took the contract out of the statute entirely. UCC section 2-201 modifies this rule by making an otherwise unenforceable contract enforceable by acceptance and receipt of goods, but only to the extent of the goods accepted and received.

   b) **Partial payment.** UCC section 2-201 treats a partial payment in the same manner as partial acceptance, for the same reason; partial payment serves as evidence of the existence of a contract, but only as to the goods paid for.

   c) **Specially manufactured goods.** Under common law, where goods were to be manufactured specially for the buyer and were not suitable for sale to others in the seller's ordinary course of business, an oral agreement was enforceable. Under UCC section 2-201 the same rule applies, but only where the seller has made a substantial beginning in the manufacture or has made commitments for the goods' procurement before being notified of the buyer's repudiation.

   d) **Estoppel.** Courts may estop either party from asserting the Statute as a defense where by word or conduct he has caused the other to rely detrimentally on the oral promise so that to deny enforcement would cause "unconscionable injury or loss."

   e) **Admission.** If the party against whom enforcement is sought admits the contract in pleadings, testimony or otherwise in court, it is enforceable but only up to the quantity of goods admitted.

   f) **Merchants.** A special exception applies to merchants which does not require a writing signed by the party to be charged. The contract is enforceable if (i) within a reasonable time, the oral agreement is confirmed in writing; (ii) the writing is sufficient to bind the sender; (iii) the writing is received by the party to be charged; and (iv) the recipient, although knowing of its contents, makes to objection to the writing.

Nebraska Builders Products Co. v. Industrial Erectors, Inc.

b. **Series of writings--Nebraska Builders Products Co. v. Industrial Erectors, Inc.,** 478 N.W.2d 257 (Neb. 1992).

1) **Facts.** Nebraska Builders Products Co. (P) was preparing a bid as a subcontractor or material supplier to the companies bidding for the general contract for construction of a building for the Omaha Public Power District ("OPPD"). P contacted Industrial Erectors, Inc. (D) regarding specifications for cranes. D told P that D would sell and install the crane systems as specified for $449,920. D noted that there were some minor exceptions

to the specifications that could be worked out with OPPD's engineer. P won a supplier contract based on D's bid, which D had in the meantime reduced twice. Although P noticed that some of the equipment was different from that specified by OPPD, D assured P that the equipment in its bid was equal to or better than that specified by OPPD. P declined to issue a purchase order, contract, or letter of intent, preferring to wait until it had signed with the general contractor. Consequently, D never issued written contracts or purchase orders to its suppliers. In the ensuing weeks, the parties exchanged various telephone calls and correspondence regarding aspects of the bid. At one point, one of D's suppliers refused to provide certain equipment without a price increase of over $100,000. D told P that to comply with all of the OPPD specs, its bid had to increase by about $150,000. P insisted on the bid price, and D refused to perform without an increase. P obtained performance from another supplier at an additional cost of $136,000. P sued to recover the increase. The trial court found for D. P appeals.

2) **Issue.** May a series of related correspondence be used to satisfy the Statute of Frauds where no one piece of correspondence would meet all the requirements?

3) **Held.** Yes. Judgment reversed.

   a) Under the Statute of Frauds, a letter may be sufficient if it evidences a contract for the sale of goods, is signed by the party against whom enforcement is sought, and specifies a quantity. The writing is sufficient if it affords a basis for believing that the offered oral evidence is based on a real transaction. Multiple writings can be considered together even if any individual writing alone would not suffice.

   b) In this case, D sent P a proposal letter and several follow-up letters confirming telephone conversations. These letters referred to equipment D was "supplying" and stated that D looked forward to working with P on the project. In one letter, D stated he assumed certain units would be furnished by others or added to the "contract." When these letters are read together, they satisfy the requirements of UCC section 2-201.

   c) The agreement also falls within the Statute of Frauds exception in UCC section 2-201(3)(b), where an oral contract may be enforced when the party against whom enforcement is sought admits in court that a contract was made. One of D's employees stated during cross-examination that "there would be an increase to the contract" if D was to comply with the specifications. This sufficed as an admission of the existence of a contract.

c. **Merchant's failure to object to writing--Thomson Printing Machinery Co. v. B.F. Goodrich Co.,** 714 F.2d 744 (7th Cir. 1983).

   1) **Facts.** Thomson Printing Machinery Co. (P) deals in used printing machinery. P's president visited the surplus machinery department of B.F. Goodrich Co. (D) and discussed the purchase of some machinery from D

for $9,000. A few days later, P sent D a printed purchase order specifying the equipment, the total price of $9,000, and terms of $1,000 deposit with the balance upon removal of the equipment by P. Although D received the purchase order, D's mailroom was unable to locate the responsible department. By the time P sought to arrange for removal of the machinery, D had sold it to someone else. D refused to recognize any contract with P, claiming alternatively that no contract had been formed and that any oral contract was unenforceable under the Statute of Frauds. P brought suit and won a jury verdict, but the district court concluded that the oral contract was unenforceable anyway. P appeals.

2) **Issue.** May a merchant assert a Statute of Frauds defense to an oral contract if he does not object within 10 days of receiving a writing in confirmation of the contract?

3) **Held.** No. Judgment reversed.

a) UCC section 2-201(2) creates a modern exception to the requirement of the Statute of Frauds when the oral contract is between merchants. A merchant who receives a writing in confirmation of the oral contract may not assert the Statute of Frauds defense unless he objects to the writing within 10 days of receipt.

b) Here, P sent a writing in confirmation that contained all the necessary information about the oral contract. The jury found that there was in fact an oral contract, so the only issue under UCC section 2-201(2) is whether D had reason to know the contents of the writing.

c) D claims that the writing was improperly addressed because it was sent to D generally and not specifically to the surplus equipment department or the person with whom P's president spoke. However, there is no doubt that D received the writing. UCC section 1-201(27) refers to notice and states that "an organization exercises due diligence if it maintains reasonable routines for communicating significant information to the person conducting the transaction and there is reasonable compliance with the routines." D had a duty to exercise due diligence.

d) The writing clearly referred to a purchase of used printing equipment, and since D had only one surplus machinery department, the mailroom should have known where to send the writing. In addition, the writing contained P's phone number, and D could have called to request further information if necessary. D's mailroom procedures were not reasonable, and its failures do not permit D to escape liability on grounds of non-receipt of the writing.

Lige Dickson Co. v. Union Oil Co. of California

d. **Promissory estoppel not applicable to Statute of Frauds cases--Lige Dickson Co. v. Union Oil Co. of California,** 635 P.2d 103 (Wash. 1981).

1) **Facts.** For many years Lige Dickson Co. (P), a general contractor, bought the oil-based products it needed from Union Oil Co. of California (D). D encouraged P to enter the asphalt paving business, which P did. The parties dealt solely by oral contracts, followed by written invoices that P paid. When the price of oil increased in 1970, D gave P an oral guarantee

against further price increases that would affect contracts P already had to provide paving at fixed, agreed sums. These contracts were listed and the amount of asphalt necessary was figured out. Almost three years later, D notified P that it was raising its prices on all future purchases. P had to buy replacement asphalt at an extra cost of over $39,000 to perform its existing contracts. P sued for breach of contract. P sued in federal court for breach of contract. The court found that although there was an oral contract, it was unenforceable due to the Statute of Frauds. P appealed to the Ninth Circuit, which in turn certified the question to the Washington Supreme Court.

2) **Issue.** May an oral promise otherwise within the Statute of Frauds be enforceable on the basis of promissory estoppel?

3) **Held.** No.

    a) The doctrine of promissory estoppel, expressed in the Restatement (Second) of Contracts section 217A, permits enforcement of a promise despite the Statute of Frauds if it induced action or forbearance by the promisee. Section 217A has not been adopted by this court, however.

    b) Other courts have distinguished between the general Statute of Frauds and UCC section 2-201. Since UCC section 2-201 establishes means for making enforceable a contract otherwise under the Statute of Frauds, promissory estoppel should not be used to broaden the means available. To do so would thwart the legislative purpose and undermine the utility of the UCC as a means of bringing uniformity among the various states in the regulation of commercial dealings.

    c) Even though at least one state has applied promissory estoppel in connection with the UCC, this is a minority position. It is not the best approach. Therefore, promissory estoppel cannot be used to overcome the Statute of Frauds in a case involving the sale of goods.

    d) Equitable estoppel based on fraud or deceit may apply in a UCC situation, but this case does not involve such allegations.

4) **Concurrence.** There is a suggestion in the record that D may have admitted a contract, so the exception of UCC section 2-201(3)(b) may apply.

B. PRECONTRACT CIRCUMSTANCES

1. **Introduction.** One of the most important contract interpretation rules is found in UCC section 2-202, the parol evidence rule. If the parties are or should be aware of a particular trade usage or course of dealing between the parties as defined in 1-205, this existing custom gives particular meaning to and supplements or qualifies the terms of the agreement. This

rule invites examination of contract language in the context of actual business practices.

Columbia Nitrogen Corp. v. Royster Co.

2. **Evidence of Custom and Usage of the Trade--Columbia Nitrogen Corp. v. Royster Co.,** 451 F.2d 3 (4th Cir. 1971).

    a. **Facts.** Royster Co. (P) contracted to sell a minimum of 31,000 tons of phosphate each year for three years to Columbia Nitrogen Corp. (D). The contract included a specific price per ton, subject to an escalation clause related to production costs. The market price of phosphate soon dropped greatly, and D ordered less than one-tenth of the contract amount, although it would have ordered the full amount at the current market price. P sold the phosphate elsewhere at a price significantly below the contract price, and sued for damages for breach of contract. D tried unsuccessfully to introduce evidence on usage of the trade and course of dealing between the parties, and the district court gave P a judgment for $750,000. D appeals.

    b. **Issue.** May evidence of usage of trade and course of dealing be admitted to show that a specific contract price was not to be binding on the parties?

    c. **Held.** Yes. Judgment reversed.

        1) D offered proof that the contract, construed in light of the usage of the trade and course of dealing, imposed no duty upon it to accept the quantities specified at the quoted prices.

        2) Although the general rule is that extrinsic evidence may not be used to explain an ambiguous contract, UCC section 2-202 authorizes evidence of usage of trade and course of dealing between the parties to explain or supplement a contract. Therefore, a finding of ambiguity is not a prerequisite to the admission of such intrinsic evidence.

        3) P claims the evidence should be excluded because it is inconsistent with the express terms of the complete contract. The test of admissibility is not completeness but whether the evidence can reasonably be construed as consistent. The contract does not prohibit use of such extrinsic evidence. Adherence to the UCC provisions reflects the reality of the marketplace and avoids overly legalistic interpretations.

    d. **Comment.** The courts have been fairly lenient in accepting trade usage and course of dealing evidence to interpret contracts. However, parties may avoid UCC section 2-202(a) by specifically excluding such customs from their agreement.

Alaskan Northern Development, Inc. v. Alyeska Pipeline Service Co.

3. **Limitation on Use of Parol Evidence--Alaskan Northern Development, Inc. v. Alyeska Pipeline Service Co.,** 666 P.2d 33 (Alaska 1983), *cert. denied,* 464 U.S. 1041 (1984).

    a. **Facts.** The president of Alaskan Northern Development, Inc. (P) began discussion with representatives of Alyeska Pipeline Service Co. (D) to buy surplus parts. P made a written letter of intent proposing to purchase the parts but not specifying a price. D replied with its letter of intent confirming the deal, with no price term, but adding the statement that it was "subject to the final approval of the owner committee." The parties later agreed to a price and filled in the blanks on D's letter of intent. However,

D's owner committee rejected the proposal. P sued, claiming breach of contract on the ground that P's owner committee was only supposed to review the proposal to determine whether the price was fair and reasonable. The trial court granted summary judgment for D on the ground that the parol evidence rule excluded extrinsic evidence to show that the owner committee's approval power was limited. The case went to trial on P's claim for reformation, but after a six-week trial, the court found that P failed to prove a specific agreement was not properly reduced to writing. P appeals.

b.   **Issue.** Does the parol evidence rule restrict external evidence that contradicts the integrated terms of a written contract?

c.   **Held.** Yes. Judgment affirmed.

   1) A court may exclude parol evidence of additional terms to a writing when two requirements are met: (i) the writing involved must be integrated, meaning the parties intended it to be a final expression of their agreement with respect to the terms included, and (ii) the evidence of a prior or contemporaneous agreement must contradict or be inconsistent with the integrated portion of the writing. Even if the parol evidence is consistent, it may be excluded if the parties would necessarily have included the provision in the writing if they had intended it to be part of the agreement.

   2) The court found that D's letter was integrated with respect to the approval clause. This finding that the contract was partially integrated, which was based on all the evidence presented, including the extrinsic evidence, is supported by that evidence and is not clearly erroneous.

   3) The parol evidence would properly be excluded if it contradicts the integrated part of the writing. An earlier agreement may help in interpreting, but it cannot contradict, a later one. The meaning asserted by the proponent of the parol evidence must be one to which the language of the writing, read in context, is reasonably susceptible.

   4) There are two basic approaches to inconsistency. One is that an additional term is not inconsistent unless it contradicts or negates a term of the writing; if it has a lesser effect, it may be proved. The other approach assesses whether there is an absence of reasonable harmony in terms of the language and the respective obligations of the party. The latter approach, which is broader, is the better one.

   5) In this case, the language used in D's letter is not reasonably susceptible to P's interpretation. The written term gave the committee an unconditional right to approval. P's parol evidence would limit that right of approval, which is inconsistent with an unconditional right.

4.   **Trade Usage to Show the Meaning of Contract Terms--Frigaliment Importing Co. v. B.N.S. International Sales Corp.**, 190 F. Supp. 116 (S.D.N.Y. 1960).

   a.   **Facts.** B.N.S. International Sales Corp. (D) contracted to sell "chicken" to Frigaliment Importing Co. (P). D shipped stewing chicken ("fowl")

Frigaliment
Importing Co.
v. B.N.S.
International
Sales Corp.

under both contracts instead of the broiling and frying chicken desired by P. P sues for breach of warranty.

b. **Issue.** To enforce a particular meaning of a common term used in a contract, must P prove either D's actual knowledge of the particular meaning or a widespread, universal usage in the particular manner asserted?

c. **Held.** Yes. Judgment for D.

1) The making of a contract depends not on the agreement of two minds in one intention, but on the agreement of two sets of external signs. What the parties said, not what they meant, is the essence of the contract.

2) P produced substantial evidence that its narrow usage of the word "chicken" is common. D, however, shows that it is relatively new in the business, did not know of this trade usage, and that in fact "chicken" is commonly used in the trade in its broadest sense, covering broilers, fryers, and stewing chickens or "fowl."

3) Furthermore, D shows that by comparing the market price and the contract price, D would have incurred a loss by shipping broilers. Thus D believed it could properly send "fowl"; P believed it would receive broilers; but P fails to meet its burden of proving that "chicken" was to be used in the narrower rather than the broader sense.

d. **Comment.** The parol evidence rule of UCC section 2-202 does not preclude use of extrinsic evidence to interpret contracts. This case illustrates the difficulty of using extrinsic evidence to give a narrow interpretation to a common general description of goods. The party seeking adoption of the narrow interpretation has the burden of production of evidence [UCC §1-202(31)] and the burden of persuasion [UCC §1-201(8)].

C. OPEN TERMS

1. **Introduction.** Sales contracts rarely cover every part of the bargain which might subsequently be a source of dispute. Sometimes the parties deliberately omit a term because it cannot be fixed at the time, although a contract is intended. More often the omission is accidental.

a. **Gap filling.** When necessary, the law will provide missing terms, derived from the following sources:

1) Express terms, written or oral, which prevail unless there are contrary UCC mandates; then

2) Course of performance; then

3) Course of dealing; then

4) Usage of trade; then

5) The UCC itself.

6) If none of the above fill the gap, the missing term will not be supplied by the court.

b. **Open quantity arrangements.** The quantity term is the one term which it is impossible for the courts to supply so that it must be included in the contract. The actual number of units need not be specified in a requirements or an output contract, however.

   1) **Requirements contract.** An agreement which specifies that the buyer will purchase from the seller all of his "needs" or "requirements" for a given commodity during a given period is a valid contract. [UCC §2-306(1)] There is no contract if the buyer agrees only to take what he "wants."

   2) **Output contracts.** If the buyer agrees to take all goods produced by a seller from a specific production unit (factory, farm, orchard, etc.) during a given period of time, the contract is enforceable.

c. **Open price arrangements.** A fixed price is not essential to a valid sales contract. When a contract is silent as to price, it is assumed that the parties intended the sale to be at a reasonable price at the time and place of delivery. [UCC §2-305(1)(a)]

2. **Disproportionate Requirements--Orange & Rockland Utilities, Inc. v. Amerada Hess Corp.**, 397 N.Y.S.2d 814 (1977).

   Orange & Rockland Utilities, Inc. v. Amerada Hess Corp.

   a. **Facts.** In December 1969, Orange & Rockland Utilities, Inc. (P) contracted to purchase its requirements for fuel oil from Amerada Hess Corp. (D) at a fixed price of $2.14 per barrel for about five years. The contract contained P's estimated requirements for the years 1970 through 1973. P reserved the right to burn as much gas as it chose by including an open requirements term. Shortly after the contract was entered, the price of fuel oil increased drastically. Within a year it reached $4 per barrel. P began notifying D of increases in its requirements until it requested about 63% more than stated in the contract. P explained it could make more money selling the gas than burning it for generating power. D then refused to supply more than the contract estimates plus 10%. D performed on this premise despite P's objections. P refused D's proposal to increase the price, while keeping it well under the market price. P bought additional oil from other suppliers. P then sued for damages consisting of the increased prices it had to pay. The trial court found that P had not incurred its increased requirements in good faith, but instead had increased consumption by increasing its sales of electricity to other utilities and by shifting from other fuels to oil, thereby spreading the savings from its contract with D to other utilities. P appeals.

   b. **Issue.** May a requirements contract be enforced against the supplier if the buyer's requirements are unreasonably disproportionate to the contract estimate?

c. **Held.** No. Judgment affirmed.

1) UCC section 2-306 provides that a requirements contract is based on good faith requirements, except that no unreasonably higher quantity than that estimated may be demanded. This rule is a departure from prior case law, and is intended to insure the expectations of the parties will be more fully realized regardless of unexpected market conditions. A buyer in a rising market may not use a fixed price requirements contract for speculation.

2) Although the term "unreasonably disproportionate" is not clearly defined, several factors should be considered: (i) the amount of the increase over the estimates; (ii) whether the seller could have reasonably forecast or anticipated the new requirements; (iii) the difference between the market price and the contract price; (iv) the fortuitousness of the market price increase; and (v) the reason for the increase in requirements.

3) Here, P's increased requirements were largely due to its sixfold increase in sales to the New York Power Pool, which in turn resulted from P's requirements contract that locked in a low price. P used the contact to become a large seller of power to other utilities, in effect making them silent partners in the contract. This shows a lack of good faith dealing.

4) In addition, after D refused to supply the requested increases, P dropped a proposal to resell gas (for which it could substitute the fuel oil) to a supplier. P never did actually use the amounts requested. In subsequent years, P shifted away from gas toward fuel oil, greatly increasing its fuel oil requirements.

5) P actually increased its demand for fuel oil to more than double the contract estimates. This demand was unreasonably disproportionate to those estimates as a matter of law. D had no reason to anticipate such an increase, and is not responsible to pay P the increased price.

Empire Gas Corp. v. American Bakeries Co.

3. **Failure to Take Any--Empire Gas Corp. v. American Bakeries Co.**, 840 F.2d 1333 (7th Cir. 1988).

a. **Facts.** Empire Gas Corp. (P), a distributor of propane, sold converters that allowed gasoline-powered vehicles to run on propane. American Bakeries Co. (D) had a fleet of over 3,000 motor vehicles and contacted P to find out about converting to propane. The parties entered an agreement for "approximately 3,000" conversions, "depending upon requirements" of D. D also agreed to buy propane solely from P for four years as long as P remains in a "reasonably competitive price posture." Within a few days, D decided against converting its vehicles and D never ordered any conversions or propane from P. P sued for breach of contract and the jury awarded P over $3 million for lost profits. D appeals.

b. **Issue.** In a requirements contract, is a buyer free to purchase nothing so long as it does not purchase the products from anyone else and is not acting out of ill will toward the seller?

c. **Held.** No. Judgment affirmed.

    1)   UCC section 2-306(1) governs requirements contracts and provides that no quantity unreasonably disproportionate to any stated estimate may be demanded. This provision protects sellers in situations where the negotiated price is advantageous and the buyer might increase requirements to resell the goods at a profit. This would allow the buyer to compete with the seller, which the parties would not have intended when they entered the contract.

    2)   UCC section 2-306(1) does not distinguish between buyers who demand more and buyers who demand less, so read literally, it prohibits buyers from taking much less than the stated estimate. But the majority approach, also the common law approach, is to treat the two situations differently and have the seller assume the risk that the buyer will not take any goods. Thus the "unreasonably disproportionate" phrase in UCC section 2-306(1) does not apply where the buyer takes less rather than more of the stated estimate in a requirements contract, and the jury should not have been instructed on this provision.

    3)   But UCC section 2-306(1) also requires the buyer to take his "good faith" requirements from the seller. D would have acted in bad faith if it had bought propane conversion units from someone other than P or made its own units, or because it wanted to hurt P for some reason. It would not have acted in bad faith if it had a legitimate business reason for deciding not to convert, such as a drop in demand for its products that caused it to reduce or abandon its fleet of delivery vehicles. But if D changed its mind for no reason, the question is closer.

    4)   If a buyer can reduce its requirements to zero, then a requirements contract is merely an option to purchase, except that the buyer cannot buy from someone else. But a requirements contract is more than a buyer's option. A requirements contract justifies a seller's expectation that the buyer will buy something like the estimated requirements unless it has a valid business reason for buying less. The buyer and seller share risks; the seller assumes the risk of a change in the buyer's business that makes continuation of the contract unduly costly, but the buyer assumes the risk of a less urgent change of circumstances such as a change in management with different priorities. A buyer does not act in good faith if it reduces the estimated requirements merely because it wants to get out of the contract.

    5)   In this case, D gave no reason for reducing its requirements to zero. Therefore, no reasonable jury could have failed to find bad faith.

d. **Dissent.** The court's instruction on the "unreasonably disproportionate" language of UCC section 2-305(1) was wrong and a new trial should be ordered. There was no evidence of either good or bad faith on the part of D. P failed to produce evidence of D's bad faith, so it failed to carry its burden of proof. Instead, the majority has imposed a presumption of bad faith without giving D an opportunity to rebut by proof of good faith.

4. **Price in the Absence of a Contract--*In re* Glover Construction Co., Inc.,** 49 B.R. 581 (W.D. Ky. 1985).

a. **Facts.** Glover Construction Co., Inc. (D) agreed to purchase vehicle washing equipment from Fleetwash for $370,000. D was to install the equipment on a construction project for the Corps of Engineers. The arrangement was set forth in a February 1982 purchase order that contained two alternative payment schemes in addition to the requirement that the total price be paid by the thirtieth of the month following the month of delivery. Fleetwash insisted that D had to choose between the two alternatives, while D claimed the alternatives were options to earn a discount. Neither party intended to be bound unless the other agreed to its own interpretation. The equipment was not delivered and in November 1982, D filed a Chapter 11 bankruptcy petition. In February 1983, Fleetwash made a partial shipment even though the parties did not agree on the price and payment terms. D sought a progress payment of about $130,000 based on the delivery, and the Corps paid the funds to the trustee. D objected to the payment of the funds to Fleetwash and Fleetwash brought this action to obtain the funds.

b. **Issue.** When one party delivers goods even though there is no contract, is the seller entitled to the price charged despite the reasonable value of the goods?

c. **Held.** No.

1) Under UCC section 2-305(4), if the parties intend not to be bound unless the price is fixed or agreed, there is no contract if the price is not fixed or agreed. In that case, the UCC does not provide for a reasonable price to make an enforceable contract. Instead, the buyer must return the goods or pay the reasonable value for them.

2) In this case, the evidence clearly shows that no contract was intended. Thus, Fleetwash is entitled to the reasonable value of the equipment delivered. The term "reasonable value" is the equivalent of the traditional doctrine of restitution used in quasi-contract situations.

3) Fleetwash, claiming the parties intended a contract but left open the price and payment terms, seeks the full $130,000. D claims the reasonable value of the equipment was between $32,000 and $34,000. The most convincing evidence is contained in a letter from Fleetwash to its attorney that explained the invoice to D would produce income of about $80,000. This means that the equipment was worth $43,000 to Fleetwash, and payment of that amount would restore Fleetwash to as good a position as it would have been in if it had never made the shipment to D.

5. **Good Faith Requirement in Establishing Price--TCP Industries, Inc. v. Uniroyal, Inc.,** 661 F.2d 542 (6th Cir. 1981).

a. **Facts.** TCP Industries, Inc. (P) was a middleman which arranged sales of butadiene from El Paso Products Co., a refinery, to Uniroyal, Inc. (D), a synthetic rubber manufacturer. P sold the butadiene to D for its cost and earned a commission from El Paso. Under the contract, P was permitted to increase the price only when El Paso increased its price, but before P's contract with D expired, El Paso discontinued its commission program. P increased its price to D contrary to the contract. The parties subsequently entered a new contract under which P was permitted to change the price upon giving no less than 15 days' notice. Other significant provisions also were changed. D bought considerably less than it had previously done, claiming the price was too high. P sued for breach of contract for D's failure to buy butadiene as agreed, and D counterclaimed for breach of the earlier contract. The jury found for P and D appeals.

    b. **Issue.** Is a price term that permits one party to change its price upon giving 15 days' notice so vague as to render the contract unenforceable?

    c. **Held.** No. Judgment affirmed.

        1) The trier of fact is responsible to determine the parties' intentions when a price term is left open. Here, the second contract significantly changed the price terms of the original contract, so the jury was not bound to rely on the prior price terms.

        2) Under UCC section 2-305(2), if the price is to be fixed by the seller, it must be fixed in good faith, which includes observance of reasonable commercial standards of fair dealing in the trade. The price set by P must be reasonable to be enforceable. The evidence shows that, although P's prices were at the high end of the industry-recognized range for the periods involved, the prices were within that range. P's price was thus reasonable.

        3) This evidence supports the jury's finding that P's price was commercially reasonable and set in good faith.

D. CHANGED CIRCUMSTANCES

    1. **Introduction.** After a contract is formed, circumstances may change. The change may have no effect; it may prompt the parties to modify the contract terms; or it may be so significant as to excuse performance.

        a. **Modification.** Should the parties choose to modify the contract, the normal contract rule requiring new consideration to make a modification enforceable is eliminated by UCC section 2-209(1). The good faith obligation prevents abuse, however. Neither party can demand a modification without legitimate commercial reason.

        b. **Impossibility.** UCC sections 2-613 through 2-616 deal with situations in which circumstances change so as to render performance impossible or commercially impracticable. UCC section 2-615 is essentially a codification of the normal contract law rules regarding impossibility of performance and frustration of purpose. A seller may be excused from performance rendered impracticable when (i) a contingency occurs, the nonoccurrence of which was a basic presumption on which the contract was made, or (ii) the seller complies with a governmental regulation or order.

Wickliffe
Farms, Inc.
v. Owensboro
Grain Co.

2. Unforeseen Circumstance Must Render Performance of Written Contractual Duty Impossible--Wickliffe Farms, Inc. v. Owensboro Grain Co., 684 S.W.2d 17 (Ky. Ct. App. 1984).

a. **Facts.** Wickliffe Farms, Inc. (P) contracted to deliver 35,000 bushels of corn at $3.70 per bushel to Owensboro Grain (D), a grain dealer. D immediately sold the 35,000 bushels for future delivery to an exporter. That summer a drought hit P's farm and P was unable to grow more than about 18,000 bushels, which it delivered to D at the agreed price. D had to buy the remaining 17,000 bushels on the market at a price of $5.54. D later set off over $19,000 against payments owed to P on separate grain contracts. P sued D for the amount due on the other contracts. D asserted a counterclaim for the loss caused by P's partial delivery of corn. The trial court granted summary judgment for D and P appeals.

b. **Issue.** If a grain supply contract does not specify where the grain is to be grown, does the seller's inability due to an unforeseen drought to grow the full contract amount on its own land relieve it from its duty to perform?

c. **Held.** No. Judgment affirmed.

1) P relied on the defense of impossibility of performance, but this defense does not apply when the impossibility related to the ability to grow the corn instead of the ability to supply it. The contract did not specify that the corn was to be grown on P's land. It only required P to supply 35,000 bushels.

2) Although UCC section 2-202 permits evidence of consistent additional terms in certain circumstances, P's claim that the corn was to be produced on its own land is not consistent with a contractual requirement to supply 35,000 bushels of corn. There was no evidence that the parties intended to contract for the production of any specific acreage. P simply failed to perform its part of the bargain.

International
Minerals &
Chemical
Corp. v.
Llano, Inc.

3. Compliance with Governmental Regulation as an Excuse--International Minerals & Chemical Corp. v. Llano, Inc., 770 F.2d 879 (10th Cir. 1985), *cert. denied*, 475 U.S 1015 (1986).

a. **Facts.** International Minerals & Chemical Corp. (P) entered into a 10-year contract to purchase all of its natural gas requirements from Llano, Inc. (D). The contract required P to take or pay for established minimum annual purchases, but also provided for adjustments if P was unable to receive gas for any reason beyond the reasonable control of the parties. During the term of the contract, New Mexico adopted more stringent particle emission standards, which required P to shut down equipment that used over one-half of its natural gas requirements. P sought a declaratory judgment that this regulatory action excused P from having to take or pay for the minimum quantity. D counterclaimed for the amounts due based on the minimum requirements clause. The trial court found for D on both issues and P appeals.

b. **Issue.** May an unforeseen change in governmental regulations which directly reduces the buyer's requirements make performance impracticable so as to excuse performance?

c. **Held.** Yes. Judgment reversed.

1) Take or pay clauses are common in requirements contracts because they compensate the seller for being ready at all times to deliver the maximum amount of gas to the buyer. In this contract, the harshness of the take or pay clause is mitigated by the force majeure and adjustment provisions.

2) The force majeure provision does not apply to this case. Even if the government regulation prevented P from taking the gas, it did not prevent it from paying for it. When a promisor can perform a contract in either of two alternative ways, the impracticability of one alternative does not excuse the promisor if performance by means of the other alternative is still practicable.

3) The adjustment provision provides that P could obtain a reduction in the minimum purchase requirements if it is unable to receive the gas. The term "unable" should be construed to mean "impracticable" as that term is used in UCC section 2-615 and the common law. Strict impossibility is not required to excuse performance, so long as unanticipated circumstances make performance vitally different from what should reasonably have been within the contemplation of both parties when they entered into the contact.

4) If performance is made impracticable due to compliance with government regulation, it may be excused. P could not have complied with the new regulation without decreasing its natural gas consumption, so the adjustment provision of the contract was properly invoked. P does not have to pay for any natural gas it did not take under the contact.

5) D claims that P complied earlier than was legally necessary, but the governmental regulation need not mandate compliance to justify an excuse from performance. A party may not cooperate with the government solely to prevent performance, but where, as here, the party recognizes the public goal and acts from willingness to effectuate that goal, its efforts cannot be considered as improper collusion done in bad faith.

4. **Good Faith Standard in Seeking Modification--Roth Steel Products v. Sharon Steel Corp., 705 F.2d 134 (6th Cir. 1983).**

a. **Facts.** Roth Steel Products (P) entered into a contract with Sharon Steel Corp. (D) to buy 200 tons of steel per month for a year at $148 per year. Shortly thereafter, the market price of steel increased significantly and D notified P that it was discontinuing the price concessions. Although it did not want to do so, P agreed to pay the contract price for the first six months and an increased price for the remaining six months because it had no alternative suppliers. In succeeding years, P bought from D at the price prevailing at the time of shipment. D's shipments were constantly late,

Roth Steel
Products v.
Sharon Steel
Corp.

and because the market price was increasing, P had to pay an increasing price. P later learned that the delivery delays were not due to shortages of production but to D's practice of providing steel to a subsidiary which sold it at premium prices. P sued for breach of the original contract and won a verdict for the difference between the contract price and the price it paid under the modification. D appeals.

b. **Issue.** If a party acts in bad faith in seeking an adjustment to a contract price, and the other party agrees to the adjustment, may the first party enforce the modification?

c. **Held.** No. Judgment affirmed in part but remanded on other grounds.

1) The UCC permits easier modification of contracts since no consideration is required as it was at common law. The only limit on modification is the general obligation of good faith. This requires evaluation of two factors: (i) whether the party's conduct is consistent with reasonable commercial standards of fair dealing in the trade, and (ii) whether the parties were in fact motivated to seek modification by an honest desire to compensate for commercial exigencies.

2) D was partially protected against raw material price increases, it expected only slim profits on the contract with P, and it had an overall profit on the contract during the first three months of performance under the original price. This evidence, however, does not justify a conclusion that D's conduct was inconsistent with reasonable commercial standards of fair dealing. A reasonable merchant may seek a modification to avoid a loss, and D's raw material costs were increasing. Even though a party has not actually suffered a loss on a contract, it may seek a modification to protect against future losses.

3) The second factor governs this case, however. D threatened not to supply P any steel if P refused to pay the increased prices. Such conduct raises an inference of bad faith that may be rebutted. D attempted to rebut the inference by citing a letter it wrote that allowed it to raise prices on a different type of steel. The significant fact is that D never advanced this justification until the litigation started; it was simply not the reason D sought the price increase.

4) Because D did not rebut the inference of bad faith, the court's finding that D acted in bad faith is not clearly erroneous and must be upheld. Because D violated the obligation of good faith, the modification is not enforceable.

d. **Comment.** The court did not reach the issue of whether the modification was voidable because P agreed to it due to economic duress.

V. PRESHIPMENT STAGE

A. SELLER'S REMEDIES FOR BUYER'S BREACH

1. **Impaired Expectation of Full Performance.** Under UCC section 2-609, either party may demand adequate assurance of due performance when there are reasonable grounds for insecurity with respect to the other's performance.

    a. **Insecurity.** When the buyer nears insolvency, the seller may have no obligation to deliver goods unless the buyer gives reasonable assurances of payment. Any other situation giving rise to insecurity may support a request for assurances as well.

    b. **Repudiation.** A party's anticipatory repudiation of some future performance due under the contract, other than the mere payment of money creates an immediate right of action by the other party. The term "repudiation" is not defined, but it normally refers to express communications as opposed to the apparent inability to perform covered by UCC section 2-609.

        1) **Aggrieved party's rights.** The aggrieved party has alternative means of responding to the other's repudiation.

            a) He may "stand on the contract" by insisting on performance, for a commercially reasonable time [UCC §2-610(a)]; or

            b) He may resort to any remedy for breach, even if he has informed the repudiating party that he would await the latter's performance [UCC §2-610(b)]; and, in either case,

            c) He is entitled to suspend all further performance on his part.

        2) **Retracting repudiation.** The repudiating party may retract and perform as agreed unless the other party has accepted the repudiation or has materially altered his position in reliance thereon. [UCC §2-611] The retraction must include any assurance justifiably demanded under UCC section 2-609.

    c. **Demand for assurance of performance.**

        1) **Grounds.** Under the UCC, either party is entitled to demand adequate assurance of performance if there are reasonable grounds for insecurity with respect to the performance of the other party. [UCC §2-609(1)] The usual grounds are potential insolvency of the other party or anticipatory repudiation by the other party followed by attempts to retract repudiation (which automatically entitles the other party to adequate assurances under UCC section 2-611(2)).

        2) **Procedure.** Adequate assurance of due performance must be demanded in writing, and the recipient must provide the

assurance in a reasonable time not exceeding 30 days. [UCC §2-609(4)]

3) **Effect of provision.** Until adequate assurances are given, the aggrieved party is entitled to suspend any performance for which he has not already received the agreed-on return. At the end of the reasonable period, failure to supply assurances is a repudiation of the contract.

4) **Standards.** Between merchants, the reasonableness of the ground given and the adequacy of the assurance received depend on factual testimony about what is customary in the trade.

5) **Partial acceptance.** Acceptance of any improper delivery or payment does not prejudice the aggrieved party's right to demand adequate assurances as to future performance. [UCC §2-609(3)]

6) **Installment sales.** UCC section 2-612 establishes a rule of substantial performance in installment sales contracts, defined as a contract that requires or authorizes the delivery of goods in separate lots to be separately accepted.

   a) **Rejecting an installment.** When the seller is to make deliveries in installments to the buyer, the buyer is privileged to reject an install-ment only if the defect in the tender substantially impairs the value of that installment. [UCC §2-612(2)]

   b) **Canceling the contract.** Only if nonconformity of one or more installments substantially impairs the value of the whole contract is there a breach of the entire contract by the seller. [UCC §2-612(3)]

Plotnick v.
Pennsylvania
Smelting &
Refining Co.

d. **Installment sale--Plotnick v. Pennsylvania Smelting & Refining Co.,** 194 F.2d 859 (3d Cir. 1952).

1) **Facts.** Plotnick (P) contracted to sell 200 tons of lead to Pennsylvania Smelting & Refining Co. (D) in several deliveries to be completed by December 25. The parties agreed that 63% of the price for each shipment should be paid shortly after each shipment was received, the full price due four weeks after each delivery. The parties had previously entered a series of contracts under which D often made late payments and P made late deliveries. P made only one delivery under this contract before December 25 and made a third delivery in March. After the third delivery, however, about 145 tons remained to be delivered. In April, D told P that it would begin buying on the open market and charge P the excess cost. P told D it would not ship any more lead until D paid for the third shipment. P brought suit for the unpaid price of the delivery and D counterclaimed for the failure to make the rest of the deliveries. The trial court found for both parties and P appeals.

2) **Issue.** Does failure to make a timely payment for a partial shipment under a contract justify the seller to refuse further shipments where the partial shipment was several months late?

3) **Held.** No. Judgment affirmed.

a) Under the Sales Act, P would be justified in refusing further shipments if D's nonpayment made it impossible or unreasonably burdensome for P to make further shipments. This was not the case here. In fact, P was actually making shipments to other purchasers for a higher price.

b) P would also be justified if D's refusal to pay created a reasonable apprehension on P's part that D might not pay for future shipments. On these facts, there was no basis for P to reasonably fear that D would not make future payments. D earnestly wanted the lead; the price was rising; and D's credit was not impaired. In addition, P had the option of shipping on sight draft if desired. There is no indication that D would have refused to honor sight drafts for the contract price.

2. **Suit for the Price.** Whether the seller is entitled to sue a breaching buyer for the full purchase price normally depends on whether the seller has delivered possession of the goods to the buyer. If he has, then an action for the full purchase price is allowed. But if the seller still has possession of the goods, he normally is limited to an action for damages; *i.e.,* he must resell the goods and sue the buyer for any loss on the resale. The exceptions are where the goods cannot be sold, either because they are specially manufactured to order or because they were destroyed or lost after the risk of loss had passed to the buyer.

3. **Contract-Market Damages.**

a. **Basic rule.** After resale under UCC section 2-706, the seller may recover against the buyer the difference between the contract price and the market price at the time and place that the goods were tendered. [UCC §2-708(1)]

b. **Buyer's repudiation--Trans World Metals, Inc. v. Southwire Co.,** 769 F.2d 902 (2d Cir. 1985).

Trans World Metals, Inc. v. Southwire Co.

1) **Facts.** Southwire Co. (D) contracted to purchase 1,000 metric tons of aluminum per month for one year from Trans World Metals, Inc. (P) for 77¢ per pound. P shipped only 750 tons the first month and made up the balance early the next month. Subsequently the market price of aluminum dropped and D canceled the contract based on P's default. P sued for damages. The jury found that D had accepted the late delivery, so P did not default. Therefore, D had repudiated the contract. P was awarded damages based on the difference between the contract and projected market prices. D appeals the damage award, claiming that P's damages should have been based on P's rate of profit on the first month's shipments projected over the life of the contract.

2) **Issue.** When the buyer repudiates the contract, is the seller entitled only to the lost profits?

3) **Held.** No. Judgment affirmed.

a) UCC section 2-708 governs the seller's damages for repudiation. The general rule in UCC section 2-708(1) is that the seller may recover the difference between the market price at the time and place for tender and the unpaid contract price together with any incidental damages, less any expenses saved by the buyer's breach. If this measure is inadequate, then UCC section 2-708(2) permits recovery based on the profit which the seller would have made from full performance by the buyer. This alternative measure of damages is often used by sellers who do not acquire the goods before the buyer repudiates.

b) D asserts that the lost profits measure should apply when the seller would be overcompensated under UCC section 2-708(1), but nothing in the language of UCC section 2-708(2) supports that theory. At any rate, there is no proof that P was overcompensated. When the parties entered into the contract, each assumed the risk of movement of the market price for aluminum. If the price had risen, D would have benefited. P should have the benefit of the drop in prices.

c) D also argues that the proper time for measuring the contract/market price differential was when D repudiated the contract, but UCC section 2-708(1) states that the proper time is the time of tender. Since the damages were awarded after the time for full performance, the damages should reflect the actual market price at each successive date when tender was to have been made. This is different from the rule for a buyer's damages for the seller's repudiation, which is based on the contract/market price differential at the time the buyer learns of the breach under UCC section 2-713(1).

d) It was inappropriate to use P's projected market prices because the actual market prices were known. However, this actually reduced the judgment because the projected prices were lower than the actual market prices.

4) Comment. The court distinguished *Nobs Chemical, USA, Inc. v Koppers Co., Inc.*, 616 F.2d 212 (5th Cir. 1980), a case in which the seller, acting as a middleman, had fixed-price contracts with both its own supplier and with the buyer. The market price in that situation was the supplier's fixed price, and awarding damages based on the open market price would have given the seller a windfall.

4. Resale to Fix Damages.

a. **Basic rule.** If the buyer resells in accordance with UCC section 2-706, he may recover the difference between the resale price and the contract price. It is not clear from the UCC itself whether the seller has the choice between a contract-resale and a contract-market recovery. Comment 1 to UCC section 2-703 states that the choice depends on the facts. The prevailing view is that the seller may use whatever measure is most favorable to him.

b. **Application--Afram Export Corp. v. Metallurgiki Halyps, S.A.**, 772 F.2d 1358 (7th Cir. 1985).

1) **Facts.** Metallurgiki Halyps, S.A. (D), a Greek steel producer, contracted to buy scrap steel from Afram Export Corp. (P) for $135 per ton. After P prepared the scrap, D's inspector found it clean but stated that D would not accept it because the price of scrap had fallen. Shortly after D rejected the scrap, P's officer called another buyer and explained he had extra scrap because of a buyer's breach. He sold about 10,000 tons of scrap to that buyer on June 4 for $118 per ton. P made a sale of about 5,000 tons on September 15 for $103 per ton. P also sold scrap on June 15 at a public sale for $102.75 per ton, designated that as the cover transaction, and sued D. All the scrap was sold from the same pile. D filed a counterclaim alleging that P had breached the contract. The district court found that P's first sales of scrap after the breach were the cover transactions, awarded damages based on that amount, and dismissed the counterclaim. Both parties appeal.

2) **Issue.** When a buyer breaches, may the seller choose any of several subsequent sales as the cover sale?

3) **Held.** No. Judgment affirmed.

    a) P's officer's conversation just after the breach indicates that the breach made that sale possible, so the revenue from that sale must be subtracted from the contract price to determine P's loss.

    b) The public sale was the next in time, but the court found that it was not made in good faith and in a commercially reasonable manner as required by UCC section 2-706(1). It consisted solely of the transfer of the scrap on P's books to the books of another affiliated corporation under common ownership with P. The scrap did not even move from P's scrap pile. This raises the inference that the sale was made only to allow P to resell the scrap at higher prices later on. Thus the September sale provided better evidence of what P actually lost.

    c) P was authorized to recover incidental damages as defined by UCC section 2-710. P claimed the interest it paid on the loan used to buy the cars that it converted to scrap. Additional interest expense is generally recoverable as incidental damages because the contract-breaking buyer, not the seller, is better able to avoid the expense and should bear the risk of its occurrence.

    d) In this case, however, P gave no evidence that it would have paid off the loan had D paid the contract price; in fact, since P seeks interest up to the date of trial, P probably did not pay off the loan even after it resold the scrap. P is actually seeking to recover its opportunity cost, or the lost interest or profit that P could have obtained by using the sales proceeds earlier. Such a loss is more of a consequential than an incidental damage. The law does not permit recovery of such damages. P is entitled only to out-of-pocket interest expenses that it would not have incurred but for the breach.

5. Lost Profits and Incidental Damages ("Personalized Damages").

    a.   Basic rule. Where other measures of damages are inadequate to put the seller in as good a position as performance would have done, damages under UCC section 2-708(2) are available. This includes lost profits and incidental damages.

R.E. Davis Chemical Corp. v. Diasonics, Inc.

    b.   Lost volume seller's damages--R.E. Davis Chemical Corp. v. Diasonics, Inc., 826 F.2d 678 (7th Cir. 1987).

        1)   Facts. R.E. Davis Chemical Corp. (P) contracted to purchase medical diagnostic equipment from Diasonics, Inc. (D). P paid $300,000 down but refused to take delivery of the equipment or pay the balance due. D resold the equipment to a third party for the same price P had agreed to pay. P sued for restitution under UCC section 2-718(2). D counterclaimed as a lost volume seller. The district court granted summary judgment for P. D appeals.

        2)   Issue. Where the buyer breaches and the seller resells the goods at the same price the original buyer was contracted to pay, may the seller recover from the buyer the seller's lost profits on the sale?

        3)   Held. Yes. Judgment reversed.

            a)   Although the issue has never been addressed by Illinois courts, courts of other states have unanimously held that a lost volume seller can recover its lost profits under UCC section 2-708(2). UCC section 2-718(2)(b) allows a buyer such as P to recover its down payment, less $500, but P's right to restitution is qualified under UCC section 2-718(3)(a) to the extent that D can show it is entitled to damages under any other Article 2 provision.

            b)   UCC section 2-706 would allow D to recover its contract price less the resale price, and UCC section 2-708(2) would allow D to recover its profit. The UCC does not clearly specify when one remedy is more appropriate than another. One approach is to allow UCC section 2-708 remedies only when UCC section 2-706 does not apply, such as when the seller does not resell in a commercially reasonable manner. This is the approach the district court took. But the better approach recognizes that the UCC remedies are essentially cumulative in nature and that a seller is not compelled to use the UCC section 2-706 resale remedy instead of the UCC section 2-708 damage remedy.

            c)   Damages for lost profits under UCC section 2-708(2) are available only if the measure of damages provided by UCC section 2-708(1) are insufficient to put the seller in as good a position as performance would have done. UCC section 2-708(1) measures damages by the difference between the contract price and the market price at the time and place for tender. A lost profits seller is one who would have made the sale represented by the resale whether or not the breach had occurred. In such a case, damages measured by UCC section 2-708(1) would not put the seller in the same position it would have been in because it still would have lost the profit on the initial sale.

    d)   On remand, D must prove both that it had the capacity to make the second sale and that it would have been profitable for D to have produced and sold two machines instead of one.

4)   **Comment.** The court noted that UCC section 2-708(2) requires the seller to give due allowance for payments or proceeds of resale. Literally applied, this would mean that in most cases, the seller would recover only nominal damages. The courts have interpreted this phrase narrowly to apply only to cases of resale of goods for scrap. This approach was adopted in this case as well.

B. SELLER'S BREACH

1.   **Introduction.** The discussions of repudiation and adequate assurances, *supra*, apply to sellers as well as to buyers. The most significant differences appear in available remedies.

2.   **Specific Performance.**

    a.   **Equity rule.** The traditional rule in equity is that a contract for the sale of chattels may be specifically enforced only where the goods in question are unique and irreplaceable, so that money damages for the seller's breach would not be an adequate remedy.

    b.   **UCC.** The UCC permits specific performance in any case where goods are unique, or in other proper circumstances, such as where the goods are in scarce or short supply.

    c.   **Application--Laclede Gas Co. v. Amoco Oil Co.,** 522 F.2d 33 (8th Cir. 1975). Laclede Gas Co. v. Amoco Oil Co.

        1)   **Facts.** Laclede Gas Co. (P) and Amoco Oil Co. (D) agreed to an arrangement to provide central propane gas distribution systems to certain residential areas until natural gas mains were extended. D, as supplier, was to provide the necessary supply facilities. P, as distributor, was to provide and operate all distribution facilities from the outlet of D's piping. P promised to pay D four cents per gallon above a particular posed price. P could terminate the agreement on 30 days' notice at the end of any year or when natural gas mains were extended. D had no right of termination. After a price dispute, D terminated the agreement, claiming it lacked mutuality. P sought an injunction against the continuing breach, but the trial court agreed with D. P appeals.

        2)   **Issue.** Is specific performance an appropriate remedy for breach of a contract involving personal property?

        3)   **Held.** Yes. Judgment reversed.

a) The law does not require that both parties be mutually entitled to specific performance for one of them to receive that remedy. All that is required is inadequacy of a remedy at law.

b) D also argues that specific performance would be difficult for the court to enforce, but the court itself has discretion to take this factor into account, and the public interest outweighs the potential burden on the court. D contends that the contract is indefinite and uncertain, but any uncertainties are resolvable.

c) Finally, D claims that P has an adequate remedy at law, so specific performance is inappropriate, especially since personalty, not realty, is involved. However, applying a practical approach to the adequacy of a legal remedy, we conclude that P could not with certainty find an alternative long-term supplier. While P has alternative propane suppliers, these provide only backup for peak shortages, not full-time residential supply.

d) Although specific performance is a discretionary remedy, when certain equitable rules have been met and the contract is fair and plain, specific performance goes as a matter of right.

3. Market-Contract Price Damages.

a. **Basic rule.** The buyer may recover against the seller the difference between the contract price and the market price at the time and place the buyer learned of the breach. [UCC §2-713(1)] If the seller refuses to deliver, the relevant place is where the buyer should have tendered the goods; if he makes a nonconforming tender, the place is the place of arrival.

Cosden Oil v. Karl O. Helm Aktiengesellschaft

b. **Anticipatory repudiation and the timing of the price differential-- Cosden Oil v. Karl O. Helm Aktiengesellschaft,** 736 F.2d 1064 (5th Cir. 1984), *reh'g denied*, 750 F.2d 69 (1984).

1) **Facts.** Karl O. Helm Aktiengesellschaft (P) sued Cosden Oil (D) for anticipatory repudiation. The district court found for P and awarded damages based on the market price at a commercially reasonable point after D informed P that it was canceling the orders. Both parties appeal.

2) **Issue.** When a seller anticipatorily repudiates a contract, should the buyer's damages be based on the market price at a commercially reasonable point after the seller notifies the buyer of the repudiation?

3) **Held.** Yes. Judgment affirmed.

a) D claims damages should be measured by the market price at the time P learned of the repudiation; P claims the market price on the last day of delivery should govern. The issue is not clearly settled by the UCC.

b) UCC section 2-713 refers to the market price at the time when the buyer learned of the breach. This has been interpreted as being (i) when the buyer learns of the repudiation; (ii) when he learns of the repudiation plus a commercially reasonable time; and (iii) when performance is due under the contract. When the buyer learns of the breach at or after the time of performance, it is clear that the damages depend on the market price at the time the buyer learns of the breach. This does not necessarily apply to anticipatory repudiation cases.

c) UCC section 2-610 permits a buyer to await performance for a commercially reasonable time after the seller anticipatorily repudiates before resorting to the remedies of cover or damages. This section must be read together with UCC section 2-713. Interpreting UCC section 2-713 to allow the buyer to wait a commercially reasonable time is consistent with UCC section 2-610. That this is appropriate is shown by UCC section 2-611, which permits a seller to retract the repudiation.

d) Giving P a commercially reasonable time to evaluate cover possibilities is also consistent with the policy of allowing the buyer to choose between cover and seeking damages. Yet the buyer may not wait until the time of performance, because he must act without unreasonable delay under UCC section 2-712(1).

c. **Limitation on market-contract price damages--Allied Canners & Packers, Inc. v. Victor Packing Co.**, 209 Cal. Rptr. 60 (Cal. Ct. App. 1984).

Alllied Canners & Packers, Inc. v. Victor Packing Co.

1) **Facts.** Allied Canners & Packers, Inc. (P) contracted to sell raisins to foreign buyers. Knowing this, Victor Packing Co. (D) agreed to sell P raisins for 29.75 cents per pound, which would give P a profit of $4,462.50 on the resale. Due to heavy rains, D's crops and those of other sources were badly damaged and D repudiated its contract with P. When the market reopened a month later, the price for raising was 87 cents per pound. P sued for breach, seeking the difference between the contract price and the market price, which was about $150,000. None of P's buyers sought to enforce their contracts, however. The trial court awarded P its lost profits, finding that P was not a buyer for its own account so that UCC section 2-713 did not apply. P appeals.

2) **Issue.** May the damages awarded to a buyer who has not covered be limited to the buyer's actual economic loss which is below the damages figured under the contract/market price formula?

3) **Held.** Yes. Judgment affirmed.

a) The contract/market price formula under UCC section 2-713 does not normally result in a damage award that reflects the buyer's actual loss. In this case, for example, P actually lost only $4,462.50, but the contract/market price formula would give P about $150,000.

b) Courts and commentators differ as to whether market damages in excess of the buyer's actual loss are appropriate for a seller's breach of delivery obligations. In effect, UCC section 2-713 acts as a statutory liquidated damage clause that deters breaches of contract.

Damages under UCC section 2-713 cannot be limited to the plaintiff's actual economic loss.

    c)   UCC section 1-106 states that the UCC remedies are intended to put the aggrieved party in as good a position as if the other party had fully performed. Some pre-UCC cases have held that a limitation to actual losses should be placed upon the contract/market price measure. Such a limitation is appropriate when the buyer has a resale contract known to the seller. In that situation, the seller would be liable for consequential damages suffered by the plaintiff; it should also be limited to those known consequential damages.

    d)   D here knew that P had a resale contract. P has not shown that it will be liable to its own buyers, and there has been no finding of bad faith on D's part, so the policy of UCC section 1-106 requires the award of damages to P be limited to its actual loss.

4. Cover and Liquidated Damages.

    a.   **Cover.** The UCC presumes that the most logical and commercially reasonable thing for the buyer to do when the seller fails to deliver goods is for the buyer to go into the market and purchase substitute goods (cover). If the buyer does so, he may recover the difference between the cover price and the contract price, as long as the cover was exercised in good faith. The choice of whether to cover rests entirely with the buyer.

    b.   **Liquidated damages.**

        1)   **Common law.** The common law rule is that the parties can liquidate (preestablish) the damages in the event of breach only in those situations where, from the nature of the case, it would be impracticable or extremely difficult to fix the actual damages.

        2)   **UCC.** The UCC sets forth a new set of standards for determining the validity of liquidated damages clauses in sales contracts. The amount of liquidated damages must be reasonable in light of the anticipated or actual harm caused by the breach, the difficulties of proof of loss, and the inability of otherwise obtaining an adequate remedy. If the sales contract fixes unreasonably large liquidated damages, the clause is considered a penalty and is deemed void.

Fertico Belgium S.A. v. Phosphate Chemicals Export Association, Inc.

    c.   **Damages for cover plus profits on resale of breaching goods--Fertico Belgium S.A. v. Phosphate Chemicals Export Association, Inc.,** 510 N.E.2d 334 (N.Y. 1987).

        1)   **Facts.** Fertico Belgium S.A. (P) contracted to purchase $4,025,000 worth of fertilizer from Phosphate Chemicals Export Association, Inc. (D) for delivery to Belgium in two shipments. D knew that P needed the fertilizer on the specified November contract dates so it could fill P's contract with Altawreed, Iraq's agricultural ministry. D notified P that the first shipment would be delivered December 4, and P notified D that the breach presented P with huge problems. P canceled the second shipment, which would also have been late. The first shipment did not arrive in Belgium until December 17 and was not off-loaded until December 21. P kept the first shipment because D had presented P's letter of credit and the issuer had honored it. To avoid breaching its contract with Altawreed, P covered by buying fertilizer from another company for $4,725,000. P renegotiated with Altawreed for a postponed delivery date and an inland direct delivery for a higher price, which P was able to meet with the cover fertilizer. P was left with D's late-delivered fertilizer which P stored until selling it to another buyer, Janssens, in March. P earned $454,000 profit on this sale. P sued D for damages. The trial court held that the increased transportation costs on the Altawreed contract were not consequential damages, that the higher price P got from the renegotiated Altawreed contract was an expense saved, and that the profits P made on the subsequent sale should reduce the damages owed by D. P appeals.

2) **Issue.** May a buyer who covers when the seller breaches by delivering goods late both recover damages for the cover and retain the late-delivered goods and resell them at a profit without accounting to the seller for the profit on the resale?

3) **Held.** Yes. Judgment reversed in part.

a) D clearly breached the contract when it did not deliver the fertilizer on time. UCC sections 2-711 through 2-713 give P the alternative of either seeking self-help of cover with recovery of damages or recovering damages only for the differential between the market price and the contract price, together with incidental and consequential damages less expenses saved. P elected to cover in this case.

b) A covering buyer may recover the difference between the cost of cover and the contract price, plus incidental or consequential damages suffered because of the breach, less expenses saved. P's additional costs of delivering the fertilizer inland would normally be consequential damages caused by D's breach and were reasonably foreseeable by D at the time of contracting. But P's customer Altawreed compensated P for these additional delivery costs, so P may not recover them from D.

c) The additional compensation Altawreed paid P is not an expense saved as a consequence of D's breach, and D is not entitled to credit for this. This compensation was for P's inland shipping agreement and was not a cost anticipated in the absence of a breach. The trial court erroneously credited this compensation in D's favor.

d) The trial court also credited D for the profits P made on its sale to Janssens. This sale was not dependent on D's breach, because P would have sought such a sale even had there been no breach by D. The UCC remedies do not squarely address the situation where the nonbreaching buyer meets its subsale obligations with the cover goods and yet acquires title and control over the late-delivered goods. However, the UCC does direct that its remedies should be liberally administered to put the aggrieved party in as good a position as if the other party had fully performed.

e) In this case, had D fully performed, P would have had the benefit of both the Altawreed contract and the Janssens sale. P's profits on the Janssens sale should not be credited to D. Accordingly, P is entitled to its differential damages of $700,000.

4) **Dissent**. The majority allows P to obtain the benefit of its bargain twice by retaining both cover damages and the profit from the sale of the late-delivered goods. Once an aggrieved buyer purchases substitute goods and sues for cover damages, it has impliedly rejected the seller's nonconforming performance and holds the seller's goods only as security for any prepayments made to the seller. A buyer such as P receives the full benefit of his bargain when it obtains cover damages. The majority has incorrectly applied a damages rule that previously applied only to aggrieved sellers who can both sue the breaching buyer for lost profits and resell the wrongfully rejected goods to another buyer at a profit, so long as the seller has an unlimited supply of standard-price goods. [UCC §2-708(2)] The rationale is that the seller would have had two sales instead of one if the buyer had not breached. But the UCC does not allow aggrieved buyers to recover profits from lost sales. In this case, if D had not breached, P would have delivered D's fertilizer to Altawreed and would have had to purchase additional fertilizer for the Janssens sale. While the Janssens sale would have been theoretically possible even without D's breach, the uncertainties of the marketplace preclude the assumption that P would have found fertilizer for the Janssens sale at the same price as it bought from D. The UCC provides that a wronged buyer may recover any down payment it made from nonconforming goods and requires the buyer to account to the breaching seller for any additional profit it has made on the resale. [UCC §2-706(6)] If D had not delivered the fertilizer, it would have been able to resell it for its own account.

d. **Cover by production of replacement goods--Dura-Wood Treating Co. v. Century Forest Industries, Inc.**, 675 F.2d 745 (5th Cir. 1982).

1) **Facts.** Dura-Wood Treating Co. (P), a producer of creosote treated hardwood cross-ties, contracted to supply ties to Smith. In partial fulfillment of this contract, P entered an oral contract with Century Forest Industries, Inc. (D) to purchase 20,000 ties for resale to Smith. D refused to deliver the ties, claiming no contract existed. Rather than purchase ties from other suppliers, P saved money by producing the ties itself. P then sued D for damages based on the cost to cover and the contract price. The trial court awarded P $100,000 and D appeals.

2) **Issue.** May a manufacturer cover by producing the replacement goods itself?

3) **Held.** Yes. Judgment affirmed.

a) The literal language of UCC section 2-712 contemplates the purchase of cover goods from outside sources. UCC section 1-102(1) states that the UCC is to be liberally construed and applied to promote its underlying purposes and policies.

b) Comment One to UCC section 2-712 states that cover is intended to provide the buyer with a remedy to enable him to obtain goods he needs to meet an essential need. Actually purchasing the cover goods from another source is not the only way to satisfy the presumption behind UCC section 2-712 that the cost of cover will approximate the market price of the undelivered goods. Covering by manufacturing goods also promotes the purposes and policies of the UCC, so P's cover is permissible. A buyer is not required to increase losses by covering through purchase from another seller when it can produce the goods itself at a lower price.

c) P in this case acted in good faith by first obtaining estimates from alternative suppliers and then determining that it could produce the ties at a lower price. P also acted within a reasonable time and produced a reasonable substitute.

d) The trial court's award included $42,000 for lost potential profits that P could have earned by producing ties and selling them to new or different customers instead of producing them as cover. Lost profits are normally consequential damages that are recoverable under UCC section 2-712. However, when these lost profits are added to the cost of producing the ties, the total is greater than the cost of simply purchasing the ties from another source would have been. D is not liable for P's failure to prevent the lost potential profits by covering on the open market.

e) The trial court also erroneously awarded P $13,000 for lost profits on its contract with Smith, but this was a double recovery since P had already been awarded the difference between the cost of cover and the contract price.

5. **Consequential Damages--Hydraform Products Corp. v. American Steel & Aluminum Corp.**, 498 A.2d 339 (N.H. 1985).

Hydraform Products Corp. v. American Steel & Aluminum Corp.

a. **Facts.** Hydraform Products Corp. (P) was a manufacturer and seller of woodstoves, a seasonal business. It sold 640 stoves in its second year. It then contracted with American Steel & Aluminum Corp. (D) to purchase enough steel for 400 stoves. D's deliveries were late and some of the steel delivered was defective. After numerous assurances that D would perform, P finally realized that D would never fully perform and it sought steel from other suppliers. By that time, it was too late in the season to locate another supplier. P sold only 250 stoves that year. P sold the woodstove manufacturing division. P then sued for breach of contract, claiming consequential damages for lost profits and a loss on the sale of the business. The jury awarded P lost profits for the year of the contract and for two years thereafter, plus the loss in value of the stove manufacturing business. D appeals.

b. **Issue.** Must consequential damages be proved with reasonable certainty to be recovered?

c. **Held.** Yes. Judgment reversed in part.

1) To be recovered by the aggrieved party, consequential damages must be reasonably foreseeable, ascertainable, and unavoidable. P's claim for the year of the breach met these requirements. D clearly should have foreseen P's lost profits on sales of up to 400 stoves, and the evidence shows that P could have sold that many. Although P did not cover, it attempted to and did everything reasonably possible to avoid the loss.

2) Lost profits on sales above 400 are not foreseeable to D, however. P never indicated to D that it expected to sell more than 400 stoves.

3) Profits lost on projected sales for the subsequent two years are too uncertain to be recovered. P was not put out of business by D's breach; it could have bought steel from another source and sold an unknown quantity of stoves in the future.

4) The loss in value of a going business is generally a recoverable consequential damage. In this case, however, to the extent the loss was based on lost profits, it was not reasonably certain. It was also duplicative of the lost profits claim. Finally, there was no evidence other than the possible lost future profits from which the jury could have determined a value, except that P's president testified that the price obtained was less than the business was worth. This is insufficient evidence to support a judgment.

VI. DELIVERY OF GOODS AND DOCUMENTS

A. RISK OF LOSS

1. **Introduction.** When goods are damaged or destroyed without fault of either party prior to delivery to the buyer, one of the parties must bear the risk of loss. Such loss could be caused by an act of God, or by some third party's negligence or wrongful act.

   a. **Pre-UCC law.** Under the Sales Act and common law, the risk of loss from accidental damage or destruction of the goods was borne by whichever party had title to the goods. This proved to be a source of uncertainty and litigation, and consequently has been rejected under the Code.

   b. **UCC approach.** As shown below, the UCC rules as to risk of loss have nothing whatsoever to do with ownership or title to the goods. As a generalization, the UCC rules follow possession of the goods, which usually means that the risk of loss passes from the seller to the buyer later than under prior law.

2. **UCC Rules in Absence of Breach.** The risk of loss from accidental damage or destruction passes as follows when there is no agreement between the parties.

   a. **Goods held by bailee (*e.g.*, a carrier or warehouseman).** If, when the sales contract is signed, the goods are in the hands of a bailee and are covered by a negotiable document of title (*e.g.*, an order bill of lading or a negotiable warehouse receipt), then risk of loss passes to B only on his receipt of the negotiable document of title covering the goods. [UCC §2-509(2)(a)] If the goods are covered by a nonnegotiable document of title, the risk of loss passes to B upon his receipt of the nonnegotiable document of title or other written directions from S to the bailee authorizing delivery of the goods to B. [UCC §2-509(c)] If the goods are not covered by any document of title, negotiable or otherwise, then risk of loss passes from S to B when the bailee tenders the goods or otherwise acknowledges that B is entitled to immediate possession of the goods. [UCC §2-509(2)(b)]

   b. **Goods shipped via carrier.** If the contract authorizes or requires the seller to ship the goods to the buyer via common carrier (as opposed to delivery by the seller's own trucks), risk of loss depends on the type of contract involved.

      1) **Shipment contracts.** A shipment contract merely requires the seller to place the goods in the hands of a carrier, not to deliver them at any particular destination. The risk of loss under such contracts passes to B upon delivery of the goods to the carrier. [UCC §2-509(1)(a)]

         a) **Commercial shipment terms.** Commercial contracts are often made in abbreviated terms indicated by mercantile symbols. This is particularly true in the area of shipment, where particular terms are widely used by businessmen to indicate whether they intend a particular contract to be a shipment contract or a destination contract.

b) **Common terms.** Use of any of the following terms indicates the contract is a shipment contract: (i) F.O.B. origin (or point of shipment) stands for "free on board" and means the seller bears the risk and expense only of putting the goods into the carrier's possession [UCC §2-319(1)]; (ii) F.A.S. stands for "free alongside" and means the seller must deliver the goods alongside or on the dock next to the vessel on which they are to be loaded, and must obtain a receipt therefor in exchange for which the carrier issues a bill of lading; and (iii) C.I.F. and C. & F. stand for "cost, insurance and freight" and "cost and freight," and represent those elements which the price includes.

2) **Destination contracts.** If the contract requires the seller to deliver the goods to a particular destination, the risk of loss passes to B only when the goods arrive at the destination and are duly tendered to B in a manner sufficient to enable B to take delivery. [UCC §2-509(1)(b)] This covers F.O.B. destination contracts or those in which the seller must transport to the destination at his expense and risk. It also covers cases where the parties make no mention of shipment by carrier, but merely agree that the seller is to "send" the goods to the buyer.

3) **Construction in favor of shipment contracts.** In practice, contracts calling for shipment of goods via carrier are usually "shipment contracts." Destination contracts are unusual. Unless the contract expressly contains an "F.O.B. destination" term or the equivalent, it will be construed as a shipment contract, so that the seller's risk ends upon delivery to the carrier.

c. **In all other nonbreach situations.** Innumerable situations may arise in which neither of the foregoing rules applies (*e.g.,* where seller is to deliver in his own trucks). Generally, the result depends on whether S is or is not a "merchant." If S is a merchant, risk of loss passes to B only when B actually receives, or takes possession of, the goods. If S is not a merchant, risk of loss passes to B upon tender of delivery by S. [UCC §2-509(3)] The reason for the difference in treatment between merchant and nonmerchant sellers is that merchants are more likely to carry insurance (and hence they should bear risk longer). [UCC §2-509, Comment 3]

Silver v. Wycombe, Meyer & Co., Inc.

3. **Seller Retains Risk When It Holds Goods at Buyer's Request--Silver v. Wycombe, Meyer & Co., Inc.,** 477 N.Y.S.2d 288 (1984).

a. **Facts.** Silver (P) ordered furniture from Wycombe, Meyer & Co., Inc. (D). When the furniture was ready for shipment, D sent invoices to P which P paid in full. P directed that only part of the furniture be shipped immediately; D was to hold the rest until further instructions. Before P sent further instructions, the furniture was destroyed in a fire not due to any negligence of D's. P's insurer paid P for the loss and sued D for reimbursement on the ground that the risk of loss never passed to P.

b. **Issue.** Where a seller never delivers goods to the buyer but holds them until the buyer gives delivery instructions, does the risk of loss pass to the buyer upon payment for the goods?

c. **Held.** No. Judgment for P.

   1) Unless agreed otherwise by the parties, risk of loss under UCC section 2-509 is determined by the manner in which delivery is to be made. Risk of loss may pass to the buyer upon tender of delivery or upon delivery to the carrier.

   2) In this case, the contract did not mention terms of delivery. However, D has established no facts to show that the risk of loss passed to P. A merchant seller cannot transfer risk of loss until actual receipt by the buyer. Therefore, D had the risk of loss and must pay.

   3) D claims the risk of loss passed because D was only a bailee after P asked D to hold the furniture. A bailment is created by delivery of the goods to the bailee, however, and D did not deliver the goods to anyone. This sale of goods may not be transformed into a bailment simply because D agreed to postpone delivery.

4. **Risk of Loss of Goods Kept in Warehouse--Jason's Foods, Inc. v. Peter Eckrich & Sons, Inc.,** 774 F.2d 214 (7th Cir. 1985).

   Jason's Foods, Inc. v. Peter Eckrich & Sons, Inc.

   a. **Facts.** Peter Eckrich & Sons, Inc. (D) contracted to purchase 38,000 pounds of pork ribs from Jason's Foods, Inc. (P). As both parties had an account in the same warehouse, delivery was to be made by a transfer of the ribs from P's account to D's. P notified D that the transfer would be made between January 10 and January 14. P phoned the warehouse on January 13 and asked that the ribs be transferred to D's account. The transfer was done immediately, but the warehouse receipt was not mailed until January 17 or 18 and D did not receive it until January 24. On January 17 the ribs were destroyed in a warehouse fire. P sued D for the contract price, but D refused to pay. The district court found that the risk of loss had not passed and granted D summary judgment. P appeals.

   b. **Issue.** Does the risk of loss on goods in a warehouse pass to the buyer upon acknowledgment of the transfer given to the seller?

   c. **Held.** No. Judgment affirmed.

   1) P claims that it lost all rights over the ribs once the warehouse transferred them to D's account, so it should not bear the risk of loss. P cites UCC section 2-509(2)(b) to support the view that once acknowledgment was given, in this case to P itself, risk of loss passed to D.

   2) UCC section 2-509(2) separates title from risk of loss. Even though title passed to D when the warehouse made the transfer, the risk of loss could not pass until the transfer was acknowledged. D did not know the goods had passed until it received the warehouse receipt.

3) Even though UCC section 2-509(2)(b) does not state that the acknowl-edgment must be to the buyer, acknowledgment to the seller would not make much sense. P did not receive any acknowledgment other than directing that the transfer be made. If the risk of loss was intended to pass when the transfer was made, the statute could have simply said so instead of requiring "acknowledgment." The Uniform Sales Act expressly required acknowledgment to the buyer for tender-ing goods that are not removed from the possession of a bailee, and the UCC was not intended to change this. Comment 4 to UCC section 2-509 indicates that the risk of loss rule is to conform with the rules of tender. Thus the risk of loss did not pass to D.

4) The policy behind risk of loss allocation is to create incentives to minimize the adverse consequences of the loss. One way to do so is through insurance, but either party could have insured the goods. The other way is to prevent the loss, but neither party had more ability to do this than the other. For that reason, the terms of the UCC and the comments are determinative.

5. **Liability Under Shipment Contract--Cook Specialty Co. v. Schrlock**, 772 F. Supp. 1532 (E.D. Pa. 1991).

a. **Facts.** Cook Specialty Co. (P) contracted to purchase a press brake from Machinery Systems, Inc. (D) for $28,000, F.O.B., D's warehouse. D obtained an insurance certificate from RTL, the carrier, with a face amount of $100,000. RTL took possession of the press brake at D's warehouse. While in transit, the brake fell from the truck, and RTL was cited by the police for not properly securing the load. P recovered $5,000 from RTL's carrier, which was the limit of RTL's policy. P sued D to recover the balance of the loss.

b. **Issue.** Under an FOB, place of shipment contract, does the seller's failure to make sure the carrier has sufficient insurance to fully cover the goods render the shipment contract unreasonable such that the seller is liable to the buyer?

c. **Held.** No. Judgment for D.

1) The term "F.O.B., place of shipment" means that the seller bears the risk and expense of placing the goods in the possession of the carrier, but under UCC section 2-509, once the goods are duly delivered to the carrier, the buyer assumes the risk of loss. To be "duly deliv-ered," the shipment contract must satisfy UCC section 2-504, which requires that the contract be "reasonable having regard to the nature of the goods and other circumstances of the case."

2) P claims that D's contract with RTL was not reasonable because it did not provide for enough insurance coverage. The only case P cited involved a shipment that was not only underinsured, but also misaddressed, shipped by fourth class mail, and inscribed with a "theft-tempting" notation. A carrier's lack of sufficient insurance, by itself, is not unreasonable. UCC section 2-504 relates to the mode of transport, such as the use of a refrigerated container for a perishable good.

3) Official Comment 3 to UCC section 2-504 notes that a shipping contract would be improper if the seller agrees to an inadequate valuation of the shipment and thus prevents the buyer from recovering from the carrier. But that does not require the seller to make sure the carrier has enough insurance to cover the full loss. In this case, RTL is still liable to P for the balance of the loss not covered by insurance.

6. **UCC Rules in Case of Breach.**

   a. **Seller's shipment of nonconforming goods.** If the goods shipped by S so fail to conform to the contract as to give the buyer the right to reject same, the risk of loss remains with the seller until cure or acceptance. [UCC §2-510(1)]

      1) **Buyer rejects.** In single-delivery contracts, any defect justifies the buyer's rejection, whereas in installment contracts, there is no right to reject unless the defect "substantially impairs" the value of the goods tendered. [UCC §§2-601; 2-612]

      2) **Buyer revokes acceptance.** A similar rule applies where the buyer only discovered the defects in the goods after accepting them, and the defect is so substantial that it justifies the buyer's revoking his acceptance. In such a case, the risk of loss is treated as having been on the seller from the beginning (to the extent that it is not otherwise covered by buyer's insurance).

   b. **Buyer's repudiation.** Where the seller has shipped conforming goods (no breach), but the buyer has wrongfully repudiated (or otherwise breached before the risk of loss has passed to him), and the seller's insurance does not cover the loss, the seller may treat the risk of loss as resting on the buyer "for a commercially reasonable period of time." [UCC §2-510(3)] This rule only applies where the seller is otherwise uninsured and has otherwise acted in a commercially reasonable manner.

7. **Allocation of Risk by Agreement.** If the parties' agreement specifies at what point the risk of loss shifts from seller to buyer, it controls. [UCC §2-509(4)] Sometimes the parties' intent may be implied from the nature of the transaction.

   a. **Sale or return.** The seller may vest the buyer with possession of the goods received for the purpose of resale. Under this arrangement, the buyer may satisfy his liability to the seller either by making payment for the goods or returning them to the seller. Until they are returned, risk of loss is with the buyer who is in possession. [UCC §2-327(2)]

   b. **Sale on approval.** The seller may vest the buyer with possession of the goods for personal use by the buyer. Under this arrangement, the risk of loss remains with the seller until the buyer signals his approval. The opposite result applies where the loss is the buyer's fault. [UCC §2-327(1)]

   c. **Consignment.** The seller (consignor) may vest the buyer (consignee) with the possession of the goods with the understanding that the consignee will act as agent for the seller in effecting sales to ultimate customers. Risk of loss remains with the consignor-seller.

8. **Insurance.** Third parties such as carriers and warehousemen are sometimes responsible for loss of or damage to goods. The question arises in such cases whether the buyer or seller, or both, have the right to sue for such loss or damage.

a. **Insurable interest.** At common law and under the Sales Act, the right to sue followed title; only the possessor of title could sue. Under the UCC, however, a seller may sue third parties for damages to the goods until they are identified to the contract, at which point the buyer obtains a right of action. Insurance law can be complex and a comprehensive examination of the issues is beyond the scope of this outline. However, the basic issues are (i) whether a particular policy covers the loss involved; (ii) how the loss should be allocated among two or more policies which cover the loss; and (iii) to what extent the insurer is subrogated to its insured's rights.

1) **Identification.** "Identified" goods are those to which the contract refers. All that identification requires is that the goods which are the subject matter of the contract have somehow been singled out from all the goods of that type in the world.

2) **Buyer's interest.** Once the goods are identified to the contract, the UCC gives the buyer "a special property and an insurable interest" in the goods. [UCC §2-501(1)] Under insurance law, the buyer must have some sort of property interest in goods before he has any right to obtain insurance thereon. If he were to procure insurance without a property interest, he would not be deemed to have an insurable interest in the goods and therefore could not collect on the insurance should the goods be destroyed. For that reason, the UCC provides him both a special property and an insurable interest in the goods.

a) **Rationale.** As soon as the buyer knows or could determine what goods he is going to receive, expectancies are created which the buyer may want to protect by insurance.

b) **Nonconforming goods.** The buyer's special property and insurable interests arise even though the identified goods are nonconforming and even though he may have an option to return or reject them.

3) **Seller's interest.** The seller has an insurable interest before sale as the owner of the goods. This interest continues after identification of the goods to the contract until title passes to the buyer and until any security interest which the seller may have in the goods (to secure payment of the price) is satisfied.

4) **Concurrent interests.** It is obvious from the above that both buyer and seller may have an insurable interest at the same time in the same goods. In such a situation, either party may, with the consent of the other, sue for the benefit of whom it may concern. However, the party who bears the risk of loss has the primary right to sue and retain whatever he recovers, since the loss is his and any recovery to offset such loss should be his as well. If the plaintiff in the suit against the third party is not the party who bears the risk of loss, and he has not made specific arrangements with the other party with

respect to splitting the recovery, then anything he obtains by way of judgment or settlement in excess of his own interest must be held as a fiduciary for the other party. [UCC §2-722]

b. **Subrogation.** Subrogation is the principle by which an insurance company, after paying the insured for his loss, takes the insured's legal position to assert claims against some other person for the loss. The other person may be the carrier, the other party to the contract, or someone else who caused the loss.

1) **Buyer insured, seller not.** If the contract requires the buyer to obtain insurance for the benefit of the seller, then a secured seller who is not insured will have a claim on the insurance proceeds. [*See* UCC §9-306(1)] If there was no contractual obligation, the insurance contract is personal to the buyer.

2) **Seller insured, buyer not.** If goods are damaged after delivery but before the buyer pays, any insurance proceeds received by the seller may reduce the buyer's liability for the price. [*See, e.g., In re* Future Manufacturing Corp., 165 F. Supp. 111 (N.D. Cal. 1958)] This is not the majority approach, however, because it would preclude the seller's insurer from enforcing its subrogation rights.

c. **Conflict between shipper's insurer and the carrier--Towmotor Co. v. Frank Cross Trucking Co.,** 211 A.2d 38 (Pa. 1965).

1) **Facts.** Frank Cross Trucking Co. (P) shipped a vehicle through Towmotor (D), a carrier. While in D's possession, the vehicle was damaged. P sued for the damages, and D answered that P had been fully insured and had recovered its loss. Under the bill of lading, any insurance on the vehicle was to benefit D, "so far as this shall not avoid the policies or contracts of insurance."

2) **Issue.** May a bill of lading which contains a clause allowing insurance to benefit the carrier operate to invalidate the insurance?

3) **Held.** No. Judgment for P.

a) The insurance policy specified that the insurance was not to benefit any carrier. This recognizes the general rule that a carrier is an insurer. Thus, in the typical case D would be liable.

b) Here, the benefit of insurance clause in the bill of lading is valid because D could have itself insured against the loss. However, the clause specifies that it is valid only so far as it does not invalidate the insurance clause. Because the insurance clause specifies that it is not to benefit a carrier, the bill of lading clause cannot take effect without invalidating the insurance clause. Therefore, D remains liable. However, any recovery against D must go to the insurer.

4) **Comment.** The benefit of insurance clause is typical of a bill of lading. The clause provided that the carrier should receive the benefit of any insurance purchased by the shipper. The effect was to take away the insurer's right of subrogation. Insurance companies responded by inserting a clause in their policies which invalidated the insurance if the insured

shipper contracted to give the carrier the benefit of the shipper's insurance. The next step was the development of the clause discussed in the *Towmotor* case.

B. DOCUMENTS OF TITLE

1. **Introduction.** Documents of title, including bills of lading and warehouse receipts, are essential to sales involving shipment by common carriers or storage in warehouses. The documents serve as receipts given to the seller for the goods, as contracts between the seller and the carrier or warehouseman, and as a substitute for the goods themselves for passage of title and creation of security interests. Article 7 governs documents of title, replacing provisions of the Sales Act, the Uniform Bill of Lading Act, and the Uniform Warehouse Receipts Act.

2. **Use of Documents of Title.** Where no credit is provided in the sales agreement, the buyer must pay when he receives the goods. [UCC §2-310(a)] When the parties are face-to-face, this presents no difficulty. When the parties deal at a distance, and shipment or warehousing is involved, a documentary exchange is necessary.

   a. **Bills of lading.** A bill of lading is issued by a carrier to the shipper of goods. On it, the carrier lists the goods received, identifies the destination, and sets forth the terms of the delivery contract. It may be either negotiable or nonnegotiable.

      1) **Nonnegotiable (straight) bills.** A straight bill of lading is one stating that the goods are consigned to a specified person but not to the person's order. [UCC §7-104]

         a) **Effect.** A straight bill is not a document of title because it is not negotiable and its possession does not establish ownership. It is merely a receipt for the goods and a contract for their carriage.

         b) **Carrier's obligation.** A carrier must deliver only to the named consignee, and may be held liable for conversion of the goods if he delivers them to someone else, even if that person was in possession of the straight bill.

         c) **Consignee's rights.** The consignee has the right to receive the goods even without surrendering the straight bill.

      2) **Negotiable bills.** A negotiable bill is a document of title because the legal possessor is entitled to possession of the goods described therein. Legal possession of a negotiable bill is tantamount to ownership of the goods. [UCC §7-403]

         a) **Types.** A negotiable bill may be either an order bill ("consign to the order of XYZ Co.") or a bearer bill ("consign to bearer"). [UCC §7-104(1)(a)]

         b) **Manner of negotiation.** A bearer bill can be negotiated by mere delivery. [UCC §7-501(1), (2)(a)] An order bill is negotiated by indorsement of the named consignee plus delivery to the party to whom the bill is being negotiated.

    c)   **Types of indorsements.** An order bill may be indorsed in blank (consignee's signature) which continues the full negotiability of the bill. It may be indorsed restrictively by naming a specific transferee, limiting negotiability to the named transferee.

    d)   **Failure to indorse.** If the transferor fails to indorse the bill properly, no rights pass, even if it was transferred for value.

    e)   **Warranties.** Negotiation constitutes a warranty that the document is genuine, that the transferor has a legal right to transfer the bill and the goods it represents, and that he has no knowledge of any fact which would impair the validity or worth of the bill.

    f)   **Carrier's obligations.** The carrier must deliver the goods to the bearer of a bearer bill, or to the lawful holder of an order bill. Upon delivery, the carrier must retrieve and cancel the bill; otherwise, the carrier would be liable to a bona fide purchaser of the spent bill.

  b.   **Shipment.** When the parties agree to a documentary sale, the seller delivers the goods to a carrier and obtains a negotiable bill, typically to his own order. Then the seller makes a sight draft for the price showing the buyer as drawee. He indorses the bill and the draft and takes them, as well as any other documents required under the contract, to his bank.

  c.   **Collection of the draft.** The seller's bank, referred to as the collecting bank and the depository bank [UCC §4-105(a), (d)], sends the draft and other documents to the buyer's bank, known as the presenting bank [UCC §4-105(e)]. Upon presentment, the buyer honors the draft and receives the bill of lading.

  d.   **Receipt of the goods.** The buyer uses the bill of lading to take possession of the goods from the carrier. Since he has already paid, his only recourse if the goods are nonconforming is to sue the seller for damages.

3.   **Misdelivery--Refrigerated Transport Co. v. Hernando Packing Co.,** 544 S.W.2d 613 (Tenn. 1976).

  a.   **Facts.** Hernando Packing Co. (P) shipped a truckload of frozen meat by the Refrigerated Transport Co. (D). The shipment was consigned "to Broward Cold Storage (acct. of J & A Trading Co.)" at Broward's business address. Broward was a public warehouse. P had sold to J & A in the past but was unaware that J & A was out of business when the order was placed by Al Hark, the son of the former owner of J & A. D trucked the meat to Broward's address but instead of delivering the entire shipment to Broward, it delivered part of the shipment to Al Hark. P sued D for misdelivery of the cargo. The trial court awarded P judgment and D appeals.

b.   **Issue.** Must a shipper deliver goods to the party named as the consignee under a straight bill of lading?

c.   **Held.** Yes. Judgment affirmed.

1)   The bill of lading here was a straight bill that was not negotiable. Delivery under such a bill may only be made to a person lawfully entitled to the possession of the goods, or the consignee named therein.

2)   Clearly, the consignee here was Broward. D's failure to present the bill of lading to an authorized representative of Broward was a breach of the contract of carriage. A carrier that fails to follow the express instructions of the shipper in making delivery acts at its peril and assumes the risk of wrong delivery.

4.   **Third-Party Claims.**

a.   **General rule.** If the bill itself is a forgery, or if its issuance was obtained by fraud or deception upon the carrier, or without the authority of the owner (*e.g.,* a thief steals the goods and obtains issuance of the bill), no rights can be created thereunder as against the true owner of the goods.

Lineburger
Bros. v.
Hodge

b.   **Stolen items--Lineburger Bros. v. Hodge,** 54 So. 2d 268 (Miss. 1951).

1)   **Facts.** Lineburger Bros. (D) grew and ginned certain bales of cotton. Carr stole the cotton, delivered it to a warehouse, and took receipts to Hodge (P) and others. P sued the warehouse for delivery of the cotton. D intervened in the suit. The trial court dismissed L's petition, found the warehouse not negligent, and awarded P the cotton. D appeals, and P cross-appeals, claiming that if D wins, P should have a claim against the warehouse for the value of the cotton.

2)   **Issue.** Does a purchaser of receipts to stolen goods have title superior to that of the original owner?

3)   **Held.** No. Judgment reversed.

a)   The warehouse was not negligent. Therefore, it cannot be liable even if P's receipts are worthless because the goods were stolen.

b)   It is clear that Carr committed larceny, because the cotton was never entrusted to Carr. Therefore, D is not estopped from claiming the cotton as against P who purchased the receipts.

c)   The statutory scheme of negotiability was intended to insure the negotiability of warehouse receipts, and a buyer must be assured that his receipts are negotiable. However, this principle must also recognize the rule that an owner cannot be divested of title by a trespasser or thief.

d)   The problem is resolved by statute by recognizing the title of the innocent buyer who buys from one to whom the receipts were entrusted by the owner. However, when the unlawful act was committed against the owners, title remains in them. The buyer must beware of buying receipts for stolen goods. Therefore, title to the cotton remains in D.

5. **Breach by a Party--Clock v. Missouri-Kansas-Texas Railroad Co. v. Crawford,** 407 F. Supp. 448 (E.D. Mo. 1976).

a. **Facts.** Crawford (D1) sold two carloads of fertilizer to Cunningham, who paid with two checks. D gave the goods to the Missouri-Kansas-Texas Railroad Co. (D2) for shipment to Eaton Agricultural Center in Indiana. D2 issued two nonnegotiable straight bills of lading to cover the goods, signed by D1. Cunningham sold the goods to Clock (P). Subsequently, the bank returned Cunningham's checks for insufficient funds. D1 issued a reconsignment order on the goods to have them sent to the Farmers Union Coop. D2 complied with the instructions. P provided replacement goods to Eaton Agricultural Center and sued D2 for conversion. When D2 filed a third-party complaint against D1, P added D1 as a defendant. P seeks damages for conversion.

b. **Issue.** May a seller who does not receive proper payment for goods already in transit direct that the goods be diverted to an alternative location, even when the seller knows that the buyer has already resold the goods?

c. **Held.** Yes. Judgment for D1 and D2.

1) A straight bill cannot be negotiated, but it can be transferred. The transferee acquires the same rights as those held by the transferor. Thus, P acquired only Cunningham's rights.

2) Under UCC section 2-703, when a buyer fails to make a payment due, the seller may withhold deliver of the goods, stop delivery by any bailee, resell and recover damages, and cancel, among other things. When Cunningham's check bounced, D1 was entitled to possession of the goods and could instruct D2 to deliver them to a different location. UCC section 7-303 permits a carrier to deliver goods to a destination other than that stated in the bill on instructions from the consignor on a nonnegotiable bill. D1 acted within his rights when he directed the alternate delivery, and D2 acted properly in complying.

3) Neither D1 nor D2 converted the goods. Conversion is an unauthorized assumption of the right of ownership, but D1 was entitled to possession of the goods. P, as a transferee under a straight bill of lading, cannot be a bona fide purchaser for value.

6. **Bailee's Non-Receipt or Misdescription.**

a. **General rule.** A careless or dishonest carrier may issue a negotiable bill showing that it has received certain goods when in fact it has not. At common law, the carrier could avoid liability by including a phrase in the bill such as "shipper's weight, load and count." If the stated measures were actually the shipper's figures, the carrier was not liable for missing goods. Under the UCC, the carrier must ascertain that something is loaded, although it need not open the package.

G.A.C. Com- b. **Carrier signs without inspecting contents--G.A.C. Commercial Corp. v.**
mercial Corp.   **Wilson,** 271 F. Supp. 242 (S.D.N.Y. 1967).
v. Wilson

1) **Facts.** G.A.C. Commercial Corp. (P) financed St. Lawrence, of which Wilson (D) was an officer, by discounting its accounts receivable. Included among these accounts receivable were 60 bills of lading. These bills were made by D on forms provided by the Norwood Railroad. D would load its goods on its own railroad siding, fill out the bills of lading, and have Norwood's agent sign the bills without inspecting the goods. The accounts receivable and the bills of lading which P discounted were false and fraudulent, and when D went bankrupt, P sued for damages. Norwood moves for summary judgment as to its liability.

2) **Issue.** Is a carrier liable to a third party financer when its agent signs straight bills of lading without inspecting the contents of the shipments?

3) **Held.** No. Judgment for Norwood.

   a) The federal statutes which govern this case make a sharp distinction between order bills of lading and straight bills. A carrier is liable to the holder of an order bill for damages caused by the non-receipt by the carrier of the goods shown on the bill. However, liability for non-receipt extends only to the owner of the goods covered by a straight bill.

   b) P in its agreement with D became the direct obligee of whatever obligations Norwood owed to D. Since D did not deliver any goods to Norwood, Norwood did not owe anything to D, and therefore did not owe anything to P. P never did own any goods within the meaning of the statute.

   c) P cannot recover on a theory of negligence; otherwise, the statutory scheme would be avoided by the form of the complaint.

   d) A straight bill is not a good risk under the federal scheme. However, P could have required order bills instead. Its error does not justify making Norwood liable.

VII. RECEIPT AND INSPECTION

A. INSPECTION, REJECTION, AND REVOCATION OF ACCEPTANCE

1. **Inspection.** Unless the parties agree otherwise, the buyer has the right to inspect the goods before payment or acceptance. [UCC §2-513(1)]

   a. **Exercise of right.**

      1) **Time.** Inspection must be made within a reasonable time after receipt of the goods or the right is lost.

      2) **Place.** The buyer may make the inspection at any reasonable place. However, the parties may contractually fix a place for inspection.

      3) **Right to test and sample.** If visual inspection is not sufficient to determine whether the goods conform, the buyer has the right to test a reasonable amount of the goods and to use and consume it in the tests, so long as his actions are reasonable.

      4) **Expense.** Expenses of inspection must be borne by the buyer, but may be recovered from the seller if the goods do not conform and are rejected.

   b. **Loss of right to inspect by contractual provision.** Provisions of the contract may be inconsistent with the buyer's right to inspect the goods prior to payment of the purchase price.

      1) **Payment against documents.** Provisions requiring the buyer to pay against shipping documents before receipt of the goods override the right to inspect before payment. [UCC §2-513 (3)(b)]

      2) **Payment C.O.D.** Where the contract calls for payment C.O.D., there is no right of inspection unless the agreement provides otherwise.

      3) **Not an acceptance.** Payment under such contractual provisions does not constitute acceptance or waiver of buyer's remedies for nonconforming goods.

2. **Inspection in Documentary Sales--Bartlett & Co., Grain v. Merchants Co.,** 323 F.2d 501 (5th Cir. 1963).

   a. **Facts.** Merchants Co. (P) contracted to buy No. 2 yellow corn from Bartlett & Co., Grain (D). The contract provided that if D loaded at Nebraska City, "'In Barge' official weights & grades" would govern. D did load at Nebraska City, where the corn was certified as No. 2 yellow. P sold the corn to Walls, to whom the corn was delivered. P paid D while the grain was in transit. When Walls received the corn, it was inspected and certified as partly No. 1 yellow corn and partly sample grade. Walls refused to accept the grain but handled it and charged P $7,000 for his services. P sued D to recover these charges. The trial court found that the original inspection was inaccurate and that because P had reserved the right "to reject shipment in event quality proves to be below contract grade," P should recover. D appeals.

b. **Issue.** Does a buyer have a right to inspect if it agrees to be bound by an inspection made at the point of shipment?

c. **Held.** No. Judgment reversed.

1) Parties may agree to be bound by an official inspection, and a buyer may not thereafter substitute its own inspection for that conducted by the agreed third party. Here, the parties agreed that the inspection made at the point of shipment would govern as to weights and grades. Therefore, P is bound by the original inspection.

2) P's reserved right to reject shipments if quality was below contract grade only gave it the right to reject if the quality measured by the original inspection did not measure up. P did not have the right to determine whether the quality was adequate.

3) The customary trade dealings support this result because prices are lowered in return for relinquishment by the buyer of the right to inspect at the destination.

3. **Right to Reject.** If the goods which the seller delivers do not conform to the contract, the buyer is entitled to reject them. [UCC §2-601] He must comply with the established rules of sales law unless the parties have agreed otherwise.

a. **Basic rules.**

1) **Notice.** To be effective, rejection must take place within a reasonable time after delivery or tender, and the buyer must notify the seller that they have been rejected. [UCC §2-602(1)]

a) **Reasonable time.** The reasonable time requirement contemplates due allowance for right of inspection, nature and size of shipment, etc.

b) **Defects known to seller.** Notice must be given by the buyer even if the seller has knowingly shipped nonconforming goods. Because the buyer might choose to accept the nonconforming goods, notice is necessary to give the seller an opportunity to cure the defect.

c) **General rejection sufficient.** The general rule is that the buyer need not specify the particular defects in the goods which he asserts as grounds for rejection. A general notice of rejection for "nonconforming goods" is sufficient. However, if the defect is ascertainable upon reasonable inspection, generalized rejection may be insufficient in two circumstances: (i) whenever the seller could have cured the defect if stated reasonably by the buyer; and (ii) when both parties are merchants and the seller has made a written statement of all defects on which the buyer proposes to rely. [UCC §2-605]

2) Effect of rejection. Where the seller has shipped defective or nonconforming goods, and the buyer has made an effective rejection thereof, the buyer's duty to pay never arises. The goods remain the property of the seller and the risk of loss also remains on the seller. [UCC §2-510(1)]

3) Duties with respect to rejected goods.

   a) Exercise of dominion. Once goods have been rejected, the buyer is under a duty not to exercise dominion over the goods. If he does use or resell the goods, the exercise of dominion is "wrongful" under UCC section 2-602(2)(a), thus entitling the seller, but it is not an acceptance unless the seller indicates he will treat it as such. [UCC §2-606(1)(c)]

   b) Duty to hold, return, or resell. The rejecting buyer having physical possession must hold the goods with reasonable care to allow the seller to remove them. [UCC §2-602(2)(b), (c)] The seller may instruct the buyer to resell the goods, and the buyer must follow the seller's reasonable instructions so long as (i) the seller has no agent or place of business at the market of rejection, (ii) the buyer is a merchant, and (iii) the buyer has possession or control of the goods. [UCC §2-603(1)] If the seller does not give instructions within a reasonable time, the buyer may take reasonable actions, including resale for the seller's account. [UCC §§2-604; 2-603(1)] The buyer is entitled to recover reasonable expenses from the seller [UCC §2-603(2)], and has a security interest in rejected goods to recover such expenses [UCC §2-711(3)].

b. Damages for bad faith rejection--Neumiller Farms, Inc. v. Cornett, 368 So. 2d 272 (Ala. 1979).

Neumiller Farms, Inc. v. Cornett

   1) Facts. Neumiller Farms, Inc. (D), a potato broker, contracted to buy 12 loads of chipping potatoes from Cornett (P), a potato farmer. The contract price was $4.25 per hundredweight, and the potatoes were to be "chipt" to D's satisfaction. D accepted three loads from P when the market price was $4.25. The price dropped thereafter to $2.00 and D declined to accept any further loads, claiming dissatisfaction. P tendered potatoes purchased from another grower whose potatoes D had accepted at $2.00, but D rejected these as unsatisfactory. D also refused P's offer to fulfill the contract from other growers' potatoes. P sued for damages and prevailed. D appeals.

   2) Issue. If acceptance is made expressly conditional upon the buyer's satisfaction, is the buyer liable for damages if he claims dissatisfaction in bad faith and rejects the seller's tender?

   3) Held. Yes. Judgment affirmed.

   a) The evidence indicates that D's claim of dissatisfaction was not made in good faith. As a merchant, D has a duty to act in good faith. Because D's rejection for dissatisfaction was not made in good faith, it was ineffectual and constituted breach of contract for which P could recover damages.

Sales & Secured Transactions - 129

c. **Cure.** Any defect in the goods tendered by the seller (in a non-installment contract may be treated as a material breach by the buyer, entitling him to reject the whole). [UCC §2-601] However, the seller may "cure" any defects in the goods tendered if he can do so within the time set by the contract for performance. If the seller cures, it constitutes sufficient performance, removing any breach resulting from the original improper delivery. [UCC §2-508]

1) **Notice.** In order for the seller to be entitled to cure, he must first notify the buyer of his intention to attempt a second conforming cure. Notice must be given "seasonably" (within a reasonable time) and need not take any particular form.

2) **Surprise rejections.** If the seller had reasonable grounds to believe that a nonconforming tender would be accepted, *e.g.,* because the buyer had accepted such tenders in the past, and the buyer suddenly rejects the tender, the surprised seller may have a further reasonable time to cure, if he notifies the buyer.

T.W. Oil, Inc. v. Consolidated Edison Co. of New York, Inc.

3) **Cure after time for delivery--T.W. Oil, Inc. v. Consolidated Edison Co. of New York, Inc.,** 443 N.E.2d 932 (N.Y. 1982).

a) **Facts.** T.W. Oil (P) bought a cargo of fuel oil having no greater than 1% sulfur content. While the cargo was at sea, P received notice from the foreign refinery that the oil actually contained only .52% sulfur. P sold the oil to Consolidated Edison (D). The sales contract described the sulfur content as .5%, pursuant to industry custom. D disclosed that it could burn oil having a sulfur content of up to 1%. After the oil shipment arrived, testing showed it contained .92% sulfur. D rejected the shipment, and the parties could not agree to a price reduction, because the market price had fallen and D refused to pay more than the latest market price. A day after D's refusal, P offered to cure the defect with a substitute delivery, but D refused this offer as well. P resold the oil elsewhere at a loss of more than $1 million. P sued for breach of contract and obtained a judgment. D appeals.

b) **Issue.** Does a seller have a right to cure after the date of performance when it has no prior knowledge of the nonconformity of the goods?

c) **Held.** Yes. Judgment affirmed.

(1) UCC section 2-508 gives a seller a right to cure a defective tender under certain circumstances. This is a limitation on the perfect tender rule, intended to promote good faith dealings in recognition of reasonable commercial standards. The right to cure safeguards a seller against surprise resulting from the buyer's sudden technicality.

(2) Cure offered when the time for performance has not yet expired is governed by UCC section 2-508(1), but cure after the date set

for performance is governed by UCC section 2-508(2). That section requires that (i) the buyer rejects a nonconforming tender; (ii) the seller must have had reasonable grounds to believe the tender would be acceptable; and (iii) the seller must have seasonably notified the buyer of the intention to substitute a conforming tender within a reasonable time.

(3) The requirements of UCC section 2-508(2) were satisfied here. P's tender did not conform to the contract and was properly rejected. P reasonably believed that the original tender would be acceptable because of its information about the sulfur content. D verified this by its willingness to accept the oil, albeit at a reduced price. P's cure offer was made the day after D's refusal to negotiate an acceptable price, a reasonable time under the circumstances.

(4) D claims that the statute should be limited to situations where a seller knowingly makes a nonconforming tender which it has reason to believe the buyer will accept. However, those courts that have considered the question have been concerned with the reasonableness of the seller's belief that the buyer would accept the goods, not the seller's knowledge or lack thereof of the defect. This is the best approach because it conforms the law to reasonable expectations and thwarts the party that seeks to escape from a bad bargain. P's belief was reasonable under the circumstances and D improperly rejected P's reasonable and timely offer to cure.

d. **Substitution of repaired for new goods is not a cure--Zabriskie Chevrolet, Inc. v. Smith,** 240 A.2d 195 (N.J. Super. 1968).

Zabriskie Chevrolet, Inc. v. Smith

1) **Facts.** Smith (D) purchased a new car from Zabriskie Chevrolet, Inc. (P). On the way home, the transmission failed to operate properly and D canceled the sale by stopping payment on the check and notifying P. P retrieved the car and replaced the transmission. P then sued on the check because D refused to take the repaired car.

2) **Issue.** Does substitution of a repaired vehicle for a new one constitute a cure under the UCC?

3) **Held.** No. Judgment for D.

a) D could rightfully reject even after taking possession if done within a reasonable time. Clearly the car did not conform to the contract because it was defective when delivered. Because D rejected the defective vehicle immediately, and the defect was substantial so as to not conform to the contract, D rightfully rejected.

b) P claims that under UCC section 2-508 it had a right to cure the nonconforming defect. A seller is protected from surprise rejections, and is given the chance to cure, if it has reasonable grounds to believe that its tender would be accepted. Such was not the case here.

    c)   Furthermore, the attempted cure was not a cure within the meaning of the UCC. A repaired vehicle's substitution for a new one is not a cure of a defect. P's attempted cure was ineffective in this case.

McKenzie v.
Alla-Ohio
Coals, Inc.

e.   **Offer of a lower price is not a cure--McKenzie v. Alla-Ohio Coals, Inc.,** 29 UCC Rep. Serv. 852, *aff'd*, 610 F.2d 1000 (D.D.C. 1979).

1)   **Facts.** McKenzie (P) and Alla-Ohio Coals, Inc. (D) conducted verbal negotiations for the sale of coal. D, a coal broker, agreed to buy coal from P to resell to its customers. To confirm the agreement, D sent P a purchase order that contained a penalty provision based on the ash content of the coal. P shipped the coal before it received the purchase order. When it did receive the order, it responded to D that the purchase order did not conform to the oral agreement, specifically with regard to the specifications and the penalty provisions. When D received the coal, tests showed that the ash level was much higher than agreed and rejected the shipment. P offered to take a lower price for the coal but D refused. P sold the coal to another buyer for a lower price. P then sued for damages. Both parties moved for summary judgment.

2)   **Issue.** May a seller cure a nonconforming tender by offering to take a reduced price?

3)   **Held.** No. Judgment for D.

    a)   Although the purchase order contained a penalty clause, this was not D's sole remedy. There is a presumption that remedies are cumulative which can only be overcome by an express statement in the writings. No such statement was contained in the purchase order.

    b)   Although the perfect tender rule of UCC section 2-601 has been diminished when the buyer suffers no damages, in this case the nonconformity was substantial. The ash content of the coal P shipped was much too high for the use of D's customers, and well beyond that agreed to. D could properly reject the shipment.

    c)   Under UCC section 2-508 a seller may cure a nonconforming tender after the time for performance if he meets the three requirements: (i) that he had reasonable grounds to believe the tender would be acceptable; (ii) that he seasonably notified the buyer of his intent to cure; and (iii) that he cures within a reasonable time.

    d)   Here, it is not reasonable that P would not know of the drastically poor quality of the coal tendered and that it could not be used by D. The only cure P attempted was to offer to take a lower price, but this is not an approved method of cure. P never offered to tender conforming coal.

    e)   D may recover damages incurred in inspecting the coal as incidental damages under UCC section 2-715(1).

4. **Timeliness of Rejection--Intervale Steel Corp. v. Borg & Beck Division, Borg-Warner,** 578 F. Supp. 1081 (E.D. Mich. 1984).

    a. **Facts.** Borg & Beck Division, Borg-Warner Corp. (D), bought steel from Barry for more than 15 years. Intervale Steel Corp. (P) is the successor to Barry. On one occasion, D ordered 22 coils of steel for use in making Belleville springs, to be used in automobile clutch assemblies. P treated the steel, but annealed it only once instead of twice. When D took the steel, it checked for dimensional accuracy and chemical content. It then began the fabrication of springs by stamping out blanks. A month later, D finished the process, but in the latter steps it discovered that the springs were cracking. D told P and stopped production. P admitted the steel was defective and authorized D to scrap the steel. P sued for the contract price less the scrap value realized by D, claiming P had accepted the steel and could not revoke acceptance.

    b. **Issue.** May a buyer reject goods after manufacturing them into parts?

    c. **Held.** No. Judgment for P, less setoff for breach of warranty.

        1) D claims it properly rejected the goods because it could not have discovered the breach of warranty any sooner than it did. But even though D acted reasonably, it did accept the steel. Under UCC section 2-606(1)(b), D did not reject the steel within a reasonable time. It had the steel for three months and stamped out all of it. Timely rejection is intended to permit the seller to make the goods conform or sell them to another buyer, but here D had manufactured the steel into parts.

        2) D's inability to inspect the goods before manufacture does not extend its time for acceptance. The remedy for buyers who accept goods with latent defects that cannot be easily detected is not rejection but an action for damages for breach of warranty.

        3) Revocation of acceptance is not available either, because D had substantially changed the condition of the goods, which prevents revocation under UCC section 2-608(2).

        4) Because D accepted the goods, D is liable for the purchase price less the scrap proceeds that it already gave P. D is entitled to withhold payment of the purchase price to the extent that is has suffered damages from P's breach, under UCC section 2-717. In this case, these damages are the difference between the scrap value of the steel and the contract price of the material, so P gets nothing.

5. **Buyer's Duty After Rejecting Goods--Borges v. Magic Valley Foods, Inc.,** 616 P.2d 273 (Idaho 1980).

    a. **Facts.** Borges (P) was a potato farmer. Magic Valley Foods, Inc. (D) inspected P's potatoes and agreed to purchase them for $3.80 per c.w.t. despite the existence of hollow heart defects in some of the potatoes. The contract provided that it would be null and void if the potatoes were unfit for fresh pack shipping, to be determined by government inspectors. All but about 5,000 c.w.t. of the potatoes were shipped under the fresh pack grade. P authorized D to attempt to blend the rest with other higher grade potatoes to bring them up to fresh pack grade standards. This did not succeed, so D processed the remaining potatoes into flakes and sold them for $1.25 per c.w.t., without notifying P. P demanded the full contract price for these potatoes, but D refused, offering to pay the $1.25. P sued and recovered a judgment based on the contract price. D appeals, claiming it never accepted the defective potatoes.

 b. **Issue.** If a buyer resells defective goods without notifying the seller, does that act constitute acceptance?

 c. **Held.** Yes. Judgment affirmed.

  1) Under UCC section 2-606(1)(c), a buyer accepts goods when he does any act inconsistent with the seller's ownership. This includes reselling the goods without notifying the seller. A buyer is liable for the contract rate for any goods accepted.

  2) The potatoes clearly did not conform to the contract and D had a right to reject them. P did authorize D to attempt to get rid of the potatoes by blending them. D claims that the subsequent resale was permitted by either UCC section 2-603(1) or 2-604. Both of these provisions apply where there are no instructions from the seller.

  3) The jury was properly instructed about UCC sections 2-603(1) and 2-604. The jury could have concluded that P's only instructions pertained to the blending option and that D acted too soon in processing the potatoes. Even if it found that a reasonable time had elapsed so as to allow D to resell the potatoes, the jury could have found that D's use of the potatoes in the ordinary course of its own business was an act inconsistent with P's ownership, and thus an acceptance of the potatoes.

6. **Acceptance.** The buyer's basic duty is to "accept and pay for" the goods. [UCC §2-301]

 a. **What constitutes acceptance.** Acceptance may occur by words or conduct by the buyer signifying his approval of the goods delivered.

  1) The most obvious acceptance occurs when the buyer, after having had a reasonable opportunity to inspect the goods, signifies to the seller either that (i) the goods are conforming, or (ii) he will take them in spite of their nonconformity. [UCC §2-606(1)(a)]

  2) Another method of acceptance is for the buyer simply to hold the goods for an unreasonable length of time without notifying the seller that he has rejected them. [UCC §2-606(1), (1)(b)] Acceptance by inaction cannot occur, however, until the buyer has had a reasonable opportunity to inspect. [UCC §2-606(1)(b)]

  3) A third method of acceptance is for the buyer to do any act inconsistent with the seller's ownership—*e.g.*, consuming the goods or selling them to others can constitute acceptance of the goods.

b. **Right to make partial acceptance.** If the seller makes a tender that in any way fails to conform to the contract (*e.g.,* part of shipment is defective), the buyer may accept any commercial unit or units and reject the rest. [UCC §2-601(c)] If he accepts part of any commercial unit, he is deemed to accept the entire commercial unit. [UCC §2-606(2)]

   1) A commercial unit is one that by commercial usage is treated as a single whole for the purposes of sale, and division of which materially impairs its character or value on the market or in use.

   2) A commercial unit may be a single article (as a machine); or a set of articles (as a suite of furniture or an assortment of sizes); or a quantity (as a bale, gross, or carload) or any other unit treated in use or in the relevant market as a single whole. [UCC §2-105(6)]

c. **Effect of complete acceptance.** Once the buyer accepts the goods, he must pay for them at the contract rate. He cannot thereafter reject the goods as nonconforming. [UCC §2-607(1), (2)] Revocation may be available, however. The buyer's acceptance does not bar a claim for damages. Where the seller is late in delivery or delivers nonconforming goods, the buyer may keep and utilize the goods, and still sue the seller for damages, or assert his claim for damages as a set-off to any action brought by the seller to recover the purchase price. [UCC §§2-714; 2-717]

d. **Acceptance by failure to properly reject--Plateq Corp. of North Haven v. Machlett Laboratories, Inc.,** 456 A.2d 786 (Conn. 1983).

   1) **Facts.** Machlett Laboratories (D) ordered specially manufactured lead-covered steel tanks from Plateq Corp. (P). The sales contract permitted D to test for radiation leaks after installation of the tanks, and P was to correct at its own expense any deficiencies. P took more time than originally contemplated, but D did not object. When P's performance was substantially complete, D noted some last-minute deficiencies, which P agreed to remedy the next day. D told P it would pick up the tanks rather than have P deliver them. Instead, D canceled the contract. P sued for the contract price and incidental damages. The trial court found for P on the ground that D had accepted the tanks. D appeals.

   2) **Issue.** Must a rejection of goods specify the grounds for the rejection in order to be valid?

   3) **Held.** Yes. Judgment affirmed.

      a) The trial court, supported by the evidence, found that P had substantially complied with the contract. Acceptance of goods occurs when the buyer after a reasonable opportunity to inspect the goods tells the seller he will take them in spite of their nonconformity or fails to make an effective rejection. [UCC §2-606(1)] The trial court found that D had a reasonable opportunity to inspect the goods and accepted them despite the remaining deficiencies.

      b) The trial court further found, as an alternative, that D failed to make an effective rejection. D's purported rejection was based on unparticularized defects and was insufficient under UCC section 2-605(1).

D claims P should have had no opportunity to cure under UCC section 2-508 because P never tendered the tanks, but D tried to cancel before P was able to tender. D's unparticularized cancellation wrongfully interfered with P's contractual right to cure any remaining post-installation defects.

7. **Revocation of Acceptance.** Normally a buyer who accepts defective or nonconforming goods must pay for them at the contract price, although he may still sue for damages. However, if the defects in the goods are "substantial," UCC section 2-608(1) permits the buyer to revoke his acceptance and makes available all the remedies open prior to acceptance.

    a. **Substantial defect.** A buyer may reject goods for any nonconformity in quality or quantity, even minor deviations, under UCC section 2-601. However, once the buyer has accepted the goods, he needs a much stronger case to justify revoking his acceptance. The buyer can revoke only if the nonconformity substantially impairs the value of the goods to the particular buyer, and only in two situations:

        1) The buyer accepted the goods knowing of the defect but on the reasonable assumption that it would be cured, and the cure has not been seasonably made. [UCC §2-608(1)(a)]

        2) The buyer accepted the goods not knowing of the defect and the acceptance was reasonably induced either by the difficulty of discovering the defect (a latent defect) or by the seller's assurances that no defects existed.

    b. **Notice.** The buyer must notify the seller of his desire to revoke acceptance within a reasonable time after the buyer discovers or should have discovered the grounds for revocation. [UCC §2-608(2)]

    c. **Condition of goods.** To properly revoke, the buyer may not have substantially consumed or detrimentally used the goods.

    d. **Effect.** If the buyer properly revokes acceptance, ownership and risk of loss to the goods revert to the seller and the buyer is relieved of any duty to pay for the goods.

Atlan Industries, Inc. v. O.E.M., Inc.

    e. **Revocation after processing the goods--Atlan Industries, Inc. v. O.E.M., Inc.,** 555 F. Supp. 184 (W.D. Okla. 1983).

        1) **Facts.** Atlan Industries, Inc. (P) supplied reground plastic to O.E.M., Inc. (D), which D used to make computer cabinets. The plastic, described as FN 215, is heat sensitive but withstands temperatures up to 205 degrees. After molding, the plastic is sent to the ultimate user, who paints the cabinets and bakes them at temperatures below 205 degrees. In accordance with the common industry practice, D tested a sample of the plastic to make sure it molded properly. D successfully molded the plastic, but when the ultimate user baked on the paint at temperatures between 130 and 170 degrees, the cabinets warped. The ultimate user rejected the goods, and D immediately notified P. P instructed D to return the material to P. P was unable to furnish FN 215 from another source, so D purchased it

elsewhere at a higher price. D also spent about $800 to inspect and re-grind the nonconforming plastic to send it back to P. P sues for the contract price, claiming D accepted the plastic. D counterclaims for damages.

2) **Issue.** May a buyer revoke acceptance even after processing the goods if the nonconformity of the goods substantially impairs the value of the goods to the buyer?

3) **Held.** Yes. Judgment for D.

   a) P contracted to sell FN 215, which does not warp at 150 degrees, but the plastic P sold did warp at 150 degrees. The plastic did not conform to the contract, so D could have rejected it. However, by processing the goods, D did an act clearly inconsistent with P's ownership, so D accepted the goods.

   b) Under UCC section 2-608(1)(b), a buyer may revoke acceptance if the nonconformity of the goods substantially impairs their value, even if he accepted the goods without discovery of the nonconformity, so long as the acceptance was induced by the difficulty of discovery before acceptance. The plastic in this case could not be used for its only reasonable use—as molded computer cabinets. This nonconformity did substantially impair the value of the plastic.

   c) In the plastic industry, the only test performed by the molder is whether the plastic molds properly. The plastic met this test. P claims that D should also have sent a sample to the ultimate user for testing. While this could have been a contractual requirement, it was not, and the industry practice does not require such testing. Therefore, D's acceptance was reasonably induced by the difficulty of discovering the nonconformity before acceptance.

   d) D provided P immediate notice of the nonconformity. Since D properly revoked acceptance, it has the same rights as it would have upon rejection, including remedies. For that reason, D is entitled to judgment on its counterclaim.

f. **Revocation not defeated by subsequent use--Johannsen v. Minnesota Valley Ford Tractor Co., 304 N.W.2d 654 (Minn. 1981).**

   1) **Facts.** Johannsen (P) had mechanical problems with the fourth gear of the transmission on his Ford Model 9600 tractor. He took it to Minnesota Valley Ford Tractor Co. (D). D told him that the transmission on the new Model 9700 had been redesigned, so P bought a new tractor. D did not tell P that Ford had sent a letter to its dealers describing transmission defects in the 9700, and that a defective tractor should be sold only if they would lose a sale otherwise. D received the tractor in July, and on its first use the transmission jumped out of fourth gear. The tractor also had other problems, including a hydraulic defect that D said it could not fix until April. P told D he wanted to return the tractor. In September, P's attorney formally notified D that P was revoking his acceptance due to the transmission and other defects. P continued to use the tractor until October, when he put it in storage after D had made three service calls. P sued for damages. D appeals a verdict for P.

2) Issue. May a buyer effectively revoke acceptance when he uses the goods after revocation?

3) Held. Yes. Judgment affirmed.

    a) D had no right to cure. Cure is limited to rejected goods by UCC section 2-508(2). It is not a proper remedy for defects that substantially impair the value of the goods, a requirement for revocation. The defects in the tractor substantially impaired its value to P, since they prevented P from farming his entire farm.

    b) P's revocation was within a reasonable time as found by the jury.

    c) Although a buyer's continued use of defective goods may be wrongful in many cases, the reasonableness of the continued use must be evaluated in light of several factors, including: (i) the seller's instructions to the buyer after revocation; (ii) the degree of economic and other hardship to the buyer from discontinued use; (iii) the reasonableness of the buyer's use as a method of mitigating damages; (iv) the prejudice to the seller; and (v) whether the seller acted in bad faith.

    d) In this case, the jury's conclusion that P's continued use was reasonable was supported by the evidence. The tractor's defects were major. D persuaded P to buy the tractor knowing that it might be defective. P only used the tractor to perform necessary jobs. In addition, the court gave D a setoff for use and depreciation of the tractor.

B. SELLER'S BREACH OF WARRANTY

1. Introduction. Warranty law has changed significantly over the years and continues to produce a significant amount of litigation.

    a. Common law approach. At early common law, breach of warranty was regarded as a tort. If the seller had used the magic words "warranty" or "guarantee," this was held to evidence his intention to be bound (*i.e.,* a promissory warranty), and his breach was considered in the nature of fraud, and hence tortious. Later the common law cases recognized that the liability for breach of warranty was really contractual in nature, and as such, it was immaterial whether there was any actual fraud or bad faith. If the words used amounted to a warranty, the seller was bound even in the absence of proof that he intended to be bound thereby. Also, the later cases rejected the requirement of special words of warranty, and were willing to imply certain warranties into every sale, even where there were not express warranties.

    b. UCC approach. The UCC, in an attempt to make clear exactly what it is that the seller has agreed to sell, recognizes express warranties [UCC §2-313], implied warranties of merchantability [UCC §2-314], and implied warranties of fitness for a particular purpose [UCC §2-315]. However, the seller is not to be held liable when it makes not warranties.

c. **Buyer's reliance on specifications--Hobson Construction Co., Inc. v. Hajoca Corp.,** 222 S.E.2d 709 (N.C. App. 1976).

Hobson Construction Co. Inc. v. Hajoca Corp.

1) **Facts.** Hobson Construction Co., Inc. (P) contracted to build a water treatment plant. The specifications required the use of a filter equal to a specified model. P purchased the specified model from Hajoca Corp. (D). D told P that the filters "should remove the iron and manganese from the water." After installation, the filters did not work adequately. P made modifications which allowed the filters to work properly, primarily by drilling more holes and by replacing plastic distributor heads with stainless steel ones. P brought suit alleging that the filters contained defects which amounted to a breach of warranty. The evidence indicated that the plastic heads were adequate for ordinary purposes but did not work under excessive water pressure as present in the treatment plant. The trial court dismissed the suit and P appeals.

2) **Issue.** Where the buyer relies on specifications but not any warranty as to fitness for the intended use, does he have a cause of action when the product does not fulfill the buyer's intended use?

3) **Held.** No. Judgment affirmed.

a) The only reason P bought the filters from D was that the contract specifications required such filters. The evidence indicated that the filters were not defective, but only that they could not operate under such extreme water pressure. The defect was in the plans and specifications, not in the filters.

b) D's only representation was that the filters met the specifications. There was no warranty of fitness for a particular purpose, and P did not rely on D's skill or judgment to furnish suitable goods. The fact that D stated that the filters "should" remove the minerals did not amount to an affirmation of fact.

2. **Express Warranties.**

a. **Affirmation or promise.**

1) **Form of warranty.** A statement of fact or promise made by the seller to the buyer in the course of negotiations, which relates to the goods and is "part of the basis of the bargain," creates an express warranty that the goods shall conform to the statement or promise made. [UCC §2-313(1)(a)]

a) **No technical words.** Contrary to the early common law rule, no magic words of warranty need be used. Any affirmation of fact or promise made in connection with the sale may be sufficient. [UCC §2-313(2)]

b) **Written or oral.** In general, an express warranty may be written or oral, and in appropriate cases may be expressed by conduct rather than words.

2) **Buyer's reliance.** The common law looked upon the buyer's reliance as the sine qua non of express warranty; unless the buyer relied, he or she could not recover. The UCC instead uses the much vaguer phrase "basis of the bargain" and reliance is no longer to be of prime significance. All statements by the seller become part of the basis of the bargain unless good reason is shown to the contrary. [UCC §2-313] Some authorities do not find any significant difference between these concepts.

3) **Seller's intent immaterial.** No intent to warrant is required. If the words used amount to a warranty, it is immaterial that the seller did not intend them as such or did not intend to be bound thereby. Liability is predicated on breach of contract, not fraud or negligence. Where the warranty is breached, the seller becomes absolutely liable. The fact that the warranty was given in good faith, or that the seller was innocent or nonnegligent in causing the breach, is immaterial. [UCC §2-313(2)]

4) **Fact vs. opinion.** A sales pitch typically includes statements of opinion about how the product is worth buying. The UCC provides that an affirmation merely of the value of the goods or a statement purporting to be merely the seller's opinion or commendation of the goods does not create a warranty. [UCC §2-313(2)] Distinguishing between statements of fact and expressions of opinion is sometimes difficult. One factor considered by most courts is the relative knowledge of the parties concerning the goods. A seller's statements are more likely to be construed as statements of fact if the buyer has limited knowledge about the goods.

5) **Time of warranting.**

a) **Statements made prior to sale.** An affirmation of fact or promise can be made at one time, and the sale at a much later date. The statement made at the earlier time will constitute express warranties only if such statements were still part of the basis of the bargain at the time of purchase.

b) **Statements made after sale.** Although at common law a statement of fact made after the sale contract closed was not an express warranty, under UCC section 2-209 a post-transaction affirmation of fact may become part of the basis of the bargain and can be deemed a modification of the contract which is effective without any new consideration.

b. **Express warranty of conformity to description.** Any description of the goods which is part of the basis of the bargain creates an express warranty that the goods shall conform to the description given. [UCC §2-313(1)(b)] This rule is similar to an implied warranty, but the UCC makes it an express warranty in order to make it more difficult to disclaim under UCC section 2-316.

1) **Description.** Any descriptive name or words used in the sale of goods constitutes a warranty that the goods delivered will conform to the general characteristics of the description. A trade term may constitute a descrip-

tion so that the seller must deliver goods which pass in the trade under the contract description.

2) **Specific goods.** There is no warranty when the parties contract with reference to specific goods; descriptive phrases then become merely a means of identification.

c. **Express warranty of conformity to sample.** If the parties have bargained on the basis of any sample or model, an express warranty arises to the effect that all goods delivered shall conform to the sample or model. [UCC §2-313(1)(c)] The whole of the goods are warranted to conform to the sample. Nonconformity of any portion of the goods is a breach of warranty to conform to the sample.

1) **Samples.** Mere use of a sample in selling does not in itself constitute a warranty that the goods shall conform to that sample. Whether the sample was part of the basis of the bargain, and hence constitutes a warranty, is always a question of fact.

2) **Models.** A model is like a sample, but differs in the sense that a sample is drawn from the mass to be sold, while a model is used by the seller to represent the goods although not drawn from the mass to be sold.

d. **Common law approach.**

1) **Description not a warranty--Chandelor v. Lopus,** 79 Eng. Rep. 3 (Exch. 1625).

Chandelor v. Lopus

   a) **Facts.** Chandelor (D), a goldsmith and jeweler, affirmed that a stone he sold to Lopus (P) was a "bezar-stone," a material formed in the stomach of certain animals which was believed to have medicinal properties. P bought the stone and later discovered it was not a bezar-stone. P sued to recover the purchase price. The trial court found for P and D appeals.

   b) **Issue.** May a seller be liable for breach of warranty when he states that the item sold is a particular item of worth but does not actually warrant that it is?

   c) **Held.** No. Judgment reversed.

      (1) All sellers affirm that their products are good, but unless they actually warrant that they are so, there is no cause of action if the product turns out not to be good.

   d) **Comment.** Bezar-stones were thought to have magical properties, depending on the user. Thus D probably could not have warranted that the stone would work for P.

2) **Representation not a warranty--Seixas v. Woods,** 2 Am. Dec. 215 (N.Y. 1804).

Seixas v. Woods

   a) **Facts.** Woods (D) was the agent for a wood company. D received wood from this company described as brazilletto, a valuable kind of wood. D advertised it as such. Seixas (P) purchased the wood, paying the high price. Later, P discovered that the wood was peachum wood, an almost worthless kind. P tendered the wood back, seeking a return of the purchase price. D refused. P sued and recovered. Neither party knew that the wood was not brazilletto. D appeals.

b) **Issue.** Does the representation that an item is of a particular type constitute a warranty that it is so?

c) **Held.** No. Judgment reversed.

(1) As in the *Chandelor* case (*supra*), there was no warranty that the wood was brazilletto. D did not know the true nature of the wood, and had no particular knowledge or expertise. Nor was a matter of judgment involved.

Sessa v. Riegle

e. **Basis of the bargain approach under the UCC--Sessa v. Riegle,** 427 F. Supp. 760 (E.D. Pa. 1977), *aff'd*, 568 F.2d 770 (3d Cir. 1977).

1) **Facts.** Sessa (P) was interested in buying a race horse from Riegle (D). P sent Maloney, a trusted agent, to inspect the horse. P also discussed the horse with D, who told P the horse was "sound." After Maloney approved the horse, P bought it. Shortly after delivery, the horse went lame. P treated the horse and cured it, but sues D for damages, including the cost of treatment.

2) **Issue.** Is a statement that a horse is "sound" an express warranty?

3) **Held.** No. Judgment for D.

a) Cases involving alleged express warranties require three steps of analysis. First, the court must determine whether the seller's words are an affirmation of fact or merely an opinion. Second, the court must determine whether the statement was part of the basis for the bargain. Third, the court must determine whether the warranty was breached.

b) The determination of the character of the seller's statements depends on the circumstances. Generally, where a horse is involved, a seller would not make a guarantee because a horse is a fragile creature. The only situation where a seller's statements about a horse's fitness may be treated as warranties is where the buyer is ignorant and depends on the seller to make a fair deal.

c) The fact that P sent a trained agent to inspect the horse indicates that D's statements were not really the basis for the bargain. In addition, D's statements were incidental to the conversation which involved primarily arrangements for delivery.

d) Finally, D did not prove that the horse was not sound at the time D shipped it.

Keith v. Buchanan

f. **No reliance requirement under the UCC--Keith v. Buchanan,** 220 Cal. Rptr. 392 (Ct. App. Cal. 1985).

1) **Facts.** Keith (P), who had never owned a yacht, attended a boat show and read literature about a sailboat described as "seaworthy." P wanted a boat that was oceangoing, and after explaining his needs, bought the boat from Buchanan (D). After P took delivery of the boat, he discovered the boat was not as seaworthy as he had been led to believe. P sued, claiming breach of express and implied warranty. The trial court granted judgment for D and P appeals.

2) **Issue.** Must a buyer prove that he acted in reliance upon representations made by the seller in order to recover for breach of warranty?

3) **Held.** No. Judgment reversed.

   a) Under UCC section 2-313, express warranties are created by an affirmation of fact made by the seller to the buyer which relates to the goods and becomes part of the basis of the bargain, and by any description of the goods which is made part of the basis of the bargain. The law of warranty is intended to determine what it is that the seller agreed to sell.

   b) A particular statement may be either an affirmation of fact or an expression of opinion. Courts have begun to increasingly construe affirmations of quality as affirmations of fact, thereby protecting consumers. A seller's statements during the course of negotiations are presumptively affirmations of fact unless the buyer could only have reasonably considered the statement as a statement of the seller's opinion. The following factors tend to indicate an opinion statement: (i) a lack of specificity; (ii) equivocal phrasing; and (iii) an indication that the goods are experimental in nature.

   c) In this case, D's sales brochures stated that the boat was a "very seaworthy vessel," and "a picture of sure-footed seaworthiness." D knew that P wanted a boat for long distance oceangoing cruises. These representations are affirmations of fact.

   d) It is not necessary for a buyer to prove reliance on the seller's representations to show that the statements became part of the basis of the bargain. A warranty statement is deemed to be part of the basis of the bargain; such representations are not part of the bargain only if the bargain does not rest at all on the seller's representations. The seller has the burden of proof on this issue, which it can meet by showing that the buyer actually knew of the true condition of the goods before making the contract.

4) **Comment.** Despite the holding in this case, many jurisdictions treat reliance and basis of the bargain as equivalent concepts. As in the *Sessa* case, the issues are (i) whether the statement was made as an affirmation of fact; (ii) whether the goods matched the statement; and (iii) whether the defect was not so obvious that the buyer should have discovered it.

g. **Seller's prediction of performance not a warranty--Axion Corp. v. G.D.C. Leasing Corp.,** 269 N.E.2d 664 (Mass. 1971).

1) Facts. Axion Corp. (P) sold three valve testing machines to G.D.C. Leasing Corp. (D) over a period of time. The first machine was a prototype and required various revisions, made by P and D together. The later two machines were to be made with the revisions, although further development and testing were required. D paid for the first two machines but refused to pay for the third unless it met a "plus or minus 5% specification." D did accept all of the machines, however. P sued for the purchase price, and D sued for breach of warranty. The trial court granted P's motions for directed verdicts on all claims and D appeals.

2) Issue. Does a specification agreed to over a year after a contract is executed constitute a basis of the bargain such that a buyer may recover for breach of warranty if the specification is not met?

3) Held. No. Judgment affirmed.

a) P made several statements of what it expected the machines to do, but these statements were more predictions than promises. These statements cannot form the basis for a warranty.

b) The 5% specification was worked out after the parties had spent many months testing and adjusting the machines. However, there was a discrepancy in the parties' understanding of what the specification meant. There was no evidence that P agreed to D's version of the specification. Therefore, the specification could not have been a basis of the bargain.

Downie v.
Abex Corp.

h. Post-sale affirmation of fact as a basis of the bargain--Downie v. Abex Corp., 741 F.2d 1235 (10th Cir. 1984).

1) Facts. The Downies (Ps) were injured when an airplane passenger loading bridge collapsed. Ps sued Abex Corp. (D), the manufacturer. D in turn filed a third-party complaint against General Motors ("GM"), which manufactured the ball-screw assembly that caused the collapse. GM had originally limited its warranties to defects in materials and workmanship. However, GM's employees told D that the assembly had a fail-safe feature that would prevent free-fall. GM also demonstrated the fail-safe features to D. GM's sales literature also referred to the fail-safe feature. The jury held GM liable on a post-sale express warranty, but the trial court granted judgment n.o.v. for GM. D appeals.

2) Issue. May warranties made after the sale become a basis of the bargain?

3) Held. Yes. Judgment reversed.

a) On these facts, a rational jury could have found that GM's representations about the fail-safe features were affirmations of fact or promises.

b) The fact that the affirmations were made after the sale does not prevent them from being part of the contract. As Official Comment 7 to UCC section 2-313 indicates, a post-sale warranty may become a modification and thus part of the contract. The post-sale representations may be intended to promote future sales. In this case, the jury could properly have found that GM made the representations to improve sales.

    c)   It is not necessary to decide whether reliance is a prerequisite for an express warranty since the evidence is clear that D did rely on GM's express warranty.

3. **Implied Warranties.** In addition to any express warranties that may be made in connection with the sale by some statement or act of the seller, the law may imply certain other warranties simply because a sale of goods has been consummated. These are the implied warranties, which are imposed by law "to promote higher standards and to discourage sharp dealings in business." They are imposed irrespective of the seller's intentions, and despite the fact that he has made no representations or promises whatsoever concerning the goods. Unless expressly negated by the parties, they arise by operation of law in every sale of goods—new or used—as part of the seller's cost of doing business.

4. **Implied Warranty of Merchantability.** In every mercantile contract of sale where it is not expressly disclaimed, the law implies a warranty that the goods shall be of "merchantable" quality. [UCC §2-314]

    a.   **Who makes the warranty.** The UCC imposes the implied warranty of merchantability only upon a seller who is a "merchant with respect to goods of that kind." [UCC §2-314(1)] This definition of merchant is narrower than that contained in UCC section 2-104(1) and presents a mixed question of fact and law. An implied warranty of merchantability arises in all sales transactions, except sales of private individuals or "occasional" sales by professionals who normally deal in other markets.

    b.   **The standard of merchantable quality.** The UCC establishes a six-part definition of merchantability. Goods must at least meet all six standards.

        1)   **Salable and usable.** The goods must be capable of passing without objection in the trade under the contract description. [UCC §2-314(2)(a)]

        2)   **Bulk of "fair average quality."** In the case of fungibles, the goods must be of "fair average quality," *i.e.*, the bulk (not the whole) of the goods must hover around the middle belt of quality. [UCC §2-314(2)(b)] This definition is particularly applicable in sales of raw materials—grains, vegetables, mineral ores, lumber—although under the UCC's extremely broad definition of fungibles [UCC §1-210(17)], it can be applied in sales of goods now not normally regarded as fungible.

        3)   **Fit for ordinary use.** Goods to be merchantable must also be "fit for the ordinary purposes for which such goods are used." [UCC §2-314(2)(c)] This is the most important standard—that the product sold pass without objection in the trade or otherwise meet normal commercial standards for products of the same type. Where a dealer buys goods from a manufacturer for resale, it means that those goods are fit for resale (*i.e.*, free of defects that cause customers to return them).

4) **Variations within normal limits.** It is also required that the goods "run, within the variations permitted by the agreement, of every kind, quality and quantity within each unit and among all units involved." [UCC §2-314(2)(d)] Thus, merchants are required to adhere to established grade tolerances in multi-unit deliveries of merchandise.

5) **Packaged per agreement.** Goods must be adequately contained, packaged, and labeled as the agreement may require. [UCC §2-314(2)(e)]

6) **Conforms to label.** To be merchantable, goods must conform to the promises or affirmations of fact made on the container or label. [UCC §2-314(2)(f)]

Agoos Kid
Co., Inc. v.
Blumenthal
Import Corp.

c. **Conformance of goods to description a requirement of merchantability--Agoos Kid Co., Inc. v. Blumenthal Import Corp.,** 184 N.E. 279 (1933).

1) **Facts.** Agoos Kid Co. (P) contracted to buy 4,000 "Bagdad goat skins dry salted" from Blumenthal Import Corp. (D). Such goat skins were subject to rot which could not be detected until introduced to the leather-making process. It was considered normal in the trade to have up to 3% of the skins rot. However, when P began to process the skins, much more than 3% were discovered to be rotten. Neither P nor D knew previously that the skins were rotten. P sued for damages on the basis of an implied warranty of merchantability and recovered. D appeals.

2) **Issue.** Is a commercial sale subject to an implied warranty of merchantability as determined with reference to the trade in general?

3) **Held.** Yes. Judgment reversed on other grounds.

a) A sale of goods by description includes an implied warranty that the goods correspond to the description. Goods are merchantable if they generally meet the description.

b) The term "Bagdad goat skins dry salted" is common in the trade and is understood to mean that no more than 3% of the skins can be rotten. In such a circumstance, P was entitled to what he ordered, and D gave an implied warranty as to quality. Because a higher percentage of the skins were rotten, P can recover.

c) However, the judgment must be reversed for consideration of a trade custom whereby P should have notified D of the defect before processing the skins.

Valley Iron
& Steel Co.
v. Thorin

d. **Seller's expertise makes it a merchant--Valley Iron & Steel Co. v. Thorin,** 562 P.2d 1212 (Or. 1977).

1) **Facts.** Thorin (D) sold equipment and supplies for the forestry trade. D approached Valley Iron & Steel Co. (P) to see if P could fabricate collars for a planting tool called a "hoedad." D showed P a sample collar and described its use, specifically stating the problem of hitting rocks during the planting process. P stated that it could make the collars and used its own judgment in deciding what metal to use. P shipped the collars to D, but D's customers found the collars unsatisfactory. D returned 80% of the collars to P and had another maker produce them. P brought suit for the value of the collars delivered. P recovered and D appeals.

2) **Issue.** Where the buyer specifically states the purpose of the items to be bought and leaves the manner of fabrication up to the seller, does the buyer have a claim of breach of warranty if the items prove unsatisfactory?

3) **Held.** Yes. Judgment affirmed as modified.

  a) For purposes of UCC section 2-314, P was a merchant because of its experience and expertise in the manufacture of metal parts. D relied on this expertise, and told P of the use of the collar. P knew that D relied on its expertise and had all the knowledge of the intended use necessary. Therefore, there was an implied warranty of fitness for the use intended by D.

  b) However, D did not return all of the collars delivered. Therefore, D must pay P the reasonable value of those collars delivered and not returned.

e. **Latent defect--Delano Growers' Cooperative Winery v. Supreme Wine Co., Inc.,** 473 N.E.2d 1066 (Mass. 1985).

Delano Growers' Cooperative Winery v. Supreme Wine Co., Inc.

1) **Facts.** The Delano Growers' Cooperative Winery (P) sold wine to Supreme Wine Co., Inc. (D), who in turn sold it under its own label to retailers. The parties followed this arrangement for five years until D began receiving returns from its customers of wine that was cloudy and contained a cottony substance. D notified P of the problem, and P promised help. When P did not help, D bought from another supplier. P later induced D to make more purchases and made four shipments. D withheld payment on the last shipment because its customers were still returning defective wine from P. P's chemist discovered Fresno mold in the wine. P told D to pasteurize, refilter, rebottle, and resell the defective wine. D did so, although it sold it at a reduced price and lost a considerable amount in processing. P sued for the contract price, and D counterclaimed. The trial court awarded damages to D, less an offset for the contract price of the fourth shipment. Both parties appeal.

2) **Issue.** If goods contain a latent defect that could be prevented by the buyer's further processing, may the latent defect constitute a breach of the implied warranty of merchantability?

3) **Held.** Yes. Judgment affirmed.

  a) The implied warranty of merchantability requires that the goods pass without objection in the trade under the contract description. P was obligated to deliver finished wine. P claims that since the wine appeared good and could be bottled, its obligation was fulfilled. P claims that all California sweet wine contains Fresno mold and that trade usage required D to add sulfur dioxide to prevent further bacterial growth.

  b) The problem with P's arguments is that none of the other wine it provided for five years contained the defects that this wine did. Nor did the wine D bought from other suppliers. P could have prevented the mold problem which rendered the wine unmarketable.

  c) The existence of a trade usage does not affect this case because the parties had a course of dealing that prevails over the usage of trade. D never had to treat the wine before. This course of dealing required P to deliver wine ready for bottling and drinking, which it did not do in this case. P's wine was not finished wine.

Doe v.
Travenol
Laboratories,
Inc.

f. Blood shield statute--Doe v. Travenol Laboratories, Inc., 698 F. Supp. 780 (Minn. 1988).

 1) Facts. Doe (P), a hemophiliac, had to take Factor VII Concentrate, which helped the clotting of blood, whenever he had surgery. In connection with the removal of a kidney stone, P was given Factor VII Concentrate manufactured by Travenol Laboratories, Inc. (D). Two months later, P was notified that a donor to the particular lot of Concentrate had died of AIDS. Two years later, a blood test showed that P had been infected with HIV. P sued D for breach of warranty, strict liability, and negligence. D moves to dismiss the first two claims as failing to state a claim upon which relief can be granted.

 2) Issue. May a person who receives a transfusion of tainted blood recover for breach of warranty or strict liability from the providers?

 3) Held. No. Motion to dismiss granted.

  a) Warranty and strict liability claims must be based on the sale of goods. The courts of most states, including Minnesota, have held that furnishing blood is a service, not a sale of goods. In addition, the state legislature has adopted a "blood shield" statute that clearly specifies that the use of any part of a body for transplantation into the human body shall be construed as a service.

  b) D participated in the use of the blood derivative, and the statute protects every person, including corporations, that participate in the use of a body part. They are therefore protected against strict liability and breach of warranty claims. Public policy supports this approach, because blood processors cannot, even with the exercise of due care, ensure that the blood supply is free from HIV. People infected with HIV may not have detectable antibodies for several weeks or months after infection. Yet, there is an important need for blood products.

International
Petroleum
Services, Inc.
v. S & N
Well Service,
Inc.

g. Used goods--International Petroleum Services, Inc. v. S & N Well Service, Inc., 639 P.2d 29 (Kan. 1982).

 1) Facts. International Petroleum Services, Inc. (P) sold used oil servicing equipment to S & N Well Service, Inc. (D). Unit No. 1 was equipped with a used diesel engine that had been approved by a diesel engine company. P used components from several other oil well servicing rigs to make this unit; only a few components were new. D knew of the used nature of the unit, and no express warranty was given. Shortly after D began using Unit No. 1, P had to install a new differential and make other repairs. The unit worked for 90 days before the engine failed and had to be rebuilt. P had the work done and charged D about $5,000. Unit No. 2 was also a used product which, at D's request, P converted from a dual axle to a single axle unit. The single axle bent shortly after D began using it. P fixed it and charged D over $1,000. The evidence showed that P knew or should have known that the single axle was inadequate. P sued for the amounts billed. D counterclaimed for breach of warranty. The trial court gave judgment for both parties, offsetting P's damages by the amount of the repairs to Unit No. 2. D appeals.

2) **Issue.** Does the implied warranty of merchantability apply to used goods?

3) **Held.** Yes. Judgment affirmed.

a) Nothing in the UCC indicates that the implied warranties do not apply to used goods. Only the state of Texas has refused to apply implied warranties to the sale of used goods.

b) UCC section 2-314 sets minimum standards of merchantability by requiring that goods to be merchantable be at least such as would pass without objection in the trade under the contract description, are fit for the ordinary purposes for which such goods are used, etc. Under this implied warranty, goods must not be suitable only for junk, but they need not be of the best possible quality either. Less is required of used goods than of new goods.

c) The applicability of the implied warranty of merchantability to used goods depends on three factors: (i) the buyer's knowledge that the good are used; (ii) the extent of the prior use; and (iii) whether the goods are significantly discounted from the price of new goods.

d) In this case, there was no evidence of price. D knew the goods were used, but neither party knew how much they had been used. Since P did make repairs to Unit No. 1, and the unit did work well for 90 days, D was not entitled to further damages for breach of the implied warranty for this unit. The court did properly give D damages for breach for Unit No. 2, since P knew the axle was not adequate for the machine.

5. **Implied Warranty of Fitness for a Particular Purpose.** If a seller has reason to be aware of the particular use of goods contemplated by the buyer, and is also aware that the buyer is relying upon the seller's judgment to select suitable goods, then an implied warranty of fitness for that particular use or purpose arises, unless specifically excluded by the seller. [UCC §2-315]

a. **Seller must have knowledge of buyer's intended use.** Under the UCC, a warranty will be implied that from all the facts and circumstances known to the seller at the time the transaction is closed, the seller should, as a reasonably intelligent person (objective test), know what the buyer's special requirements are and that the buyer is relying on him to supply those requirements.

1) **"Single-use" goods.** Although goods may have but one use, such as shoes, no warranty for a particular purpose automatically arises; such a warranty would be simply duplicate the ordinary purposes warranty. Yet if the buyer makes known to the seller some special or unique contemplated use (*e.g.*, mountain climbing), then the warranty of fitness for that special purpose would arise.

2) **Merchant or nonmerchant seller.** Unlike the implied warranty of merchantability which applies only to sales by merchants, the fitness warranty may apply to any sales transaction, merchant or no merchant.

b. **Buyer's reliance essential.** Unlike the merchantability warranty, the fitness warranty requires that the buyer must in fact rely on the seller's superior skill or judgment as part of the transaction. Thus, if the sales contract is based on plans and specifications furnished by the buyer, he cannot claim reliance on the seller's selection of the goods, and there is no implied warranty of their fitness for the buyer's purpose.

c. **Seller must select or furnish goods.** The seller must wither select or furnish the goods. Often the seller does both, but many situations involve self-service stores, such as supermarkets, in which case the furnishing of the goods suffices.

Van Wyk v. Norden Laboratories, Inc.

d. **Particular purpose same as ordinary purpose--Van Wyk v. Norden Laboratories, Inc.,** 345 N.W.2d 81 (Iowa 1984).

1) **Facts.** Norden Laboratories, Inc. (D) sold a live-virus vaccine to a veterinarian. The veterinarian then inoculated cattle belonging to Van Wyk (P). Most of the cattle became sick with the illness that the vaccine was designed to prevent, and many of them died. P sued for breach of warranty. The trial court submitted only the theory of liability based on the implied warranty of fitness for a particular purpose. The jury found for P and D appeals.

2) **Issue.** Does an implied warranty of fitness for a particular purpose arise solely because the buyer's particular purpose is the same as the ordinary purpose for which the product is furnished?

3) **Held.** No. Judgment reversed.

a) The implied warranty of fitness for a particular purpose under UCC section 2-315 differs from the implied warranty of merchantability, or fitness for ordinary purposes, under UCC section 2-314. The UCC section 2-315 warranty is based on the buyer's special reliance on the seller to provide goods to meet a specific use. The buyer must prove that (i) the seller had reason to know of the buyer's particular purpose; (ii) the seller had reason to know the buyer was relying on the seller's skill or judgment to furnish suitable goods; and (iii) the buyer in fact so relied on the seller.

b) In this case, P had no direct dealings with D; the vaccine was applied by a veterinarian who exercised his own judgment. The fact that P's particular use for the vaccine was the same as the ordinary use for the product does not by itself give rise to an implied warranty of fitness for a particular purpose. P must show that he relied on D's expertise, and that D knew he did. P is unable to show this, so the court erred in submitting this theory to the jury.

c)   In some cases, a buyer's particular purpose may be the same as the product's ordinary purpose. For both types of warranties to arise, however, the buyer must still meet the burden of proof required for each type of warranty.

e.   **Seller's expertise--Lewis v. Mobil Oil Corp.**, 438 F.2d 500 (8th Cir. 1971).

Lewis v. Mobil Oil Corp.

1)   **Facts.** Lewis (P) bought used hydraulic equipment to operate his sawmill. The equipment was in good condition, but P did not know what kind of oil to use in it. P dealt with Rowe, an agent of Mobile Oil Corp. (D), and asked Rowe what oil he should use. Rowe supplied a particular product that had no chemical additives. P's equipment did not operate properly and eventually broke down. P replaced it and, based on Rowe's further assurances, continued to use D's oil. After going through several pumps, P was visited by another agent of D, who recommended a different oil containing certain additives. When P began using this oil, he experienced no further problems. P sued for damages suffered by the use of the nonadditive oil. The jury found for P and D appeals.

2)   **Issue.** Does a warranty of fitness for a particular purpose arise where the seller knows of the buyer's needs and the buyer relies on the seller's expertise?

3)   **Held.** Yes. Judgment affirmed.

a)   An implied warranty of fitness may arise where (i) the seller has reason to know the use for which the goods are purchased and (ii) the buyer relies on the seller's expertise in supplying the proper product.

b)   Here, it is obvious that P relied on D because P did not know about the oil used and sought reassurances from D on several occasions. At the same time, D knew what P was using the oil for because P specifically told D.

c)   D says that P did not provide sufficient information about his equipment. However, where the buyer relies on the seller's expertise, the seller must obtain any further information necessary before making a recommendation. P would not know what information D needs.

d)   D also claims that P's equipment contained abnormal features which may have caused the problems. However, there is no evidence that P's equipment was unique or abnormal in the respects mentioned by D. Also, the implied warranty covered P's equipment as it was, and D should not have undertaken to supply P if it could not supply oil suited to P's equipment.

4)   **Comment.** An implied warranty of merchantability, or even an express warranty, could probably have been asserted as well.

C. WARRANTY LITIGATION PROBLEMS

1. **Introduction.** A buyer seeking to recover must prove (i) the seller made a warranty, (ii) the breach of the warranty, and (iii) the damages caused by the breach. The buyer must also comply with UCC notice provisions, avoid improper use of the goods, and sue before the statute of limitations expires.

2. **Notice.** In order to recover for breach of warranty, the buyer must plead and prove that he gave the seller notice of the breach within a reasonable time after such breach was discovered. If he fails to do so, the buyer's right to recover against the seller in a warranty action will be entirely barred. [UCC §2-607(3)(a)]

   a. **Form of notice immaterial.** No particular form of notice is required; it may be written or oral.

   b. **Content.** The notice need not contain any claim of damages or threat of litigation, so long as it informs the seller that the transaction is troublesome and bears watching. However, some courts require precision in identifying the existence and nature of the claimed breach.

   c. **Time limits on claims.** If the warranty stipulates the time period for assertion of claims, it may be upheld as "part of the contract," provided the period selected is reasonable.

      1) Such periods do not apply to latent defects undiscoverable within the period.

      2) Courts do not enforce time limits which are so short (*e.g.,* between 10 and 15 days after purchase) as to cause the buyer's remedy to fail of its essential purpose—*i.e.,* the ability to make a claim for defective goods. [Neville Chem. Co. v. Union Carbide Corp., 294 F. Supp. 649 (1968)]

   d. **Failure to give notice--Standard Alliance Industries v. Black Clawson Co.,** 587 F.2d 813 (6th Cir. 1978).

      1) **Facts.** Standard Alliance Industries (P) bought a large machine from Black Clawson Co. (D). D agreed to manufacture the machine to meet P's special needs and made express performance warranties, although D disclaimed any implied warranties. D also agreed to repair or replace any defective parts in the first year. Soon after P accepted the machine, difficulties arose. D sent its employees to P's plant where they worked on the machine for five months with D's help. D's employees left P's plant, and 11 months later, P sued for damages on a warranty theory. The jury found that D breached both the performance warranties and the repair warranties. D appeals, claiming that P failed to give notice.

      2) **Issue.** Must a buyer give separate notice to the seller of the breach of separate warranties?

3) **Held.** Yes. Judgment reversed.

a) Notice is a condition precedent to recovery. The notice need not be as specific as that required for rejection, but it must inform the seller that the buyer considers the transaction to be troublesome.

b) Here, there is sufficient evidence to support the jury verdict that P notified D of the breach of the performance warranties. However, D made a significant attempt to remedy the breach and claims that it believed the machine was operating properly when its employees left P's plant.

c) There is evidence to support the conclusion that D knew that the machine did not operate properly after its employees left. The question remains, however, whether P ever notified D that D breached its repair warranty.

d) The evidence shows that after D's employees left P's plant, D was never told that anything was wrong until P filed suit. Under the circumstances, P was required to give notice of this separate breach.

e) The fact that D may have known that it was in breach of the repair warranty does not absolve P of the duty to give notice. Notice serves the purpose of promoting negotiated settlement and gives the seller a chance to cure the breach. It informs the seller that the buyer considers him in breach, a fact the seller may not know even if it knows it is in breach. Therefore, notice was a condition precedent to P's recovery which was not met.

f) The evidence indicates that D may have been prejudiced by the lack of notice because the machine was dismantled six weeks after P filed suit and D was deprived of the chance to gather evidence.

g) Additionally, the high standard of good faith imposed on merchants requires that P inform D that its repair efforts had failed. Notice of the first breach cannot extend to a second, distinct breach.

3. **Proof of Breach.**

a. **Introduction.** In an action for breach of warranty, the buyer must always show that the breach was the proximate cause of the loss he sustained. [UCC §2-715(2)(a), (b)] It is not sufficient that the buyer demonstrate that the defendant's breach of warranty could have been one of several possible causes of the damage; rather, he must prove that the breach of warranty is the proximate cause of the injury.

b. **Use of circumstantial evidence--Chatfield v. Sherwin-Williams Co.,** 266 N.W.2d 171 (Minn. 1978).

Chatfield v. Sherwin-Williams Co.

1) **Facts.** Chatfield (P), a professional painter of farm buildings, asked an agent of Sherwin-Williams Co. (D) whether D's "Commonwealth Ranch Red" paint would be good and troublefree. The agent replied that the paint was "tried and true" and would be good barn paint. P bought the paint and used it on 11 farms. P did not follow the instructions on the label which required addition of a large percentage of linseed oil for the first coat. P stated that when he used that much, the paint wrinkled. Instead, he added oil as dictated by his own judgment. P gave some the paint to his father, also a professional. Within a few months, the color of the buildings P painted began to fade. D's chemist investigated and indicated that P had done good work but he could not determine why the paint faded. D later told P that fading was to be expected because of the poor quality of the paint. P sued for damages. At trial, D's chemist gave a scientific explanation for the fading, the essence of which was that if P had followed the instructions, the paint may not have faded. P's father testified that the paint he used also faded, but that another batch of Commonwealth Ranch Red did not fade when used the same way. The jury found that P was 15% negligent and that D's breach of warranty was 85% of the cause of the damage. The court gave the full amount of damages to P and D appeals.

2) **Issue.** May breach of warranty be proved from circumstantial evidence?

3) **Held.** Yes. Judgment affirmed.

   a) D claims that P did not prove that the paint faded because of an inherent defect. However, proof of a breach of warranty may be made by circumstantial evidence. P showed that the paint faded uniformly even where he added different amounts of oil. P also showed that D said the fading could be expected with the quality of paint involved. Such evidence is sufficient to support the jury verdict. P did not need to have the paint analyzed by experts.

   b) Causation may also be shown by circumstantial evidence as it was here.

   c) D claims that P should be barred from recovery because he did not follow the instructions. However, this was one of the factors considered by the jury. The jury could determine whether P acted negligently, and whether this negligence was the cause of his injury. There was evidence that P worked in a professional manner.

   d) The jury was also adequately instructed on mitigation of damages.

   e) Finally, the principle of comparative fault has not been applied in Minnesota to breach-of-warranty actions, and the question was not argued below. Therefore, the judgment is affirmed.

4. **Statute of Limitations.** The UCC provides a four-year statute of limitations on

actions to enforce rights under any contract of sale; this includes actions for breach of warranty. [UCC §2-725(1)] Warranty actions do present unique issues, however.

a. **Accrual of action.** The statute commences to run on "breach" of the warranty obligation. This is deemed to occur when delivery is made or tendered, even though the buyer may not actually know of it at that time. [UCC §2-725(2)]

   1) If it takes more than four years for the buyer to discover the breach of warranty, no action is available, despite his diligence in suing once he found out.

   2) Exception: a different rule applies where the warranty expressly extends to future performance, such as a guarantee of product use. In such cases only, the cause of action accrues from the date the breach is or should have been discovered, rather than from the date of delivery.

b. **Tolling.** The UCC does not alter the normal rules on when a party may be estopped to plead the statute as a defense, or circumstances under which the statutory period is tolled. [UCC §2-725(4)] A defendant's merely promising or attempting to repair the defective goods is not enough by itself to toll the statute of limitations.

c. **Conflict between statutes of limitation.** Many state statutes of limitation provide for shorter periods within which actions for personal injury or property damage must be brought than the UCC provides. Courts that treat warranty actions as a type of tort action apply the general tort statutes of limitations, but most courts apply the UCC statute to pure warranty actions, giving the plaintiff the benefit of the longer statutory period.

d. **Time of discovery--Standard Alliance Industries, Inc. v. Black Clawson Co.,** 587 F.2d 813 (6th Cir. 1978).

   1) **Facts.** The facts are set forth *supra*. This portion of the opinion deals with the statute of limitations claim. The contract contained a clause that specified that any action for breach must be brought within one year of the accrual of the cause of action. D appeals, asserting that this clause bars P's action because D gave P notice that the machine was defective on December 27, 1967, but P did not sue until May 29, 1969.

   2) **Issue.** Where an express warranty extends for a specific period, does the statute of limitations begin to run at the time the breach is discovered, if it is within the warranty period?

   3) **Held.** Yes. Judgment reversed.

      a) Under the UCC, a cause of action accrues when the breach occurs. The problem here is determining when the breach occurs when a defective product is delivered.

      b) P claims that there is no tender of the machine until the machine is made to operate correctly. Therefore, there was no tender until P's employees finished working on the machine in June 1968. However, the UCC gives two definitions of tender. One is an offer coupled with the present ability to perform; the other is an offer of goods as if in fulfillment of the contract even though there is a defect. The term "tender" as used in UCC section 2-725(2) is the latter definition. Otherwise, the statute of limitations would extend indefinitely until the defect was corrected, making it not a true limitation. Therefore, a tender occurs when the product is delivered, defective or not.

   c)   The next question is whether the statute of limitations is meant to run from delivery or from the time the defect is discovered. Where an express warranty extends into the future, as it does here, it must extend to future performance. Here, D warranted the machine for one year. This means that P had one year in which to discover any defects. The statute began to run when the defect was discovered, if within the one-year period. Therefore the statute began to run on December 27, 1967, and P's action is time-barred.

   d)   There is no statute that tolls the limitation period during attempts to repair, so D's attempts to repair do not affect the running of the statute.

   e)   P could still sue for failure to fulfill the repair warranty, if it gave proper notice.

4)   Comment. Where an express warranty does not extend into the future, the statute of limitations on both it and any implied warranties begins to run at delivery.

Spring Motors **5.   Limitations of Warranty--Spring Motors Distributors, Inc. v. Ford Motor**
Distributors,   **Company,** 489 A.2d 660 (N.J. 1985).
Inc. v.
Ford Motor   **a.   Facts.** Spring Motors Distributors, Inc. (P) bought 14 trucks manufactured
Company   by Ford Motor Company (D) for a total price of $265,029.80. As P had required, the trucks were equipped with Clark transmissions. D provided a form warranty to repair or replace any defects in material or workmanship, but excluded all other express or implied warranties. Clark gave D a warranty as well that specifically stated Clark would in no event be liable for incidental, consequential, or special damages. P leased the trucks to a customer, but the transmissions began failing within a few months. Eventually, after spending considerable money in repairs, P sold the trucks to its customer. Alleging breach of warranties as well as negligence and strict liability, P sued four years and one month after it took delivery of the trucks. P sought recovery of consequential damages including the expenses of towing, repairing and replacing parts, lost profits, and the decrease in market value of the trucks due to the defective transmissions. The trial court found that the four-year statute of limitations under UCC section 2-725 had expired and that the state six-year statute of limitations for negligence and strict liability did not apply. It dismissed the warranty claim for lack of privity. The court of appeals reversed the dismissal of the tort claims, and the state supreme court granted D's petition for review.

   b.   Issue. Is a commercial buyer entitled to pursue a cause of action for economic loss caused by the purchase of defective goods based on negligence or strict liability when its cause of action under the UCC is barred by the statute of limitations?

c. **Held.** No. Judgment reversed.

1) The UCC is a comprehensive system for determining the rights and duties of buyers and sellers with respect to contracts for the sale of goods. It provides for various warranties, and allows the parties to modify warranties or exclude them altogether. Subject to the unconscionability doctrine, the parties may also agree to limit or exclude consequential damages. The UCC recognizes the freedom of parties to choose their own contract provisions.

2) These UCC rules overlap the tort doctrine of strict liability. Strict liability has been adopted by tort law to permit recovery by consumers for damages caused by defective products. One of the purposes of this doctrine was to allocate risk to the manufacturer, who can prevent defects and spread the cost of the risk among all its customers. The doctrine was applied to permit recovery of economic loss in *Santor v. A. & M. Karagheusian, Inc.*, 207 A.2d 305 (N.J. 1965). In *Seely v. White Motor Co.*, 403 P.2d 145 (Cal. 1965), the court disagreed with Santor and held that a consumer could not recover for economic loss under strict liability. Most courts follow *Seely* instead of *Santor*.

3) Recovery under the UCC is generally less beneficial to buyers than strict liability because (i) privity may be required, (ii) notice to the seller of a breach of warranty is required, and (iii) a seller may limit or disclaim liability under the UCC but not under strict liability. However, the UCC fulfills a different function than strict liability, which was adopted in response to inadequacies in sales law with respect to consumers. Parties acting under the UCC have comparable bargaining power and can allocate risk as they see fit. In fact, in this case P was able to have D install the transmissions it desired.

4) Because the policies behind strict liability do not apply to commercial parties having comparable bargaining power, a commercial buyer may seek recovery for economic loss only under the UCC. Thus P can only seek its remedies under the UCC, which are time-barred in this case by the four-year statute of limitations.

5) P's negligence claim is subject to similar analysis as its strict liability claim. A seller does not have a duty of care that includes protection against the buyer's purely economic loss. Economic interest are not normally entitled to protection against mere negligence. Disputes over economic losses are more appropriately resolved under contract law.

6) P has not challenged the trial court's dismissal of its warranty claim for lack of privity. However, the absence of privity between a supplier and the ultimate purchaser does not preclude extension of the supplier's warranties through the manufacturer to the purchaser. UCC section 2-318, Alternative A, eliminates the requirement of horizontal privity, but does not specifically address vertical privity. Yet without applying strict liability to commercial economic loss cases, it is consistent with *Santor* to eliminate the requirement of vertical privity in this type of case. This is

especially true here where P specifically requested Clark transmissions and should be protected by Clark's warranties. Of course, P's warranty suit is time-barred.

D. REMEDIES FOR BREACH OF WARRANTY

1. **Introduction.** If a breach of warranty occurs prior to acceptance of the goods, or upon revocation of acceptance, the breach is treated as any other failure to perform the contract. Once the buyer has accepted the goods, the UCC provides that the buyer may recover any loss in value of the goods because of the breach [UCC §2-714(2)] plus consequential and incidental damages where proper [UCC §2-714(3)].

2. **Direct Damages.** The standard measure of value in goods is the difference, at the time and place of acceptance, between the value of the goods accepted and the value they would have had if they had been as warranted.

   a. **Price.** The price of the goods has nothing to do with fixing damages (except that were there is no open market in the goods, the price may be evidence of their value). Thus, where the market price has fluctuated upward or downward from the price at which B bought, and he still elects to accept the goods and sue for breach of warranty, he gets the benefit of the bargain to which he was entitled under the contract—the difference between the value of the goods he should have received and those in fact received.

Soo Line
Railroad Co.
v. Fruehauf
Corp.

   b. **Interest expenses not recoverable--Soo Line Railroad Co. v. Fruehauf Corp.**, 547 F.2d 1365 (8th Cir. 1977).

      1) **Facts.** Soo Line Railroad Co. (P) contracted to buy 500 railroad cars from Fruehauf Corp. (D). P found cracks in the cars, but D refused to repair them. It cost P more than $500,000 to repair the cars. P sued for breach of warranty. The jury awarded P damages for the difference in value between the cars as accepted and their value if they had been built according to contract specifications. This verdict was based in part on the testimony of Klingel, a vice president of P, who testified that the diminution in value was about $2,000 per car at the least, and $4,000 at most. The jury awarded damages on this point of $1,951. D appeals.

      2) **Issue.** May the cost of financing during repair be considered as part of the diminution in value in computing damages?

      3) **Held.** No. Judgment affirmed.

         a) Klingel's opinion was based in part on the cost of repair, on the higher maintenance costs after repair, and on the lost interest incurred while the cars were being repaired. The last element is not a proper factor in diminution of value. The diminution measure is intended to determine the market value of the cars as delivered as compared with what their value would have been if made in conformance with the contract. This measure does not include interest incurred while not being able to use the cars.

b) D objects that Klingel was not an expert. However, he was in charge of determining the value of P's rolling stock and was familiar with the problems involved.

c) The jury was adequately instructed as to the law, and there was substantial evidence to support the verdict.

c. **Limitation of remedy--Hill v. BASF Wyandotte Corp.,** 696 F.2d 287 (4th Cir. 1982).

Hill v. BASF Wyandotte Corp.

1) **Facts.** Hill (P), a soybean farmer, purchased the herbicide, Basalin, manufactured by BASF Wyandotte Corp. (D). P purchased Basalin instead of his regular herbicide because D's sales agent told P that it should be used just like the regular herbicide and would do the same job at a lower cost. The label on each can of Basalin had instructions, a disclaimer of any warranties other than the one expressly stated, and a limitation of remedies other than direct damages for breach of that warranty. It also contained an invitation to return the product if the terms were not acceptable. P used the herbicide but it did not work effectively. P sued D for breach of warranty and misrepresentation, claiming direct and consequential damages. At the retrial after a mistrial, the judge instructed the jury that D's agent's oral warranty could bind D and that consequential damages could be imposed. The jury found for P and D appeals.

2) **Issue.** Is a consumer bound by a disclaimer of warranties on the label of a product?

3) **Held.** Yes. Judgment reversed and remanded.

a) P admitted he read the label before using the Basalin. Since he had notice of the disclaimer as an express condition of the sale, the sales agent's oral statements cannot vary the terms of the conditions of sale. [UCC §2-202] P knew he could have returned the product if he did not want to accept the sale conditions.

b) Under UCC section 2-719, a seller can limit remedies so long as the limitation is not unconscionable, or not intended to be exclusive, or does not fail of its essential purpose. P does not claim the limitation was unconscionable. He does assert that the limitation was not to be exclusive, but the label clearly states that damages in no case would exceed any direct damages, and P chose not to return the product knowing of this limitation.

c) It cannot be said that the remedy failed of its essential purpose since that concept applies where the limitation of remedy involves repair or replacement that cannot return the goods to their warranted conditions, an exception that does not apply to this case.

Hill v. BASF
Wyandotte
Corp.

d. **Measure of damages--Hill v. BASF Wyandotte Corp.,** 311 S.E.2d 734 (S.C. 1984).

    1) **Facts.** *See* preceding case. After the Fourth Circuit Court of Appeals reversed and remanded the case, holding that only the written warranties on the label applied and that the limitation of remedies on the label was valid, the trial court certified this question to the Supreme Court of South Carolina.

    2) **Issue.** In a herbicide failure case, where there is a valid limitation of consequential, special, or indirect damages, is the measure of actual damages the value that the crop would have had if the product had conformed to the warranty, less the value of the crop actually produced, less the expense of preparing for market the portion of the probable crop that was prevented from maturing?

    3) **Held.** Yes.

        a) The following South Carolina statute applies: "Where the buyer has accepted goods and given notification, he may recover as damages for any nonconformity of tender the loss resulting in the ordinary course events from the seller's breach as determined in any manner which is reasonable." Thus, we hold that the measure of actual damages is the value that the crop would have had if the product had conformed to the warranty less the value of the crop actually produced, less the expense of preparing for market the portion of the probable crop that was prevented from maturing.

        b) D argues that this formula includes lost profits and that lost profits are a consequential damage barred by the limitation of remedies on the labels of the herbicide. We disagree. The court in *W.R. Grace and Co. v. LaMunion,* 138 S.E.2d 337 (S.C. 1964), noted that the destruction or loss of a mature crop, which has a realizable value in excess of the cost of harvesting, processing, and marketing, results in a monetary loss to the owner, regardless of whether the farming operation would otherwise have been profitable. If the measure of damages we have adopted includes an element of lost profits, such inclusion is merely coincidental as the measure covers the direct loss resulting in the ordinary course of events from the alleged breach of the warranty.

3. **Incidental and Consequential Damages.**

    a. **Incidental damages.** The buyer may recover any costs or expenses reasonably incurred incidental to the seller's delay or delivery of defective goods, *e.g.,* storage, inspection charges, return freight, costs of cover, etc. [UCC §2-715(1)]

    b. **Consequential damages.** Often the loss of value of goods will represent only a part of the buyer's loss. The UCC follows the rule of *Hadley v. Baxendale,* 156 Eng. Rep. 145 (1854), and imposes liability where the seller at the time of the contract had reason to know of additional loss that would result from a failure to meet the buyer's needs or requirements. [UCC §2-715(2)(a)] The breach must actually be a substantial cause of the loss, and the loss must be proven with reasonable certainty.

1) **Economic loss.** In appropriate cases, consequential damages may include any of the following: loss of profits from expected resale of goods, loss of operating profits due to disruption of business, and damage to goodwill or business reputation. A retailer who is held liable to a customer for breach of warranty of merchantability will normally have the same cause of action over against the wholesaler of manufacturer who supplied the product. Whatever damages the retailer is forced to pay his customer are recoverable as consequential damages in his action against the wholesaler or manufacturer.

2) **Noneconomic loss.** Even noneconomic losses may be recoverable as consequential damages under appropriate circumstances. For example, in personal injury cases consequential damages may include medical expenses and pain and suffering.

3) **Cover.** When consequential damages are claimed on account of the nonavailability of the goods bargained for, rather than on account of injuries or losses sustained through their use, then to whatever extent such damages could have been prevented by "covering" with goods from another source, damages are limited to the cost of "cover."

c. **Retailer's reimbursement of customers' losses may be consequential damages--Nezperce Storage Co. v. Zenner,** 670 P.2d 871 (Idaho 1983).

Nezperce
Storage Co.
v. Zenner

1) **Facts.** Due to a shortage of spring wheat, Nezperce Storage Co. (P) bought 2,000 bushels of wheat was supposed to be spring wheat from Zenner (D), a wheat farmer. P in turn resold part of the wheat to eight farmers who planted it. In fact the wheat was a mixture of spring and winter wheat and the crops failed. P paid out $84,000 to settle the farmers' claims. P sued D for indemnification. The jury found that D had breached an express warranty. D appeals.

2) **Issue.** Does a retailer's loss due to his compensating his customers for their damages caused by a defective product constitute consequential damages recoverable from the supplier for breach of warranty?

3) **Held.** Yes. Judgment affirmed.

   a) Under UCC section 2-715(2)(a), consequential damages include any loss (i) resulting from needs the seller knows of, or has reason to know of, at the time of contracting and (ii) which could not reasonably be prevented by cover or otherwise. The jury specifically found that D knew of the shortage of spring wheat and that P was buying the wheat for resale as spring wheat. The jury also found that P acted reasonably in reselling the wheat without performing more tests than it did.

   b) Under state law, one who sells seeds which are incorrectly labeled without obtaining a grower's declaration of kind is subject to penalties. D claims it was entitled to an instruction on negligence per se because P violated this statute. However, the statute is intended to protect P's customers, not D, P's supplier. In fact, D was the one who supplied mislabeled seed. D cannot claim that P's failure to properly label the seed should reduce P's damages.

Lewis v.
Mobile
Oil Corp.

d. **Recovery of lost profits--Lewis v. Mobile Oil Corp.,** 438 F.2d 500 (8th Cir. 1971).

1) **Facts.** The facts are set forth *supra*. This portion of the opinion deals with the award of damages. P recovered as damages the costs incurred in repairing and replacing mechanical parts damaged by the improper oil, the cost of the excess oil used, lost profits during the time he used the oil, and lost profits after D provided the proper oil because P could not operate at full capacity due to the financial drain of the use of the wrong oil. D appeals.

2) **Issue.** Are lost profits recoverable in a suit for breach of warranty?

3) **Held.** Yes. Judgment affirmed in part and remanded in part.

a) The first question is whether P can recover lost profits for the entire 30-month period in which he used the wrong oil. D claims P should have taken some steps to solve the problem sooner than he did. Although there is a duty to mitigate damages, P did not know the oil caused the problem here. P relied on D's expertise. There is no indication that P acted in bad faith. The only way P could have mitigated his damages would have been to consult an independent expert, but under the circumstances, P acted reasonably in relying only on D.

b) Lost profits may be a proper element of damages in a suit for breach of warranty if the seller had reason to know of them. But where a breach of warranty is involved, lost profits are foreseeable if they are proximately caused by and are the natural result of the breach. The seller is assumed to know that defective goods will disrupt the buyer's business with the probability that profits will be lost. Therefore, P may recover lost profits.

c) P introduced evidence of lost sales and of past profits. This evidence is sufficient to support an award.

d) However, P may not recover for profits lost after the proper oil was supplied on the theory that the breach caused a drain on his financial resources and prevented him from operating at full capacity. The cause of these lost profits was inadequate capitalization for which D is not liable. Because the record does not suffice to determine what a proper award should be, the case must be remanded.

4) **Rehearing.** P's profits before the breach ranged from $8,000 to $11,000. During the time he used the wrong oil, P's profits were about $4,800 per year. In the period immediately after, P's profits were about $20,500 per year. The jury awarded $80,000 for lost profits. There is no proof to support this award if confined to the 30-month period. Therefore, a new trial on the issue of damages is necessary.

Delano
Grower's
Cooperative
Winery v.
Supreme
Wine Co.,
Inc.

e. **Lost goodwill--Delano Grower's Cooperative Winery v. Supreme Wine Co., Inc.** 473 N.E.2d 1066 (Mass. 1985).

   1) **Facts.** The facts are set forth *supra*. D also appealed from the award of damages for injury to P's business reputation.

   2) **Issue.** May an injured party recover damages for lost goodwill in a suit based on breach of warranty?

   3) **Held.** Yes. Judgment affirmed.

      a) P suffered a decline in sales after it began receiving returns of the defective wine it had bought from D. The master found that the main reason for this was D's defective wine. This finding is supported by the evidence presented.

      b) P presented testimony of a business appraiser who valued P's business at $593,700, including goodwill and assets worth $237,092. P's president testified that P's value was $500,000. The judge in finding that the loss of goodwill attributable to D's breach was $100,000 relied on a variety of factors. Even though the damages were not proved with mathematical certainty, the findings are supported by the record.

      c) Some jurisdictions do not permit recovery for lost goodwill under UCC section 2-715, frequently because of its speculative nature. However, when a seller knows that substantially impaired goods provided for resale could affect continued operations and established goodwill, the buyer's loss of goodwill caused by the seller's breach should be recoverable as consequential damages.

4. **Disclaimer of Warranty.** At common law, acceptance of the goods was deemed to be a waiver of any claim for breach of warranty. The Sales Act abrogated this rule and the UCC does not reinstate it. However, if a buyer actually inspects the goods before entering the sales contract, he cannot later claim a breach of express or implied warranties as to any patent defect. [UCC §2-316(3)(b); Comment 8]

   a. **Contractual disclaimers.** Contractual disclaimers of express and implied warranties present numerous difficult issues and have given rise to considerable litigation. Courts generally are hostile to warranty disclaimers. UCC section 2-316, which covers disclaimers, has been narrowly construed in most cases.

      1) **Express warranties.** Because under UCC section 2-316(1) a disclaimer is inoperative if it is unreasonable, whenever an express warranty is made by the seller as part of the bargain, he will be bound by the warranty. Any express representation by the seller becomes part of the bargain under UCC section 2-313, and a disclaimer would be unreasonable if it disclaimed a warranty created by the same document as the disclaimer. Consequently, for all practical purposes express warranties may not be disclaimed.

2) **Implied warranties.** Because implied warranties arise separately from any agreement of the parties, the parties have greater latitude to limit or disclaim liability arising therefrom.

    a) **By custom or usage.** The UCC specifically recognizes that implied warranties may be excluded or modified by course of dealing or performance between the parties, or by custom and usage in the trade generally. [UCC §2-316(3)]

    b) **By catch-phrase disclaimers.** Another method of exclusion sanctioned by the UCC is the "catch-phrase" disclaimer; *e.g.,* buyer accepts item "as is" or "with all faults." Such language is sufficient by itself to alert the buyer that he must assume the risk, and all implied warranties are excluded. [UCC §2-316(3)(a)]

    c) **By specific disclaimers.** A seller may include disclaimers in the contract, but the requirements of UCC section 2-316 must be satisfied. If the disclaimer pertains to the implied warranty of merchantability, it must mention that term and be conspicuous. If the disclaimer applies to the implied warranty of fitness for a particular purpose, it must be in writing, it must mention the word "fitness," and it must be conspicuous.

    d) **By limiting remedies.** The UCC permits the parties to specify what remedy shall be available in the event of breach, and to make such remedy exclusive. [UCC §2-719(1)(b)] A provision limiting a seller's liability to repair or replacement of defective parts, in lieu of all other warranties, express or implied, is generally effective as a disclaimer of any other fitness or merchantability warranties. [Seely v. White Motor Co., 403 P.2d 145 (Cal. 1965)]

3) **Limitations.** A disclaimer may be effective only as to the warranty (contract) claim. It will not bar an action for negligence or strict tort liability where a defective product has caused personal injury or property damage, including damage to the product itself.

4) **Failing of its essential purpose.** If a limited warranty fails of its essential purpose, the clause is disregarded and the buyer is free to pursue his remedies under other provisions of the UCC. Under UCC section 2-719(2), an exclusive remedy fails of its essential purpose whenever as a result of circumstances arising after the inception of the contract it operates to deprive a party of a substantial benefit of the bargain. A common example of such a limited warranty is the "repair or replace" clause. It is not necessary to show that the warrantor's conduct in failing to repair is negligent or willfully dilatory or in bad faith, so long as the failure to repair or replace within a reasonable time deprives the buyer of a substantial benefit of its bargain.

Martin v. Joseph Harris Co., Inc.

b. **Industry-wide limitation of damages unconscionable--Martin v. Joseph Harris Co., Inc.,** 767 F.2d 296 (6th Cir. 1985).

    1) **Facts.** Martin and another commercial farmer (Ps) ordered cabbage seed from Joseph Harris Co., Inc. (D). D's order form, like that of all other seed sellers, included a disclaimer of the implied warranty of merchantability and limited Ps' remedies for breach of any warranty or contract to the purchase price of the seed. Several months later, Ps received D's catalog which included a notice that D would no longer "hot water" treat cabbage seed as it had in the past to prevent black leg, a seed-borne disease. About two months after Ps planted their seed, D notified them that the seed was infected with black leg. Ps' crops were partially destroyed, but Ps made an above-average profit on their crop due to the increased market price caused by the shortages of cabbage. Ps sued for negligence and breach of implied warranty. The court granted Ps a judgment n.o.v. on the implied warranty issue, and a second jury awarded Ps a total of $52,000. D appeals.

2) **Issue.** May a seller disclaim the implied warranty of merchantability and limit the buyer's remedies to the purchase price of the goods when all such sellers include similar provisions and the goods contain a latent defect that the seller could have prevented?

3) **Held.** No. Judgment affirmed.

a) Although UCC section 2-316 specifically provides for exclusion or modification of the implied warranty of merchantability by disclaimer, such disclaimers are still limited by UCC section 2-302, which applies to any clause of a contract. Thus a disclaimer may be unconscionable.

b) Commercial contracts are only rarely unconscionable because business parties normally do not have such one-sided relationships that one can impose unconscionable terms on the other. However, a circumstance may arise in which one party has no realistic alternative, no option but to accept the other's terms or do without. If so, and the challenged term is not substantively reasonable, then the term may be found unconscionable.

c) Some of the factors to be considered in determining unconscionability are (i) the relative bargaining power of the parties, (ii) the relative economic strength of the parties, and (iii) the alternative sources of supply. In this case, D is a large national seed producer and distributor while Ps are independent farmers. All seed distributors used exclusions such as D's, so Ps had no realistic alternative suppliers.

d) In this case, D's salesman did not inform Ps of the legal effect of the clauses. Nor did D inform Ps that it had discontinued the hot water treatment it had been using for 26 years. The defect was latent because the disease is not detectable until after the crop develops. D could have prevented the defect.

e) If D's disclaimer were enforced, Ps could lose their livelihood even though they had no notice of, control over, or ability to detect the defect. At the same time, D would lose only a few hundred dollars despite having had the ability to prevent the disease. The trial court's finding of unconscionability is adequately supported.

Cayuga Har-
vester, Inc.
v. Allis-
Chalmers
Corp.

c. **Consequential damages exclusion separate from limited warranty--Cayuga Harvester, Inc. v. Allis-Chalmers Corp.**, 465 N.Y.S.2d 606 (1983).

1) **Facts.** Cayuga Harvester, Inc. (P), a corn grower, bought a harvester manufactured by Allis-Chalmers Corp. (D) from a dealer for $142,213. The written purchase order contained a limited repair and replacement warranty and, in paragraph I, an exclusion of consequential damages. The harvester malfunctioned and prevented P from effectively harvesting its crop. P sued, claiming the limited remedy failed of its essential purpose and that it should therefore be entitled to consequential damages. The trial court granted summary judgment for D on the breach of warranty claims and found that paragraph I was not unconscionable as a matter of law. P appeals.

2) **Issue.** Is a consequential damage exclusion enforceable even when the limited warranty provision in the contract is found to have failed of its essential purpose?

3) **Held.** Yes. Judgment affirmed on this issue, reversed as to the summary judgment.

   a) Whether a limited remedy fails of its essential purpose under UCC section 2-719(2) is normally a fact question for the jury, but only after the plaintiff makes a prima facie showing. In this case, P did make a prima facie showing through its evidence of the numerous breakdowns and several thousands of dollars worth of warranty claims submitted to D by its dealer. For that reason, the grant of summary judgment is reversed, and P is not precluded from recovering the normal measure of damages, which under UCC section 2-714(2) is the difference between the value of the goods as accepted and the value they would have had if they had been as warranted.

   b) If the limited warranty is found to have failed of its essential purpose, P claims the consequential damages exclusion in paragraph I should also be disregarded because the two are mutually dependent. There is a divergence of authority on this issue, but in determining whether paragraph I would remain effective, it is relevant to this case that D did not act in bad faith and that P would be entitled to damages under UCC section 2-714(2).

   c) D claims the limited warranty and paragraph I are unrelated and independent. The two clauses do have separate purposes and can be separately enforced, so the plain meaning supports D's approach. Each clause is tested by a different standard; the limited warranty is valid unless it fails of its essential purpose, while the exclusion clause is enforceable unless it is unconscionable.

   d) It would not be reasonable to apply P's construction of these clauses because that construction would subject D to potential liability many times the value of the machine despite D's good faith efforts to repair the machine. D would not reasonably have intended to assume such risks.

   e) The UCC permits the parties to shape their remedies.

Under UCC section 2-719(3), consequential damages may be excluded unless the exclusion is unconscionable. In this case, the exclusion is not unconscionable because P is left with a fair quantum of remedy that the parties could reasonably have intended. P is a large commercial grower and did not lack a meaningful choice due to poor bargaining position.

5. Special Rules for Consumers.

a. Introduction. The implied warranties of merchantability and fitness for a particular purpose have been expanded by statute, insofar as they apply to sales of "consumer goods"—those purchased primarily for personal, family, or household purposes, including major purchases such as automobiles and mobile homes.

1) The Magnuson-Moss Warranty Act. This federal statute, codified at 15 U.S.C. section 2301, was intended to make warranties on consumer goods more readily understandable and enforceable. It does not require a seller to give any warranty of consumer goods, but it provides certain protections when a warranty is given.

a) Disclosure. If any written warranty is given on consumer products costing more than $10, it must be conspicuously designated as either a "full warranty" or as a "limited warranty." This applies to advertisements as well as warranty cards accompanying the product.

b) Privity. A consumer is allowed to recover under a warranty regardless of privity of contract between the consumer and warrantor. Recovery against all warrantors of the produce is permitted.

c) Disclaimer. A disclaimer of implied warranties may not be included in a written warranty.

d) Remedies. The Act expands the consumer's remedies for breach of warranty and permits recovery of attorneys' fees. A consumer must have the option of receiving a refund or replacement without charge of a defective or malfunctioning product or part after the warrantor has made a reasonable number of attempts to repair.

2) FTC rules. The Federal Trade Commission has promulgated rules which specify what information is to be contained in the text of the warranties and what methods of presale disclosure will be acceptable. [16 C.F.R. §§701-702]

3) State legislation. The Magnuson-Moss Act sets a minimum standard with respect to consumer goods transactions. It does not preclude the states from adopting more protective statutes, however, and many states have in fact adopted statutes that provide more protection to consumers.

b. **Interaction between federal and state law--Ventura v. Ford Motor Corp.,**
433 A.2d 801 (N.J. Super. 1981).

1) **Facts.** Ventura (P) bought a new Ford from Marino Auto, a dealership
which had disclaimed the implied warranty of merchantability. Ford
Motor Corp. (D), the manufacturer, provided a limited warranty. Paragraph 7 of the purchase order included an agreement that the selling dealer
would promptly perform and fulfill all terms and conditions of the owner
service policy, but it also provided that there were no warranties, express
or implied, except the one expressly given to the buyer upon delivery. The
car was defective and P sued both Marino Auto and D. The trial court
found that D breached its warranty but that P failed to prove damages
against D. It also allowed P to revoke acceptance despite the warranty
disclaimer. P recovered attorney's fees from D under the Magnuson-Moss
Act and recovered the purchase price less an allowance for use from
Marino Auto. Marino Auto was awarded a judgment against D. D
appeals.

2) **Issue.** Are state law remedies available when a disclaimer valid under
state law is invalidated by federal law?

3) **Held.** Yes. Judgment affirmed.

   a) The disclaimer of implied warranty of merchantability contained in
   paragraph 7 complies with the UCC and is valid under state law.
   However, paragraph 7 constitutes a written limited warranty under
   the Magnuson-Moss Act because in it the dealer agrees to make
   warranty repairs. Since federal law prevails over state law, the
   disclaimer of implied warranties contained in the paragraph is invalid
   and the implied warranty accompanies the limited warranty.

   b) Because the disclaimer of implied warranties is invalid, Marino Auto
   was liable to P for its breach of the implied warranty. P could
   revoke his acceptance and claim a refund as permitted by UCC
   sections 2-608 and 2-711. This state law remedy is available for
   breach of the implied warranty even though the Magnuson-Moss Act
   would permit a refund of the purchase price only for breach of a full
   warranty.

   c) P also could have recovered the purchase price from D for breach of
   D's manufacturer's warranty. The remedies of revocation of acceptance and a refund of the purchase price are available to a buyer
   against a seller in privity. When D as the manufacturer gives a warranty to induce the sale, the same type of remedy is available. The
   warranty creates a direct contractual obligation to the seller.

   d) D claims the award of attorney's fees was improper because D was
   not given adequate notice of the defects and because P did not receive
   a judgment directly against D. The notice requirement of the Magnuson-Moss Act was satisfied by P's attempts to have D's dealer
   repair the car. Even though the court did not award P damages
   against D, it did find that D breached its warranty and that the value
   of the car was substantially impaired. P was entitled to at least
   nominal damages, and the court's failure to award nominal damages
   to which the attorney's fees could be attached is not prejudicial to D.

VIII. CREDITOR DISPUTES OVER POSSESSION OF GOODS SOLD

A. RIGHTS IN GOODS IN ANOTHER'S POSSESSION

1. **Introduction.** Title to goods is an important prerequisite to protection against claims to the goods made by third parties. Under the Sales Act, title was also critical in determining which party bore the risk of loss and whether the seller could sue for the price. The UCC has generally eliminated this reliance on title. [UCC §2-401] When a transaction falls within Article 2, title is relevant only if the specific provision involved refers to title. Two important provisions that do involve title are UCC section 2-403 (power to transfer) and UCC section 2-312 (implied warranty of title).

2. **True Owner's Claim.** The common law protected the true owner by providing that a purchaser acquires only such title as the vendor had. This rule was adopted in UCC section 2-403(1).

   a. **Void title.** Even an innocent purchaser for value acquires no valid title if he purchases from one who is not the owner and has no authority to sell, such as a thief or bailee.

   b. **Entrusted goods exception.** If goods are entrusted to a merchant who deals in goods of that kind, under UCC section 2-403(2) the merchant automatically has the power to transfer all the rights of the entruster to a buyer in the ordinary course of business, regardless of lack of express authority. A common example is a consignment to a merchant.

   c. **Voidable title.** If the seller has voidable title, a good faith purchaser takes complete and valid title. A person may acquire voidable title by obtaining the goods with a bad check, or through fraud or imposture.

   d. **Good faith purchase from holder of void title ineffective--Inmi-Etti v. Aluisi,** 492 A.2d 917 (Md. 1985).

   Inmi-Etti v. Aluisi

   1) **Facts.** While she was visiting her sister in the United States, Aluisi (P) ordered a new Honda from a dealer. P then returned home to Nigeria. The certificate of title was issued in P's name, but a friend named Butler took delivery and removed the car without permission. Butler attached the car after winning a summary judgment when P failed to respond to his claim that P was an absconding debtor. Inmi-Etti (D), a deputy sheriff, executed the writ of attachment but left the car with Butler. Butler sold the car to Pohanka, a dealer, by representing himself as the dealer and by obtaining a fraudulent certificate of title. Pohanka later resold the car. When P returned to the United States, she had Butler's judgment set aside and then she sued Butler, Pohanka, and D. The trial court granted summary judgment against Butler and for Pohanka and D. P appeals.

2)   Issue. May a good faith purchaser obtain title from a transferor who has void title?

3)   Held. No. Judgment reversed as to Pohanka.

a)   Conversion does not have to be a forcible dispossession of personal property. Any distinct act of ownership or dominion exerted by one person over another's personal property in denial of his right or inconsistent with it is a conversion. By selling the car, Pohanka committed a conversion unless it had valid title.

b)   Pohanka's title to the car depends on whether Butler had void or voidable title when he sold it to Pohanka. The UCC does not define voidable title, and none of the specific subsections of UCC section 2-403(1) apply to this case. Non-UCC state law is therefore determinative.

c)   Commentators suggest that voidable title is obtained only when the owner of the goods voluntarily transfers them. This approach is supported by the case law. When goods are obtained against the will of the owner, only void title results.

d)   In this case, Butler never received a voluntary transfer of title. For that reason, his title was void and Pohanka obtained no title through its purchase from Butler. The erroneously issued certificate of title Butler had was prima facie evidence of title, but it could not divest the true owner of her title to the car.

e)   The fact that Pohanka was a good faith purchaser for value does not assist because Butler had no title. Nor does it matter that Pohanka converted the car with innocent intent; it still converted the car and is liable for damages based on the fair market value of the car at the time of conversion.

Johnson & Johnson Products, Inc. v. Dal International Trading Co.

e.   No duty to inquire about title--Johnson & Johnson Products, Inc. v. Dal International Trading Co., 798 F.2d 100 (3d Cir. 1986).

1)   Facts. Dal International Trading Co. (D) was an instrumentality of the Polish government. D contracted with J & J Ltd., the British subsidiary of Johnson & Johnson Baby Products Co., to purchase baby products and toothbrushes. D allegedly represented that it would distribute the products in Poland only, and received a lower than normal wholesale price. The products were delivered to D at a West German factory. However, D delivered the products to Quality King, an American distributor that participates in the gray market, or goods imported outside the manufacturer's normal distribution system. Pursuant to normal gray market practices, the shipping labels were stripped from the shipping cartons to obscure the identity of supply sources. Due to the low price D paid, Quality King was able to offer the goods to American retailers at prices below those charged by Johnson & Johnson Products, Inc. (P), the American distributor. P sought an injunction against the sale, distribution or other disposition of the goods on the ground that D had obtained the goods by misrepresentation and had only voidable title. The district court granted a preliminary injunction on the ground that Quality King had a duty to inquire about the fraud because of the suspicious circumstances of the sale, and that since it failed to so inquire, it was not a good faith purchaser. Quality King appeals.

2) **Issue.** Does a buyer have a duty to inquire about a possibly voidable title if its purchase is made under suspicious circumstances, even if it has no actual knowledge or suspicion of a defect in the title of the goods?

3) **Held.** No. Judgment reversed.

a) A good faith purchaser may acquire good title from a seller with voidable title under UCC section 2-403(1). However, if the buyer does not act in good faith, he acquires only voidable title and may have to surrender the goods to the defrauded party.

b) Quality King probably had reason to suspect that P would not approve of the sale of British products to an American distributor. This does not mean that Quality King would know or suspect that D obtained the goods through fraudulent misrepresentation. If D actually intended to distribute the goods in Poland when it contracted for them, and changed its mind after entering the contract, then D would have good title and at most could be liable for breach of contract. This issue cannot be resolved on the basis of the evidence presented.

c) Quality King's participation in the gray goods market does not, by itself, raise an inference that it knows or suspects that there is a defect in the title of the goods. Removal of shipping labels and other practices can be explained by the middlemen's need to keep sources unknown to avoid being bypassed in later transactions.

d) The good faith purchaser doctrine is intended to promote commerce by allowing parties to buy and sell without making expensive investigations as to title. To impose a duty to investigate under the circumstances of this case would undermine this important policy. A party who subjectively suspects that title is flawed may have a duty to investigate, but a party may not be judged as to good faith by facts he or she might have uncovered through investigation.

3. **Secured Party Claims.**

a. **Introduction.** The normal protection given by a perfected security interest does not survive a sale to a buyer in the ordinary course of business under UCC section 9-307(1) if the interest was created by the seller. Under section 1-201(9), the buyer must (i) buy goods out of inventory in the ordinary course of business, (ii) give new value, and (iii) not know that the sale violates the terms of the security agreement.

b. **Entrustment by the secured party--Executive Financial Services, Inc. v. Pagel,** 715 P.2d 381 (Kan. 1986).

1) **Facts.** Tri-Country, a John Deere dealership, sold three tractors to Executive Financial Services, Inc. (P) and then leased them back through Mohr-Loyd Leasing, a partnership. P perfected its security interest by filing, but Tri-Country retained possession of the tractors. Tri-Country sold the leased tractors to Pagel (D) and other buyers, who in turn granted John Deere purchase money security interests in them, which John Deere perfected by filing. Mohr-Loyd Leasing defaulted on the leases and P sued to recover the tractors. Ds won a summary judgment and P appeals.

2) **Issue.** May a security interest in entrusted goods not created by the seller be extinguished under UCC section 2-403(2) if the entruster created the security interest?

3) **Held.** Yes. Judgment affirmed.

   a) Ds cannot take free of P's security interest under UCC section 9-307(1) because Mohr-Loyd created P's security interest, not Tri-Country which sold the tractors to Ds. Under UCC section 2-403(2), however, P may have lost its interest if it entrusted the tractors to Tri-Country.

   b) Under common law, entrusting goods to a merchant who dealt in goods of the kind did not prevent the owner from recovering them from a bona fide purchaser for value. UCC section 2-403(2) reversed this rule by giving the merchant power to transfer all the entruster's rights to a buyer in the ordinary course of business. The theory is that the dishonest merchant harms both the entruster and the buyer, and that the entruster should bear the loss.

   c) Some commentators and courts have adopted the view that a buyer cannot rely on UCC section 2-403(2) if he does not qualify under section 9-307(1) because only Article 9 governs security interests. UCC section 9-306(2) provides that a security interest continues despite sale unless the secured party authorizes the sale or unless Article 9 otherwise provides. This approach would apply where the entruster and the secured party are different entities, because the buyer only acquires the entruster's interests.

   d) In this case, P was both the secured party and the entruster. P knew that the tractors would remain in the dealer's lot; although P expected Mohr-Loyd to lease the tractors to farmers, it entrusted them by failing to segregate them from the dealer's other inventory. All the buyers were buyers in ordinary course. Consequently, Tri-Country transferred all of P's interests to Ds.

   e) P claims that one of the buyers actually received the tractor in satisfaction of Tri-Country's debt to the buyer. If this were so, that buyer would not have been a buyer in ordinary course under UCC section 1-201(9). However, it appears that the buyer acquired the tractor in an even exchange for another tractor, which makes it a buyer in ordinary course of business.

B. SELLER'S WARRANTY OF TITLE

1. **Introduction.** Under UCC section 2-312, a seller warrants that the title conveyed shall be good and that its transfer is rightful, and that the goods shall be delivered free from any security interest or other encumbrance not known to the buyer. This warranty may be excluded or modified. It does not arise at all in situations where the buyer should reasonably know the seller makes no claim of title.

2. **Breach Despite Transfer of Good Title--Sumner v. Fel-Air, Inc.,** 680 P.2d 1109 (Alaska 1984).

   a. **Facts.** Fel-Air, Inc. (P), an air taxi operator, bought a Piper Navajo aircraft from Sumner (D), a commercial airplane dealer, for $105,000. P made a down payment by transferring a smaller airplane to D, and agreed to pay the balance in $2,000 monthly installments. The Navajo subsequently needed repairs requiring it to be left at Seattle Flight Service on two occasions. While the Navajo was in the shop the second time, P was notified that another company, Century Aircraft, Inc., was the actual owner of the plane and that D was only a lessee with an option to purchase. Seattle Flight Service filed a mechanic's lien and P stopped making payments. D paid the lien and retrieved the Navajo. D then put the documents of title in escrow to be given to P upon payment of the balance of the purchase price and the cost of the lien. P sued for damages caused by D's breach of implied warranties of merchantability and title. D counterclaimed for the amount of the lien he paid and asked that P's payments be treated as an offset for rent for the use of the Navajo. The trial court found for P. D appeals.

   b. **Issue.** May a seller breach the warranty of title even when he does transfer good title to the buyer?

   c. **Held.** Yes. Judgment affirmed.

      1) The evidence supports the trial court's finding that the sale included an implied warranty of title under UCC section 2-312. The fact that Century's interest was reflected on FAA files does not give P constructive notice that D did not have title. To defeat the warranty, UCC section 2-312 requires actual knowledge by the buyer or circumstances which would reasonably lead the buyer to conclude the seller does not have title.

      2) Under UCC section 2-403, D had been entrusted with the Navajo and thus could transfer to P all of Century's rights, including its good title. While this would satisfy the first part of the warranty of title, it does not satisfy the requirement that the transfer be rightful.

      3) D's lease-purchase agreement did not include authorization by Century for the sale of the Navajo. Therefore, D breached the warranty of title. D's breach created a shadow on the transaction that could not be removed without careful interpretation of

investigation to determine that all the necessary requirements of UCC section 2-403(b) were met.

Jones v.
Ballard

3.   Auctioneer's Warranty of Title--Jones v. Ballard, 573 So. 2d 783 (Miss. 1990).

a.   **Facts.** Luckey delivered a backhoe to Jones (D), an auctioneer, under a consignment agreement whereby D would receive a commission of 8%. D conducted the auction and sold the backhoe to Ballard (P) for $10,500, without disclosing the consignment relationship. P spent $1,000 to fix up the backhoe and then sold it to Black for $15,000. A police officer subsequently determined that the backhoe had been stolen four days before the auction. The officer returned the backhoe to the true owner, and P had to refund the $15,000. When D refused to reimburse P, P sued, alleging that D had impliedly warranted that he had title to the backhoe when he auctioned it off. P moved for summary judgment, and the trial court granted the motion. D appeals.

b.   **Issue.** Does an auctioneer who sells goods on consignment but does not disclose the consignment relationship or otherwise disclaim ownership of the goods make a warranty of title?

c.   **Held.** Yes. Judgment affirmed.

1)   The parties to an auction sale may contract regarding the quality of title that passes from the auctioneer, but there was no contract between P and D in this case except for the successful bid and the payment by P of the money.

2)   The general rule is that an auctioneer who fails to disclose his principal is deemed to warrant title to the goods he sells. To avoid making this warranty, the auctioneer must disclose the name of the principal. The rationale is that an auctioneer is in a better position than the bidders to ascertain the title to property being sold which would indicate the true owners.

3)   In this case, P offered his affidavit that the name of the owner and seller of the backhoe was never disclosed to him. D offered no evidence to contradict P's affidavit.

Universal
C.I.T. Credit
Corp. v. State
Farm Mutual
Automobile
Insurance Co.

4.   Warranty Does Not Extend Beyond Immediate Buyer--Universal C.I.T. Credit Corp. v. State Farm Mutual Automobile Insurance Co., 493 S.W.2d 385 (Mo. 1973).

a.   **Facts.** Banning, a car dealer, bought a used car from the Auction Co. Banning then sold the car to Sensenich. Universal C.I.T. Credit Corp. (P) financed this sale and State Farm Mutual Automobile Insurance Co. (D) insured the car. The car was demolished in a collision and during the investigation, it was discovered that the car had been stolen. Sensenich refused to make further payments and revoked his acceptance of the car. Banning requested the Auction Co. to satisfy Sensenich's demands, but the company refused. P sued Sensenich and D, then settled with D. Sensenich brought in Banning as a third party D, and Banning brought in the Auction Co. The trial court gave judgment for P against Sensenich, for

Sensenich against Banning, and for Banning against the Auction Co. The court also awarded Banning attorneys' fees. Banning went out of business and Sensenich sought to have the Auction Co. held liable directly to him. The Auction Co. appeals.

b.   **Issue.** Does an implied warranty of title run with the goods sold?

c.   **Held.** No. Judgment affirmed.

   1)   Sensenich may not claim against the Auction Co. The warranty of title on personalty extends only to the immediate buyer, unlike a covenant for title to land. Only the parties to the contract are involved in the title to personalty. Because there was no personal injury as there is in other breach of warranty cases, there is no compelling reason to do away with the requirement of privity.

   2)   The Auction Co. was properly held liable to Banning because it did not disclose its principal before making the auction sale. The general rule is that an auctioneer is liable as seller and is held to the burdens of an implied warranty of title unless it discloses the name of the principal at the time of sale.

   3)   The Auction Co. claims it should not be liable for attorneys' fees. However, under the common law a buyer may claim as consequential damages those expenses, including attorneys' fees, which he incurs in defending title after having notified the seller that a third party is claiming adversely. This rule is not changed by the UCC. Section 2-715(2)(a) allows consequential damages which the seller had reason to know. Here, the Auction Co. knew that Banning would resell the car and would have to defend itself if there was a breach of the warranty of title.

5.   **Damages for Breach--Menzel v. List,** 246 N.E.2d 742 (N.Y. 1969).

Menzel
v. List

a.   **Facts.** Menzel (P) bought a painting by Chagall in Belgium in 1932 for about $150. The Germans removed the painting when they invaded, and its location was unknown until 1955 when Perls bought the Chagall from an art gallery in Paris for $2,800. Perls relied on the gallery's reputation and did not inquire about the Chagall's history. Later that year Perls sold the Chagall to List (D) for $4,000. In 1962 P noticed the Chagall in a book of reproductions and demanded that D return the painting to her. D refused, and P started a replevin action. D impleaded Perls. The jury found for P against D, and for D against Perls, requiring Perls to pay D the current value of the Chagall of $22,500. D returned the painting to P. Perls appealed. The Appellate Division reduced the judgment against Perls to $4,000 plus interest from the purchase date. D appeals, and Perls cross appeals, claiming the interest should have accrued only from the date of P's judgment.

b.   **Issue.** When a seller breaches the warranty of title, are damages to be determined as of the date of the original sale instead of the date the buyer's enjoyment is interfered with?

c. **Held.** No. Judgment reversed.

   1) There is no consistent case law that establishes a rule as to the proper measure of damages for breach of the implied warranty of title and quiet enjoyment. Perls asserts that D should be limited to recovery of the purchase price as in the case of breach of warranty of quiet possession of real property. This remedy constitutes a rescission and restitution, however; under general contract law principles, the buyer should be able to seek damages that will put him in as good a position as he would have been in had the contract been kept.

   2) D can only be put in as good a position as he would have had if Perls had not breached the warranty of quiet enjoyment if he recovers the value of the painting at the time when his quiet enjoyment was interfered with; namely, when P won a judgment. D would have had a painting worth $22,500. Permitting D to recover only the purchase price would place him in the same position he would have been in had the sale never been made. D is instead entitled to the benefit of his bargain.

   3) Perls could have avoided this result by making proper inquiries, or by informing D of the uncertainty as to title, or even by specifically modifying or excluding the warranty.

   4) Since D's damages are to be determined as of the date D lost possession, interest should run from the date of P's judgment.

C. CLAIMS TO GOODS IN BUYER'S POSSESSION

1. **Introduction.** Various remedies are provided under the UCC to protect a seller who, though under an obligation to deliver goods to the buyer, has either not been paid or has good reason to believe that he will not be paid.

2. **Right to Withhold Delivery or Demand Cash Payment.** At common law, and under the Sales Act, the seller was deemed to have an implied-in-law "lien" on the goods as security for the unpaid purchase price. The UCC abandons any such notion, and instead simply provides that, under appropriate circumstances, a seller is entitled to withhold delivery of the goods [UCC §2-703(a)] or demand cash payment for them notwithstanding an earlier agreement for credit [UCC §2-702(1)].

   a. **Circumstances authorizing seller to demand cash.** If the buyer becomes insolvent and the seller learns of it, then irrespective of any credit term in the contract the seller is privileged to demand payment in cash, both for goods previously delivered and for goods delivered thereafter, and to withhold future deliveries until such cash payment is forthcoming. [UCC §2-702(1)]

   b. **Circumstances authorizing seller to withhold delivery.** An unpaid seller who is still in possession of the goods may withhold delivery when the buyer (i) wrongfully rejects; (ii) rescinds (*i.e.*, revokes acceptance); (iii) fails to make a payment when due; or (iv) anticipatorily breaches the contract. [UCC §2-703(a)] The seller loses his right to withhold delivery once he transfers possession of the good to the buyer. However, he may acquire another right—reclamation—which is also of great significance.

c. **Possession retained by seller--*In re* Black & White Cattle Co.,** 783 F.2d 1454 (9th Cir. 1986).

1) **Facts.** Black & White Cattle Co. (P) operated two calf raising and feed lot facilities. Granada Corp. (D) and other entities would buy feeder cattle, hire third parties to feed and raise them, and then sell them for beef. P and D executed a cattle feeding agreement on July 17 whereby P would buy 6,000 day-old calves for Ds' customers who would be the "owners." This included 1,204 cattle P had previously bought for D pursuant to an oral agreement. These cattle were not identified until several months later when they reached the feed lot. Several months later, P filed a Chapter 11 bankruptcy petition. It then filed an adversary proceeding seeking to have Ds' interest in the 1,204 cattle declared invalid. The court granted P partial summary judgment because Ds had failed to comply with California Civil Code section 3440 which requires actual delivery to and possession by a buyer. D appeals.

2) **Issue.** Must a court consider the customs and practices of a particular industry before deciding whether a seller's retention of possession after the sale is commercially reasonable?

3) **Held.** Yes. Judgment reversed in part.

    a) Ds claim that since P bought the cattle as Ds' agent, Ds always had title and P never did. P actually bought the calves in its own name, spending its own funds and paying with its own checks. P took possession and branded them with its own brand. It bore the risk of loss. The calves were not identified to the contract until much later. For this reason, P had title until the July 17 contract transferred title retroactively.

    b) Constructive delivery may satisfy the statutory requirements for certain kinds of property and situations which make it impracticable to make actual physical delivery. Segregation and labeling are not enough either if delivery is practicable. The cases deciding this issue have held that for cattle, constructive delivery is not sufficient.

    c) Under UCC section 2-402(2), a merchant seller's retention of possession after sale is not fraudulent if the seller retains the goods in good faith, in a current course of trade, and for a commercially reasonable time after the sale or identification. After concluding that UCC section 2-402(2) restates section 3440, the bankruptcy court determined that P kept possession of the cattle for longer than a commercially reasonable time. However, UCC section 2-402(2) is intended to provide greater protection to buyers. There is sufficient evidence that P's retention of possession was commercially reasonable that the court should not have awarded summary judgment.

3. **Reclamation of Goods.**

   a. **Prior law.** At common law and under the Sales Act, where the buyer obtained possession of the goods by defrauding or deceiving the seller (*e.g.*, by misrepresenting his ability to pay), the unpaid seller's "lien," could be asserted against the buyer and any successor in interest to the buyer, except a bona fide purchaser.

   b. **UCC.** The UCC recognizes an unpaid seller's right to reclaim goods in two situations: (i) cash sales, where the buyer pays by check at the time of delivery, but the check is returned for nonsufficient funds [UCC §2-507(2)]; and (ii) credit sales, where, after delivery of the goods to the buyer, the seller discovers that the buyer is insolvent [UCC §2-702(2)]. In either event, the seller may reclaim the goods by demanding their return within 10 days after the buyer receives them. [UCC §2-702(2)]

      1) **Buyer's insolvency.** The seller's right to reclaim exists in all cases where the buyer is in fact insolvent at the time he receives the goods, regardless of whether the buyer knew or should have known of the insolvency, or whether he made any representations at all to the seller with respect to his financial condition.

         a) **Effect of misrepresentation as to solvency.** If the buyer did misrepresent his solvency to the particular seller, in writing, within three months prior to the delivery in question, then the 10-day limit on demand for reclamation does not apply. [UCC §2-702(2)]

         b) **Insolvency defined.** A person is insolvent within the UCC's meaning of the word if he has ceased to pay his debts in the ordinary course of business, or cannot pay his debts as they become due, or is insolvent within the meaning of the Federal Bankruptcy Act. [UCC §1-201(23)] A person is insolvent under the Bankruptcy Act simply if his liabilities exceed his assets. [11 U.S.C. §1(19)]

         c) **Compare with cash sales.** When a cash sale is involved and the buyer's check later bounces, the seller can reclaim regardless of the buyer's solvency.

      2) **Enforcement of the right.** The right of reclamation is exercised by a written demand for return of the goods. If the buyer refuses to honor the demand, then an action for possession of personal property—replevin or claim and delivery—will lie to recover it.

         a) **Self-help not authorized.** Unless the buyer voluntarily turns the goods over to the seller, the seller must institute appropriate legal actions or proceedings.

         b) **Comment.** The seller need only make his written demand within the 10-day period. He does not lose his right to reclaim if he fails to obtain the goods within the 10 days.

3) **Reclamation as election of remedies.** Successful reclamation of goods excludes all other remedies. [UCC §2-702(3)] For example, the seller cannot thereafter sue for loss of profits on the sale.

4) **Rights of third parties.**

    a) **Bona fide purchasers.** Transfer to a bona fide purchaser cuts off the seller's right of reclamation. If the buyer has transferred possession of the goods to a purchaser for value without notice of the seller's rights, the purchaser prevails over the seller as to possession of the goods. [UCC §2-702(3)]

    b) **Secured creditors.** A secured creditor who advanced money in the past and obtained a perfected security interest covering the debtor's after-acquired goods is generally treated as a "good faith purchaser" under UCC section 2-702(3) and hence prevails against the unpaid seller of the goods who attempts to reclaim them. Consequently, the right of reclamation is ineffective when the buyer finances his inventory, because lenders typically require that inventory loans cover both present and future inventory.

c. **Timeliness of reclamation--Holiday Rambler Corp. v. First National Bank & Trust Co. of Great Bend, Kansas,** 723 F.2d 1449 (10th Cir. 1983).

Holiday Rambler Corp. v. First National Bank & Trust Co. of Great Bend, Kansas

    1) **Facts.** Holiday Rambler Corp. (P), a recreational vehicle manufacturer, determined that the financial condition of one of its dealers, Kansas Kamper, was poor after a new buyer acquired control. P decided to provide campers to Kansas Kamper on a c.o.d. basis and accepted its company checks. P delivered four campers and accepted four checks drawn on Kansas Kamper's account with the First National Bank & Trust Co. of Great Bend, Kansas (D). Kansas Kamper then went to D for a loan, using the campers as collateral. After paying off some of its loans to D, Kansas Kamper had insufficient funds in its account with D to pay the checks made out to P, and the checks were dishonored. P resubmitted the checks and they were again dishonored. Kansas Kamper filed for bankruptcy after it had sold three of the campers in the ordinary course of business and paid off the notes and security agreements with D. P sued D for the value of the checks. The district court granted summary judgment for D on the ground that D had valid perfected security interests in the campers with priority over P and that D had not committed fraud in collecting the debt which wiped out Kansas Kamper's account with D. P appeals.

    2) **Issue.** Does a seller lose its rights to reclaim goods sold if it does not do so within 10 days of the time the buyer takes possession?

    3) **Held.** Yes. Judgment affirmed.

        a) A buyer's rights to dispose of goods is conditional upon the seller's right of reclamation; if P had a right to reclaim the campers, D could not have received enforceable security interests until Kansas Kamper obtained rights in the collateral.

b) Under UCC section 2-702, a seller who discovers that a buyer received goods on credit while insolvent may reclaim the goods within 10 days of the buyer's receipt. This right extends to sellers who accept bad checks. Thus P had a right to reclaim when Kansas Kamper's check was dishonored.

c) P's right to reclaim expired because it failed to repossess the campers for several months after delivery. The 10-day limitation of UCC section 2-702 applies to UCC section 2-507(2).

d) If D's security interest had been fraudulently obtained, it would not have had priority over P's claim. D did nothing to induce P to accept uncertified checks from Kansas Kamper. D's knowledge that the campers were not paid for when it extended credit and acquired a security interest does not constitute fraud. P simply failed to use the protections provided for by the UCC.

D. BULK SALES

1. **Introduction.** Special formalities are required in connection with "bulk transfers"—transfers by a merchant of some substantial part of his inventory other than in the ordinary course of business. These requirements appear in Article 6 of the UCC. The purpose is to afford the merchant's creditors notice of the impending transfer so that they will have the opportunity to protect themselves by asserting their claims against the seller or his stock in trade. The law applicable to bulk sales is, therefore, really not a part of the law of Sales, but rather within the realm of creditors' rights.

   a. **Covered businesses.** The bulk sales statutes are aimed primarily at transfers by a retail merchant whose principal business is the sale of inventory. Service establishments such as restaurants, farms, barber shops, etc., are generally outside the bulk sales laws even though the sale includes some stock of merchandise. Some states have enlarged the scope to include certain service types of businesses, however.

   b. **Covered transfers.** The bulk sales statutes apply generally to any transfer by a merchant of all or a major part of his inventory, other than in the ordinary course of business. [UCC §6-102(1)] Normally this means that more than 50% of the inventory is transferred. It also applies to transfers of a merchant's equipment if made in connection with a bulk transfer of the inventory.

   c. **Notice requirement.** The UCC requires the seller to prepare a list of his creditors [UCC §6-104(2)], and requires the buyer to send written notice of the sale to each creditor listed by the seller, or otherwise known to the buyer. [UCC §§6-105; 6-107(3)]

   d. **Creditors protected.** All of the seller's existing creditors, having fixed claims at the time of the bulk sale, are protected by the bulk sales statutes. [UCC §6-104(2)]

e. **Effect of noncompliance.** If the bulk seller and buyer fail to comply with the statute, the transfer to the buyer, even though he is a good faith purchaser, is void as against the seller's creditors. [UCC §6-105] The seller's creditors can then seize the goods by judicial process in satisfaction of their debts as if the transfer had never been made. However, if the bulk buyer transfers the goods to a subsequent good faith purchaser for value before the bulk seller's creditors catch up with them, then the innocent subvendee gets good title as against the seller's creditors. [UCC §6-110(2)]

2. **Transfer to Settle Creditor's Security Interest--Ouachita Electric Cooperative Corp. v. Evans-St. Clair,** 672 S.W.2d 660 (Ark. Ct. App. 1984).

a. **Facts.** The National Acceptance Co. ("NAC") had loaned over $2 million to two St. Clair companies and took a security interest in all of their assets. Evans-St. Clair (D) purchased machinery, equipment tools and other property, but no inventory, from the St. Clair companies. D paid NAC $200,000 cash and signed a promissory note for another $500,000. NAC reduced the St. Clair companies' debt by $700,000 and agreed not to collect from them should D default on its note. D also was entitled to purchase the St. Clair companies' inventory, although it could also be sold to anyone else. D actually bought about one-third of the inventory over a period of time to meet its own manufacturing needs, but not in bulk. Ouachita Electric Cooperative Corp. (P) had provided electricity to the Arkansas St. Clair company and sought to collect the $37,676.80 bill from D on the ground that its purchase of the assets constituted a bulk transfer. The trial court found for D and awarded P judgment against the Arkansas company. P appeals.

b. **Issue.** May a debtor's transfer of property to a third party in settlement of a creditor's security interest be outside the bulk transfer rules?

c. **Held.** Yes. Judgment affirmed.

1) Transfers in settlement or realization of a lien or other security interest are not subject to the bulk transfer rules. The transfer in this case satisfied NAC's security interest.

2) It is not necessary that the transfer be made to the holder of the security interest, so long as the transfer is for the benefit of the holder. The purpose of the rule is to prevent merchants from selling out and disappearing without paying creditors. When the transfer settles a security interest, there is no cash for the merchant to take.

3) P was not prejudiced by this transaction. If P had levied on the collateral held by St. Clair, the proceeds from the sale would have been subject to NAC's prior security interest, and the debt to NAC was larger than the available collateral. Alternatively, St. Clair could have transferred the property to NAC.

4) Article 6 does not apply to agreements to purchase inventory in the future such as the one here. Until the goods are actually transferred, the seller retains possession and is subject to levy by the seller's creditors.

5) Nor was there a preponderance of the evidence to show that the sale was a fraudulent transfer. Varying valuations of the property were offered, but the findings of no fraud are supported by the evidence. P did not prove that a greater price could have been obtained.

E. LEASES

1. **Introduction.** Reflecting the increasing importance of leasing in commerce, Article 2A has been adopted by more than half of the states. Many of its provisions mirror those contained in Article 2 on sales.

2. **Distinguishing a Lease from a Security Interest.** A key issue is distinguishing between a lease and a security interest. UCC section 2A-103(1)(j) defines a "lease," and UCC section 1-201(37) defines a "security interest." The difference is important. A transferor who creates a security interest instead of a lease must file under Article 9 to protect its interest, but a lessor does not have to.

   a. **Reversionary interest.** A key to distinguishing a lease from a security interest is whether the transferor retains a reversionary interest, which is an economically significant interest the lessor has at the end of the lease term.

   b. **Inclusion rules.** Because the lessor has no reversionary interest, a transfer creates a security interest where:

      1) the lessee pays the lessor for the right to use and possess the goods; and

      2) the lessee's obligation is for the term of the lease not subject to termination by the lessee; and

      3) the following is satisfied:

         a) the original term of the lese is equal to or greater than the remaining economic life of the goods;

         b) the lessee is bound to renew the lease for the remaining economic life of the goods or is bound to become the owner of the goods;

         c) the lessee has an option to renew the lease for the remaining economic life of the goods for no additional consideration or nominal consideration upon compliance with the lease agreement; or

         d) the lessee has an option to become the owner of the goods for no additional consideration or nominal additional consideration upon compliance with the lease agreement.

   c. **Exclusion rules.** UCC section 1-201(37) also contains exclusion rules, providing that a transfer does not create a security interest merely because any of the following circumstances or conditions are present:

1) the present value of the consideration the lessee is obligated to pay the lessor for the right to possession and use of the goods is substantially equal to or is greater than the fair market value of the goods at the time the lease is entered into;

2) the lessee assumes risk of loss of the goods, or agrees to pay taxes, insurance, filing, recording, or registration fees, or service or maintenance costs with respect to the goods;

3) the lessee has an option to renew the lease or to become the owner of the goods;

4) the lessee has an option to renew the lease for a fixed rent that is equal to or greater than the reasonably predictable fair market rent for the use of the goods for the term of the renewal at the time the option is to be performed; or

5) the lessee has an option to become the owner of the goods for a fixed price that is equal to or greater than the reasonably predictable fair market value of the goods at the time the option is to be performed.

3. **Formation, Priorities, and Remedies.**

   a. **Formation.** Much of Article 2A follows Article 2 with regard to formation of lease contracts. Generally, Article 2A allows freedom of contract in forming leases. However, there are special provisions for consumer leases.

   b. **Priority.** A lessor's interests in its reversionary interest, in its leasehold interest in the lessee, and in its right to rent are protected against the lessee's creditors and the lessee's buyers and sublessees. The lessor does not have to file the lease contract or a financing statement, unless the leased property is a fixture. There are specific rules regarding creditors, buyers and sublessees that affect creditors who supply services or materials with respect to the leased goods and buyers in the ordinary course of business.

   c. **Remedies.** The Article 2A remedies for lessors are comparable to the sellers' remedies contained in Article 2. A lessee's remedies are comparable to a buyer's remedies.

   d. **Lessor's remedies--Honeywell, Inc. v. Lithonia Lighting, Inc.**, 317 F. Supp. 406 (N.D. Ga. 1970).

      1) **Facts.** Honeywell, Inc. (P) leased computer equipment to Lithonia Lighting, Inc. (D). The parties had disagreements over performance, and D terminated the lease. P sued for breach. The court found that D had breached. D claimed that P's damages should be reduced by the amount of rentals that P could have received by leasing the equipment to someone else. D's evidence on that issue consisted of

proof that P disassembled the equipment and sold some of the parts to other customers. P argues that its damages should not be so reduced.

2) **Issue.** To reduce damages for the money the nonbreaching party could have received by leasing the goods to a third party, must the breaching party offer evidence that the goods in fact could have been leased?

3) **Held.** Yes. Damages not reduced.

a) D had the burden to show a potential reduction in the damages award by proving P could release the property. D merely showed that P sold some of the parts. But the evidence suggested that there was little or no market for used equipment of the kind D leased, and there was no evidence that P would not have had an adequate supply of the parts he sold if D had not returned the equipment.

b) P is entitled to recover the net profit it would have realized on the balance of the contract, measured by deducting from the gross rental due for the balance both the direct costs (*e.g.,* maintenance, depreciation, amortization, taxes, insurance) and the indirect costs (*e.g.,* marketing support, operating expenses) that P would have incurred in performing if D had not breached.

4) **Comment.** This case was not decided under Article 2A.

4. **Finance Leases.**

a. **Introduction.** Article 2A provides for special leases called "finance leases" that are created by financing institutions. A finance lease is a true lease and not a security interest, but it has unique aspects. A finance lease typically arises after a lessee identifies goods and negotiates terms of purchase with the supplier. The lessee then contacts a financing institution, which actually purchases the goods and leases them to the lessee. The supplier's promises and warranties run to the lessee as a third-party beneficiary of the sales contract between the supplier and the financing institution. The lessor normally disclaims all warranties to the lessee and requires an irrevocable obligation to pay the rent.

Angelle v.
Energy Build-
ers Co., Inc.

b. **Lessor's duty to provide possession--Angelle v. Energy Builders Co., Inc.**, 496 So. 2d 509 (La. Ct. App. 1986).

1) **Facts.** Angelle (P) needed a Low Group Pressure ("LGP") tractor, equipped with a KG blade, to bid on a contract to clear swamp land. P discovered that Energy Builders Co., Inc. (D) had an LGP tractor and a KG blade. P contacted General Leasing Services, Inc. ("GLS"), which agreed to purchase the equipment from D and lease it to P. GLS paid $65,000 for the equipment and leased it to P for approximately $3,000 per month. The lease provided that GLS would not be liable for damages "if for any reason the supplier delays or fails to fill the order." It further provided that "lessee shall accept such equipment if delivered in good repair," and that "no defect

or unfitness of the equipment shall relieve Lessee of the obligation to pay rent." GLS assigned its rights under the lease to Heller, a creditor. D delivered the tractor to P, but did not include the KG blade. When D did send a KG blade, it did not fit the tractor. P never got a satisfactory KG blade, but made payments to GLS totaling over $21,000. P sued GLS and D for breach of contract, based on the failure to provide a KG blade. Only GLS was served, however, and it was in a bankruptcy reorganization that allowed Heller to enforce the lease. Heller intervened, seeking cancellation of the lease and damages for nonpayment. P added Heller as a defendant and sought the return of the payments it had made. The trial court found that there had never been a valid lease because P had never received the KG blade, so Heller was not entitled to damages. The court also dismissed P's claim for a refund. Both parties appeal.

2) **Issue.** Where a lessor has not provided the lessee with peaceable possession of the leased equipment, may the lessee be held liable for payments?

3) **Held.** No. Judgment affirmed.

   a) To perfect a lease, there are three requirements: a thing, a price, and consent. Delivery of the item is not essential to the perfection of the contract. Because the contract between P and GLS contained all three elements, it was a perfected lease contract.

   b) Heller's right to receive payments under the lease depends on GLS's rights under the lease. The lease provided that GLS made no warranties and that no defect in the equipment would relieve P of the obligation to pay rent. Lessors may properly renounce warranties against defects and unfitness in this manner. However, the parties may not waive fundamental obligations, such as the lessor's obligation to deliver the leased property. The right of peaceable possession is guaranteed by state statute and cannot be waived.

   c) In this case, P made efforts to obtain the necessary KG blade, but was unable to get one. By not delivering all the leased property, GLS breached the contract and P is not required to make rental payments. As GLS's assignee, Heller has no right to the payments, either.

   d) P seeks a refund of its payments, but nothing in the record shows that the payments went to Heller. Heller was an assignee of the lease for security purposes, and as such, Heller is not liable to P for payments P made to GLS.

4) **Comment.** This case was not decided under UCC Article 2A.

c. **Financing lessor as buyer--Midwest Precision Services v. PTM Industries Corp.**, 887 F.2d 1128 (1st Cir. 1989).

Midwest Precision Services v. PTM Industries Corp.

   1) **Facts.** PTM Industries Corp. (D) desired to buy a grinder from Midwest Precision Services (P). P was to customize the machine to suit D's needs. D contacted Shawmut Bank to finance the deal, and entered into a dollar option lease whereby Shawmut would lease the machine to D for 60

months. At the end of the lease, D could buy the grinder for $1. Shawmut gave P a purchase order for the grinder. The order stated that it was the "complete and exclusive statement of the agreement." Shawmut was to pay $345,500 for the grinder, and P agreed to deliver it directly to D. P expressly warranted the machine and gave both Shawmut and D the right to enforce the warranties. Shawmut could cancel the purchase order with no liability unless within 90 days P had delivered the grinder and Shawmut had received from D a "signed acceptance certificate" acknowledging receipt of the grinder in good condition. P never knew the terms of the lease between Shawmut and D. P modified the grinder and shipped it to D. D inspected it and declared it was damaged. D refused to accept delivery, and rejected P's offers to cure any damage. One hundred and one days after issuing the purchase order, Shawmut canceled the agreement. P sued D. D moved to dismiss on the ground that Shawmut, not D, was the real party in interest. P named Shawmut as a defendant. By this time, D became insolvent. The jury found for P, finding that Shawmut breached the purchase order contract, that D caused P damages by breaching its separate contract with P, and that both breaches occurred on the day D rejected the grinder. P and Shawmut appeal.

2) **Issue.** May a financing lessor be deemed a buyer of the goods leased?

3) **Held.** Yes. Judgment affirmed. New trial on damages ordered.

a) Under UCC section 2-103(1)(a), a "buyer" is a person who buys or contracts to buy goods. Shawmut claims that it was a financing agent in a three-party transaction and should not be treated as a buyer.

b) Commercial leasing arrangements are often set up as tripartite deals involving a supplier, a lessee, and a lessor. The lessor may be a bank that performs no procurement functions, but merely purchases the property as selected and negotiated for by the lessee. The supplier delivers the goods directly to the lessee, who makes the lease payments to the bank. The bank thus buys the equipment from the supplier and leases it to the lessee.

c) In suits by a lessee against the lessor for breach of warranty, it makes a difference whether the lessor is a "merchant lessor" or a "finance lessor," but the distinction in this case is irrelevant because D has not made a claim against Shawmut. Instead, P has sued Shawmut on the purchase order. Under the terms of that agreement, including the one giving Shawmut the power to directly enforce P's express warranties, Shawmut is clearly a buyer.

d) The purchase order provided that Shawmut could terminate if it had not received D's signed acceptance certificate. This provision delegated to D the task of performing Shawmut's duties to accept the machine and permit cure. D wrongfully rejected the machine. Shawmut claims that it was not liable for D's wrongful rejection; because it never received a "signed acceptance certificate" from D, it could terminate the agreement. But the purpose of that language was to protect Shawmut against P's nonperformance, not to create a technical barrier to P's right to payment. The focus is not on Shawmut's receipt of D's signed certificate, but on whether Shawmut received the performance to which the certificate must attest. P did meet its obligations, and Shawmut must meet its payment obligation.

e) The trial court did make mistakes in the damage instructions, and a new trial on damages is necessary.

4) Comment. The court noted that even if the contract had more explicitly excused Shawmut from the buyer's normal duty to accept and pay for conforming goods and to permit cure when appropriate, public policy might have invalidated the provision. UCC section 2-508 has a goal of avoiding injustice to the seller by reason of a surprise rejection by the buyer. Note that this case was not decided under Article 2A.

F. LETTERS OF CREDIT

1. **Introduction.** Letters of credit are used principally in international commerce, and replace to some extent the financing through documents of title, such as bills of lading, in internal commerce. In a letter of credit transaction, the buyer obtains a local bank's guarantee to a foreign seller that the goods will be paid for upon tender of a proper set of documents.

   a. **Firm payment against documents.** By issuing the letter of credit, the buyer's bank obligates itself to pay the amount specified in the letter of credit (the price) upon receipt of proper documents.

      1) The bank is obligated to pay, even if it knows or suspects that goods being delivered by the seller do not conform to the contract. [UCC §5-114(1)]

      2) Only if the buyer obtains a court order enjoining the bank from making payment is the bank privileged not to honor the letter of credit. [UCC §§5-114(2)(b); 2-512(b)] A few states, including California, have eliminated this provision of the UCC, leaving it unclear whether a court would issue an injunction against payment.

   b. **Documents must conform.** The documents must conform to the terms stated in the letter of credit, or the bank is not required to honor the letter. [UCC §5-109(2)] However, it has been held that if some of the documents conform to the terms of the credit and others do not, the bank must honor the credit if the invoice is in proper form even though there may be errors in some of the other documents, such as the bill of lading or the insurance certificate.

   c. **Whether credit irrevocable.** A letter of credit can be drawn to be revocable by the bank at any time prior to the presentation of the documents to it; or it may be drawn to be irrevocable. Where a contract calls simply for a letter of credit, a presumption arises that it means an irrevocable letter of credit unless it is expressly agreed otherwise. [UCC §2-325(3)]

   d. **Effect of furnishing a letter of credit.** Where the contract calls for payment by a letter of credit, and the buyer has furnished a proper letter of credit, his obligation to pay is suspended. [UCC §2-325(2)] Thereafter, only if for some reason the letter of credit is dishonored may the seller demand direct payment from the buyer. [UCC §2-325(2)]

2.   Issuer's Duty to Pay.

Banco Es-
panol de
Credito v.
State Street
Bank & Trust
Co.

a.   Buyer's duty to establish standards--Banco Espanol de Credito v. State Street Bank & Trust Co., 385 F.2d 230 (1st Cir. 1967), *cert. denied*, 390 U.S. 1013 (1968), *appeal after remand*, 409 F.2d 711 (1st Cir. 1969).

1)   Facts. Lawrence obtained two irrevocable letters of credit from State Street Bank & Trust Co. (D) to finance the purchase of clothing from a Spanish supplier. Banco Espanol de Credito (P) was the correspondent bank. The letters of credit required signed invoices, customs invoices, inspection certificates, and full sets of clean on board bills of lading. D informed Lawrence that requiring an inspection certificate without naming an inspector was risky, but Lawrence told D that an inspector would be named in a later amendment. This was done. However, Lawrence gave Supervigilancia, the named inspector, conflicting instructions about what it was to inspect. Finally Supervigilancia issued two certificates of inspection based on inspections of samples provided by the manufacturer. When the documents were presented to P, P honored them and made payment. D then refused to accept the drafts on the ground that the inspection certificates did not conform to the orders as required by the terms of the letters of credit. The trial court found for D and P appeals.

2)   Issue. Does the buyer have a duty to establish in the letter of credit specific standards for inspections of the goods to be delivered?

3)   Held. Yes. Judgment reversed and vacated.

a)   An issuing bank's duty to honor a demand for payment is governed by statute. Under UCC section 5-114(1), an issuer must honor a draft which complies with the terms of the relevant credit regardless of whether the goods conform to the underlying contract.

b)   Documents submitted incident to a letter of credit must be strictly construed. However, the courts must balance the integrity of international transactions with the need for flexibility so that undue technical errors as to ancillary matters do not defeat the deal.

c)   Since the buyer initiates international transactions, the procedure is structured by the buyer. When buyers are interested in quality assurance, they establish inspection requirements in the letters of credit, but these need to be specific enough to accomplish the intended purpose.

d)   In this case, Lawrence sent Supervigilancia conflicting instructions as to how to inspect the goods. Supervigilancia relied on the seller's representations as to the appropriateness of the samples. It could do nothing more. Since Lawrence failed to establish a more reliable assurance of authenticity, P was entitled to rely on the inspection.

b. **Strict compliance--Courtaulds North America, Inc. v. North Carolina National Bank,** 528 F.2d 802 (4th Cir. 1975).

1) **Facts.** For the account of its customer Adastra, the North Carolina National Bank (D) issued a series of letters of credit making funds available upon the drafts of Courtaulds North America, Inc. (P). The letters required that the drafts be accompanied by commercial invoices describing the goods as 100% acrylic yarn. When P presented the last of the drafts, the accompanying invoices stated that the goods were "Imported Acrylic Yarn." The packing lists stapled to the invoices stated that the goods were 100% Acrylic. As it had in the past when documents were deficient, D contacted Adastra to determine whether Adastra would waive the discrepancies, but Adastra was undergoing bankruptcy and could not waive without the trustee's consent. D refused to honor the draft. P sent amended invoices that complied with the letter of credit, but the letter had expired. D returned the documents and P sued. The trial court granted summary judgment for P. D appeals.

2) **Issue.** Must the terms of a letter of credit be complied with strictly even though the documents presented with the draft, taken together, demonstrate that the goods involved are what was called for in the letter of credit?

3) **Held.** Yes. Judgment reversed.

a) The drawee bank which issues a letter of credit deals only with documents, not merchandise. Its duties are established by the letter of credit, not by the contract between its customer and the seller. Accordingly, the seller who is the beneficiary of the letter of credit must meet precisely the terms of the credit to obtain performance.

b) The letter of credit in this case clearly required that the invoice state that it covered 100% acrylic yarn. P claims that the invoices were sufficient when considered in connection with the packing lists, since these lists were actually detailed explanations of the invoices. However, the banking trade only treats as invoices documents clearly labeled as invoices.

c) If D had honored the draft despite the discrepancy, it might have been liable to the trustee in bankruptcy. It could also have been subject to a claim from P that P shipped the yarn to Adastra because of D's assurance of credit, so that D would be liable for P's loss.

d) D's past practices of honoring drafts despite discrepancies does not change the result because on each of those occasions, D obtained the consent of Adastra. D did not waive the strict compliance requirement.

c. **Timeliness of claim--Marino Industries Corp. v. Chase Manhattan Bank, N.A.,** 686 F.2d 112 (2d Cir. 1982).

1) **Facts.** Marino Industries Corp. (P) sent construction materials to a job site in Saudi Arabia at the request of Bautechnik, a West German firm. Bautechnik's German bank had issued two irrevocable letters of credit which Chase Manhattan Bank (D) confirmed. Partial payments were to be

made upon shipment and upon receipt at the destination. The letters of credit required that the signatures of a representative of the joint venture or of the freight forwarder would be accepted. The German bank told D that only one of three signatures would be acceptable, but P was never informed about this. P submitted the certificates on October 15, and D's employee made a discrepancy sheet two days later, but D did not return these to P until December 2, the day after the letter of credit expired. D then told P it would not make payments because its claim was not timely presented. P sued, but the trial court found for D. P appeals.

2) **Issue.** May a correspondent bank refuse to pay on the ground that the submitted claim is not timely when the seller submits a defective claim in a timely manner but the bank does not notify the seller of the defects until the letter of credit expires?

3) **Held.** No. Judgment reversed.

a) While letters of credit are strictly construed, the letters must specify precisely and clearly the requirements for payment. Ambiguities are resolved against the bank.

b) The letter of credit in this case did not indicate that only one of three specific signatures would be acceptable. The trial court did not determine whether the signature in the certificates P presented was in fact that of a representative of the joint venture, so this issue must be decided on remand.

c) In order for P to receive payment, it must have presented certificates of inspection as required by the letter of credit. D found defects in these certificates, but it did not inform P until after the letter had expired. While D was entitled to a reasonable time to examine the documentation, it should have returned the items to P to allow correction of the deficiencies. By not doing so, D made it impossible for P to comply in a timely manner, and D should not be allowed to rely upon the defects as a justification for refusing payment.

Manufacturers Hanover International Bank Corp. v. Spring Tree Corp.

d. **Beneficiary bears risk of nonconforming documents--Manufacturers Hanover International Banking Corp. v. Spring Tree Corp.**, 752 F. Supp. 522 (D. Ma. 1990).

1) **Facts.** Spring Tree Corporation (D) contracted to sell cocoa to a Hong Kong trading company. The Hua Chiao Commercial Bank ("HCCB") issued the letter of credit, and Manufacturers Hanover International Banking Corp. (P) acted as negotiating bank at D's request. After making a final shipment, D delivered a draft to P for the full amount of the letter of credit. D submitted the required supporting documents. P transmitted the documents to HCCB, disclaiming any responsibility for their validity or accuracy. P paid D. HCCB refused to accept the documents because they did not conform to the terms of the letter of credit. P asked D for the return of the money it paid D. D refused, and P sued. Both parties move for summary judgment.

2) **Issue.** Where there is a dispute over a letter of credit, should the beneficiary bear the financial cost instead of the negotiating bank?

3) Held. Yes. P's motion granted.

  a)   Under UCC section 5-111, a negotiating bank has the right to rely on the beneficiary's warranty that the documents it submits satisfied the requirements of the letter of credit. The negotiating bank has recourse against the beneficiary for proceeds advanced to the beneficiary if the issuing bank dishonors the draft because the documents do not comply with the letter of credit.

  b)   Under the circumstances, D must reimburse P, regardless of the dispute between D and the issuing bank regarding whether the issuing bank properly dishonored the documents.

e.   Beneficiary's duty to provide conforming documents--Philadelphia Gear Corp. v. Central Bank, 717 F.2d 230 (5th Cir. 1983).

Philadelphia
Gear Corp. v.
Central Bank

  1)   Facts. United Machinery Services, Inc. ("United") contracted to sell goods to Philadelphia Gear Corporation (P). United's bank, Central Bank (D), issued a $4.5 million letter of credit in favor of P as beneficiary. The letter required P to present an inland bill of lading evidencing shipment of specified goods. The letter was subject to the Uniform Customs and Practices for Commercial Documentary Credits, contained in ICC Pub. 290, which provided, inter alia, that banks will refuse documents presented to them more than 21 days after the issuance of the shipping documents. ICC Pub. 290 also requires banks that reject documents to give prompt notice to that effect, "stating the reasons therefor," and either hold the documents at the disposal of the remitting bank or return them to such bank. An issuing bank who fails to do so is precluded from claiming defects in the documents presented. The relationship between United and P deteriorated, and P presented drafts on the letter of credit to D. D returned them to P's intermediary bank with a notice stating that they were being returned "due to their noncompliance with the terms of the relevant credit." D refused to provide a more definite statement of its reasons for rejection. P sued to recover on the drafts. The district court found that P's tendered drafts failed to conform to the letter of credit, that the defects were curable, that P knew about some of the defects, and that D neither returned the supporting documentation to P's drafts nor informed P's intermediary bank that D would hold the documentation on file for its inspection. The court held that D's dishonor of the drafts was wrongful and required D to pay them. D appeals.

  2)   Issue. Where a beneficiary presents nonconforming documents and the issuing bank rejects them but does not specify a reason other than general noncompliance, is the beneficiary entitled to payment anyway?

  3)   Held. No. Judgment reversed.

  a)   The district court focused on the issuer's duty to pay, and because D failed to provide specific reasons for dishonoring P's drafts, required D to pay them. However, D's dishonor puts at issue the adequacy of P's performance, which must be the primary focus of analysis.

  b)   The doctrine of strict compliance is based on the commercial reality that an issuer who pays on nonconforming documents loses its right to reimbursement from its customer. Rejection of the strict compliance doctrine would undermine the viability of letters of credit, because it would force issuers to assume the risks of the underlying contract's nonperformance and possible judicial realignment of its obligations under the letter of credit. Strict compliance means that there can be no wrongful dishonor when the drafts presented are nonconforming and the issuer gives timely and sufficient notice of dishonor.

c) The district court found that P's drafts were all defective. Some were accompanied by documents other than inland bills of lading; others were stale (*i.e.,* more than 21 days old). P claims that the documents were stale because of its agreement with United, but D cannot be required to consider the underlying contract unless the letter of credit expressly incorporates it, which this letter of credit did not. D was not required to amend the terms of the letter of credit, and did not act in bad faith either in declining to amend the credit or in rejecting facially nonconforming documents.

d) P also claims that it should recover because the defects in its documents were curable and D had a duty to notify it of the precise defects. But under a letter of credit, the issuer's obligation to pay is entirely conditioned on the beneficiary's performance, including the delivery of specified documents. Under UCC section 5-111, a beneficiary warrants, in presentation, that its drafts conform to the conditions of the credit. By knowingly tendering nonconforming drafts, P breached this warranty. The court cannot hold that a beneficiary could knowingly tender nonconforming drafts and then recover on them because it was not advised of the defects.

e) On remand, the court should determine which of the drafts P knew were defective.

4) **Dissent.** The court holds that a knowing tender of defective drafts absolves the issuing bank of its duty to give notice of the defects and of its duty to return the drafts and supporting documentation. This is an incorrect approach. The rules regarding treatment of a letter of credit are not based on subjective knowledge of the parties, but require compliance with clear procedures. The procedures for dishonoring a draft are intended in part to allow the beneficiary an opportunity to cure. If the issuing bank fails to specify the defects, the beneficiary cannot cure. D should not be excused from its obligations, even if P knew of the defects. Introducing the beneficiary's state of mind into the law will make dealing with letters of credit more unpredictable.

3. Issuer's Right to Dishonor Because of Fraud.

a. **Introduction.** Under UCC section 5-114(2), an issuer acting in good faith may honor a draft despite notification from its customer of fraud, forgery or other defect not apparent on the face of the document. However, a court may enjoin the bank from honoring the document. Courts have applied varying standards in deciding cases under this section.

b. **Payment enjoined due to seller's fraud--Sztejn v. J. Henry Schroder Banking Corp.**, 31 N.Y.S.2d 631 (1941).

1) **Facts.** Sztejn (P) purchased bristles from Transea Traders, an Indian corporation. J. Henry Schroder Banking Corp. (D) issued an irrevocable letter of credit to Transea upon which Transea could draw for a specified portion of the purchase price. Transea fraudulently shipped worthless material and rubbish but obtained the documents called for in the letter of credit. Transea drew a draft under the letter of credit which it presented, along with the specified documents, to the Chartered Bank. The Chartered Bank presented these to D for payment. P sued for an injunction against payment. D moves for dismissal.

2) **Issue.** May payment under a letter of credit be enjoined where the seller's fraud is made known to the issuing bank before there is a presentment for payment?

3) **Held.** Yes. Motion denied.

   a) Generally, a letter of credit is independent of the sales contract and the issuing bank must pay upon presentation of documents, not goods. The issuing bank may not refuse to pay merely because the buyer and seller dispute the quality of the goods shipped.

   b) However, where the seller commits fraud which is made known to the issuing bank before drafts and documents are presented for payment, the principle of independence should not be extended to protect the seller. The bank need not recognize a fraudulent document as complying with the letter of credit.

c. **Scope of extrinsic evidence considered--Colorado National Bank of Denver v. Board of County Commissioners of Routt County, Colo.**, 634 P.2d 32 (Colo. 1981).

1) **Facts.** Woodmoor obtained approval from the Board of County Commissioners of Routt County, Colo. (P) to develop a subdivision. This approval was conditioned on Woodmoor's agreement to complete roads as indicated in the design specifications. The Colorado National Bank of Denver (D) issued letters of credit to secure Woodmoor's obligation. These letters of credit allowed P to draw upon D for a total of about $350,000 upon submission of a duly signed statement by P that the improvements were not made in accordance with the subdivision agreement. Woodmoor never build the roads, and P submitted the required documents to D for payment. D dishonored the drafts. P sued for the face amount. In defense, C claimed that P would receive a windfall if D paid the drafts. P's motion in limine to exclude evidence beyond the terms of the letters of credit and the demands made on the letters of credit was granted by the court. The trial court found for P and D appealed. The court of appeals affirmed. D appeals.

2) **Issue.** In a suit for dishonor of drafts drawn on letters of credit, may the court exclude evidence concerning matters beyond the four corners of the letters of credit and the demands made on the letters of credit?

3) **Held.** Yes. Judgment affirmed.

   a) The letters of credit D issued in this case were standby letters of credit. Although this type of letter of credit is used to secure the bank's customer's performance to a third party, it differs from a suretyship contract because D's liability rests upon the letter of credit instead of upon the underlying contract.

   b) The commercial vitality of the letter of credit is its independence from the underlying contract. The issuing bank is obligated to honor an apparently conforming draft or demand for payment, unless a required document is forged or fraudulent or there is fraud in the transaction. The documents in this case were not fraudulent. Nor was there any fraud in the transaction between Woodmoor and P.

   c) If D wanted to require actual completion of the roads before it had to pay P, D could have required additional conditions in the letters of credit. P fully satisfied the requirements stated in the letter of credit and D cannot litigate the performance of the underlying contracts.

Cromwell v.
Commerce &
Energy Bank

d. **Proof that beneficiary committed fraud necessary--Cromwell v. Commerce & Energy Bank**, 464 So. 2d 721 (La. 1985).

   1) **Facts.** Cromwell (P) and other investors purchased limited partnership interests in C.I., Ltd., which had been formed by C.E., Inc., the general partner. Ps paid $250,000 for each unit, but only $20,000 in cash. Ps each gave one demand note for $30,000 and another demand note for $200,000, secured by a $200,000 standby letter of credit issued by the Commerce & Energy Bank (D) and other banks. The partnership was a blind pool; according to the Private Placement Memorandum ("PPM"), C.I., Ltd. was to invest the proceeds in unspecified real estate and generate tax advantages for Ps. The letters of credit permitted the beneficiary to draw a draft if accompanied by certification that a default exists under any loan of C.I., Ltd., or any indebtedness of Ps which the letter of credit secured. C.I., Ltd. obtained loans of about $7.8 million, secured by the letters of credit and security interests in the demand notes. The proceeds of the loans were mostly used to invest in other related limited partnerships, although the largest single investment was the purchase of a hotel. After a series of negotiations, C.I., Ltd. obtained a $10 million line of credit from European American Bank ("EAB"). During the negotiations, EAB had reservations and made credit reference checks, but it was ultimately satisfied that C.I., Ltd. was a satisfactory credit risk. About seven months after EAB made the loan, it declared C.I., Ltd. to be in default. Two months later, EAB drew drafts on Ds for payment under the letters of credit. Ps sought a preliminary injunction preventing Ds from honoring the drafts on the ground that there was fraud in the transaction under UCC section 5-114(2). The trial court found that EAB had knowledge of facts pertaining to C.I., Ltd.'s business dealings that constituted fraud and thus should have known of the fraud being perpetrated upon Ps. The court of appeal reversed, holding there was no fraud under UCC section 5-114(2). Ps petitioned to have the trial court's judgment reinstated.

2) **Issue.** To prove fraud in the transaction, must there be evidence that the beneficiary of the letter of credit participated in the fraud?

3) **Held.** Yes. Judgment reversed.

a) A court has authority to enjoin the honor of a letter of credit if there is fraud in the transaction. The first transaction involved is the contract between the customer and the issuing bank. Another transaction is the sale and delivery of goods, or, in the standby case, a contract or performance or a loan by the beneficiary bank to a borrower, secured by the customer's letter of credit.

b) It is critical to the efficiency of the letter of credit that the courts recognize the letter of credit is independent of the primary contract of sale between the buyer and the seller. When the documents accompanying the draft are genuine and conform to the requirements of the letter of credit, the letter must be honored.

c) In *Sztejn v. J. Henry Schroder Banking Corp.* (*supra*), the beneficiary was involved in active fraud as an agent for the seller-beneficiary which committed the fraud. The seller-beneficiary could not profit from its own fraud. Similarly, when fraudulent documentation is presented with drafts drawn on a standby letter of credit, payment was properly enjoined because the beneficiary was relying on fraud. [Shaffer v. Brooklyn Park Garden Apartments, 250 N.W.2d 172 (Minn. 1977)] However, the phrase "fraud in the transaction" means more than just fraudulent documentation.

d) When a customer obtains a letter of credit, he assumes the risk that payment may be made even when the beneficiary has not properly performed the underlying contract. However, this risk does not include making payment to a beneficiary who engages in fraudulent conduct in the underlying contract.

e) In this case, the underlying transaction is the loan EAB made to C.I., Ltd. If in making the loan EAB committed fraud with respect to Ps, it cannot profit from the fraud. Here, despite the trial court's findings, EAB did not commit fraud. EAB made adequate investigation of C.I., Ltd. The PPM sufficiently disclosed the risks involved in the investment and did not provide EAB with knowledge of fraud when compared with C.I., Ltd.'s actual business deals. EAB may have had knowledge of problems, but this does not rise to the level of fraud or knowledge of fraud.

4. **Commercial and Standby Letters of Credit.**

a. **Introduction.** Standby letters of credit differ from commercial letters of credit. The beneficiary of a commercial letter may draw on the letter by presenting the specified documents showing that the beneficiary has performed and is entitled to the funds. A standby letter requires the production of documents showing that the customer has defaulted on its obligation to the beneficiary. This default triggers the beneficiary's right to draw down on the letter.

b. **Equitable subrogation.** Equitable subrogation arises where property of one person is used to discharge an obligation owed by another under such circumstances that the other would be unjustly enriched by the retention of the benefit thus conferred. The first person is entitled to be subrogated to the position of the obligee. Before a claimant may assert the remedy of equitable subrogation, it must satisfy five requirements:

(i) the claimant paid the creditor to protect his own interests;

(ii) the claimant did not act as a volunteer;

(iii) the claimant was not primarily liable for the debt (secondary liability);

(iv) the entire debt has been satisfied; and

(v) allowing subrogation will not cause injustice to the rights of others.

Tudor Development Group, Inc. v. United States Fidelity and Guaranty Co.

c. **No equitable subrogation for issuer of standby letter of credit--Tudor Development Group, Inc. v. United States Fidelity and Guaranty Co.**, 968 F.2d 357 (3d Cir. 1992).

1) **Facts.** The United States Fidelity and Guaranty Co. (D) issued performance bonds of nearly $3 million for the construction of a multi-family residential development by Susquehanna Construction Corporation ("SCC") under contract with Green Hill Associates ("Associates"), which was the owner and developer of the project. Tudor Development Group, Inc. (P) was Associates' general partner on the project. To begin work on the project, Associates needed the approval of the Township and agreed to complete certain improvements on the site. Associates obtained an irrevocable standby letter of credit from Dauphin whereby Dauphin would pay the Township over $1 million upon certification that the site improvements had not been completed as required. Associates agreed to reimburse Dauphin if Dauphin honored the letter of credit, but did not assign Associates' rights in D's bonds. Dauphin did receive a collateral note from P and an assignment of the proceeds of performance bonds issued by Wausau. SCC eventually defaulted under its contract with Associates, and Associates defaulted in its obligation to do the site improvements. The Township issued its draft for $800,000 against the Dauphin letter of credit. Dauphin paid on the draft but did not get reimbursed by Associates. After SCC's default, P and Associates sued D for the proceeds of D's performance bonds. Associates settled its claims with D, and about $600,000 of the settlement was paid into court pending resolution of the various claims. Associates asserts a claim against the fund as obligee under D's bonds. Dauphin claims it is equitably subrogated to Associates' interest in the fund. The district court did not allow Dauphin an equitable interest, and Dauphin appeals.

2) **Issue.** Is the issuer of a standby letter of credit entitled to the remedy of equitable subrogation?

3) **Held.** No. Judgment affirmed.

a) Associates was the customer in the letter of credit transaction. The subdivision agreement between Associates and the Township was the underlying contract, and the Township was the beneficiary. Dauphin, as issuer, was obligated under the letter of credit to honor the Township's demand for payment upon its certification that Associates had not made the improvements. Once Dauphin honored the letter, Associates had an immediate obligation under UCC section 5-114(c) to reimburse Dauphin.

b) UCC section 5-114(c) does not provide the manner for reimbursement, but leaves this issue for the parties to negotiate. The agreement between Associates and Dauphin provided for reimbursement and also gave Dauphin as security assignment rights in Associates' rights under the Wausau performance bond and P's promissory note. Dauphin apparently seeks equitable subrogation because its other security is inadequate.

c) The minority position allows an issuing bank the remedy of equitable subrogation, but the majority position does not. There are some similarities between guarantees and letters of credit, but they have distinct legal characteristics and the available remedies should remain distinct. A guarantor's obligation is secondary, but the issuer of a letter of credit has a primary obligation. The issuer satisfies its own obligation, not that of the customer, so it does not fulfill the requirement of satisfying the debt of another. Having paid its own debt, the issuer cannot step into the shoes of the creditor to seek subrogation.

d) Article 5 of the UCC reflects an intention to keep the law of guarantee and the law of letters of credit separate. While UCC section 5-109 suggests that an issuer may be subrogated to the customer's rights against the beneficiary, in this case, Dauphin seeks subrogation rights against a stranger to the letter of credit, not against the beneficiary of the letter.

e) The equities in this case also argue against giving Dauphin the remedy of equitable subrogation. Dauphin contracted for an assignment of rights in the Wausau bonds and a promissory note from P as its security. It also received a large annual fee for issuing the letter of credit. It could have contracted for an assignment of rights in D's bonds but did not do so. The courts should not be used to rewrite a contract to give Dauphin more security than it bargained to receive. Dauphin also has legal remedies of suing P on the note and suing Associates directly under the Reimbursement Agreement and under UCC section 5-114(c).

4) **Dissent.** The majority rule is not the best approach. Even though Dauphin was "primarily" liable in the sense that it had to pay the Township on demand, it was "secondarily" liable in the sense that its obligation arose only after Associates failed to satisfy its obligation. Thus, it is in fact satisfying a debt for Associates. The letter of credit served the same economic role as a performance bond would have. The UCC does not require the majority approach, either.

The cornerstone of the law of letters of credit is the independence principle, and allowing an issuer to subrogate to the rights of its customer would not undermine the independence principle. The argument that the issuer could have contracted for more security applies to every guaranty or suretyship contract and would virtually eliminate equitable subrogation if broadly applied. On balance, the best rule would be to allow equitable subrogation on a case-by-case basis to deal with the unexpected. On remand, the trial court should be allowed to consider the equities.

In re Valley Vue Joint Venture

d. **Subrogation to creditor bank's rights--*In re* Valley Vue Joint Venture,** 123 B.R. 199 (E.D. Va. 1991).

1) **Facts.** Valley Vue Joint Venture (D) obtained a short-term loan for about $4.5 million from Ameribanc to buy land for a housing development. D had Rodgers, one of its contractors, furnish a guaranty and letter of credit to Ameribanc. The guaranty agreement between D and Rodgers provided that Rodgers waived subrogation with respect to its guaranty, and acknowledged that it had no recourse against D in the event that the letter of credit is drawn upon for D's default. Rodgers never gave Ameribanc a guaranty, but did cause a $1 million standby letter of credit to be issued for Ameribanc's benefit. D refinanced the Ameribanc loan with the Bank of Baltimore, secured by a deed of trust on the property that D acquired with the Ameribanc loan proceeds. The Bank of Baltimore also received an additional $1 million standby letter of credit from Rodgers. D defaulted on its loan, and the Bank of Baltimore drew the full amount of the letter of credit. Rodgers reimbursed Sovran Bank, the confirming bank, for the $1 million paid to the Bank of Baltimore. D filed for bankruptcy under Chapter 11. Rodgers filed a proof of claim asserting subrogation to the Bank of Baltimore's rights. D objects to the proof of claim.

2) **Issue.** Is the party who arranges for the issuance of a letter of credit entitled to be subrogated to the rights of the creditor bank that draws on the letter of credit?

3) **Held.** Yes. Judgment for Rodgers.

a) D claims that Sovran Bank's obligation was a primary obligation, not a claim of a creditor against D, and that Rodgers could not acquire any greater rights than Sovran Bank had.

b) Other courts have held that an issuer who pays a standby letter of credit is not entitled to be subrogated to the rights of the beneficiary under 11 U.S.C. section 509(a) because the payment under the letter of credit satisfies a debt for which the issuer was primarily liable, thus failing one element of the basic test for equitable subrogation set forth in *In re Kaiser Steel Corp.*, 89 B.R. 150 (D. Colo. 1988). But while the issuer of a standby credit is satisfying its primary obligation, it is in fact satisfying a debt for which a person other than the issuer is primarily liable. The issuer is not primarily liable on the debt supported by its standby credit.

c) The *Kaiser* test is unrealistic and should not be followed. Instead, where a standby letter of credit is used to support a loan from the beneficiary to the debtor, a confirming bank that honors the credit and reduces the debtor's obligation to the beneficiary is an entity that is liable with the debtor on a claim of a creditor against the debtor as required by 11 U.S.C. section 509(a). It has thus satisfied a debt for which it is not primarily liable under general equitable principles of subrogation. A nondebtor account party who reimburses a confirming bank is entitled under general equitable principles to be subrogated to the rights of the confirming bank.

d)   In this case, D had the primary liability to repay its loan. Sovran Bank's liability was primary only regarding its duty to the Bank of Baltimore to honor the letter of credit. The parties intended that, by honoring the letter of credit, Sovran Bank would reduce a debt that D was primarily liable for.

e)   The equitable requirement that a party seeking subrogation not be "primarily liable" is intended to prevent a person who received the loan proceeds from the creditor from being subrogated to the creditor's rights against a guarantor after the debtor has satisfied its own obligations. The term "primarily liable" has a different meaning in the letter of credit context, where it reflects the independence principle that makes the issuer's obligation independent of the underlying commercial transaction.

f)   A standby letter of credit is not a guaranty, because the issuer's obligation is independent of the underlying transaction. But this difference does not preclude the application of subrogation principles to issuers. Neither equity nor 11 U.S.C. section 509(a) requires a party seeking subrogation to be a surety or guarantor. Instead, the equities favor allowing an issuer and a nondebtor account party of a standby letter of credit the right to subrogation. The comparative equities of the issuer and the debtor whose loan is supported by the standby credit favor the issuer, since the proceeds of the standby credit are used to reduce the debtor's debt. Accordingly, Rodgers is entitled to subrogation.

TABLE OF CASES

(Page numbers of briefed cases in bold)

Notes

Notes

Notes

Notes

Notes

Notes

Publications Catalog

Gilbert Law Summaries are the best selling outlines in the country, and have set the standard for excellence since they were first introduced more than twenty-five years ago. It's Gilbert's unique combination of features that makes it the one study aid you'll turn to for all your study needs!

Accounting and Finance for Lawyers
TBA

Basic Accounting Principles; Definitions of Accounting Terms; Balance Sheet; Income Statement; Statement of Changes in Financial Position; Consolidated Financial Statements; Accumulation of Financial Data; Financial Statement Analysis.
ISBN: 0-15-900382-2   Pages: 136 $16.95

Administrative Law
By Professor Michael R. Asimow, U.C.L.A.

Separation of Powers and Controls Over Agencies; (including Delegation of Power) Constitutional Right to Hearing (including Liberty and Property Interests Protected by Due Process, and Rulemaking-Adjudication Distinction); Adjudication Under Administrative Procedure Act (APA); Formal Adjudication (including Notice, Discovery, Burden of Proof, Finders of Facts and Reasons); Adjudicatory Decision Makers (including Administrative Law Judges (ALJs), Bias, Improper Influences, Ex Parte Communications, Familiarity with Record, Res Judicata); Rulemaking Procedures (including Notice, Public Participation, Publication, Impartiality of Rulemakers, Rulemaking Record); Obtaining Information (including Subpoena Power, Privilege Against Self-incrimination, Freedom of Information Act, Government in Sunshine Act, Attorneys' Fees); Scope of Judicial Review; Reviewability of Agency Decisions (including Mandamus, Injunction, Sovereign Immunity, Federal Tort Claims Act); Standing to Seek Judicial Review and Timing.
ISBN: 0-15-900000-9 Pages: 300 $19.95

Agency and Partnership
By Professor Richard J. Conviser, Chicago Kent

Agency: Rights and Liabilities Between Principal and Agent (including Agent's Fiduciary Duty, Principal's Right to Indemnification); Contractual Rights Between Principal (or Agent) and Third Persons (including Creation of Agency Relationship, Authority of Agent, Scope of Authority, Termination of Authority, Ratification, Liability on Agents, Contracts); Tort Liability (including Respondeat Superior, Master-Servant Relationship, Scope of Employment). Partnership: Property Rights of Partner; Formation of Partnership; Relations Between Partners (including Fiduciary Duty); Authority of Partner to Bind Partnership; Dissolution and Winding up of Partnership; Limited Partnerships.
ISBN: 0-15-900327-X Pages: 142 $16.95

Antitrust
By Professor Thomas M. Jorde, U.C. Berkeley, Mark A. Lemley, University of Texas, and Professor Robert H. Mnookin, Harvard University

Common Law Restraints of Trade; Federal Antitrust Laws (including Sherman Act, Clayton Act, Federal Trade Commission Act, Interstate Commerce Requirement, Antitrust Remedies); Monopolization (including Relevant Market, Purposeful Act Requirement, Attempts and Conspiracy to Monopolize); Collaboration Among Competitors (including Horizontal Restraints, Rule of Reason vs. Per Se Violations, Price Fixing, Division of Markets, Group Boycotts); Vertical Restraints (including Tying Arrangements); Mergers and Acquisitions (including Horizontal Mergers, Brown Shoe Analysis, Vertical Mergers, Conglomerate Mergers); Price Discrimination — Robinson-Patman Act; Unfair Methods of Competition; Patent Laws and Their Antitrust Implications; Exemptions From Antitrust Laws (including Motor, Rail, and Interstate Water Carriers, Bank Mergers, Labor Unions, Professional Baseball).
ISBN: 0-15-900328-8   Pages: 193 $16.95

Bankruptcy
By Professor Ned W. Waxman, College of William and Mary

Participants in the Bankruptcy Case; Jurisdiction and Procedure; Commencement and Administration of the Case (including Eligibility, Voluntary Case, Involuntary Case, Meeting of Creditors, Debtor's Duties); Officers of the Estate (including Trustee, Examiner, United States Trustee); Bankruptcy Estate; Creditor's Right of Setoff; Trustee's Avoiding Powers; Claims of Creditors (including Priority Claims and Tax Claims); Debtor's Exemptions; Nondischargeable Debts; Effects of Discharge; Reaffirmation Agreements; Administrative Powers (including Automatic Stay, Use, Sale, or Lease of Property); Chapter 7- Liquidation; Chapter 11- Reorganization; Chapter 13-Individual With Regular Income; Chapter 12- Family Farmer With Regular Annual Income.
ISBN: 0-15-900245-1   Pages: 356 $19.95

Business Law
By Professor Robert D. Upp, Los Angeles City College

Torts and Crimes in Business; Law of Contracts (including Contract Formation, Consideration, Statute of Frauds, Contract Remedies, Third Parties); Sales (including Transfer of Title and Risk of Loss, Performance and Remedies, Products Liability, Personal Property Security Interest); Property (including Personal Property, Bailments, Real Property, Landlord and Tenant); Agency; Business Organizations (including Partnerships, Corporations); Commercial Paper; Government Regulation of Business (including Taxation, Antitrust, Environmental Protection, and Bankruptcy).
ISBN: 0-15-900005-X   Pages: 295 $16.95

California Bar Performance Test Skills
By Professor Peter J. Honigsberg, University of San Francisco

Hints to Improve Writing; How to Approach the Performance Test; Legal Analysis Documents (including Writing a Memorandum of Law, Writing a Client Letter, Writing Briefs); Fact Gathering and Fact Analysis Documents; Tactical and Ethical Considerations; Sample Interrogatories, Performance Tests, and Memoranda.
ISBN: 0-15-900152-8   Pages: 216 $17.95

Civil Procedure
By Professor Thomas D. Rowe, Jr., Duke University, and Professor Richard L. Marcus, U.C. Hastings

Territorial (personal) Jurisdiction, including Venue and Forum Non Conveniens; Subject Matter Jurisdiction, covering Diversity Jurisdiction, Federal Question Jurisdiction; Erie Doctrine and Federal Common Law; Pleadings including Counterclaims, Cross-Claims, Supplemental Pleadings; Parties, including Joinder and Class Actions; Discovery, including Devices, Scope, Sanctions and Discovery Conference; Summary Judgment; Pretrial Conference and Settlements; Trial, including Right to Jury Trial, Motions, Jury Instruction and Arguments, and Post-Verdict Motions; Appeals; Claim Preclusion (Res Judicata) and Issue Preclusion (Collateral Estoppel).
ISBN: 0-15-900272-9   Pages: 447 $19.95

Commercial Paper and Payment Law
By Professor Douglas J. Whaley, Ohio State University

Types of Commercial Paper; Negotiability; Negotiation; Holders in Due Course; Claims and Defenses on Negotiable Instruments (including Real Defenses and Personal Defenses); Liability of the Parties (including Merger Rule, Suits on the Instrument, Warranty Suits, Conversion); Bank Deposits and Collections; Forgery or Alteration of Negotiable Instruments; Electronic Banking.
ISBN: 0-15-900367-9   Pages: 222 $17.95

Community Property
By Professor William A. Reppy, Jr., Duke University

Classifying Property as Community or Separate; Management and Control of Property; Liability for Debts; Division of Property at Divorce; Devolution of Property at Death; Relationships Short of Valid Marriage; Conflict of Laws Problems; Constitutional Law Issues (including Equal Protection Standards, Due Process Issues).
ISBN: 0-15-900235-4   Pages: 188 $17.95

Conflict of Laws

By Dean Herma Hill Kay, U.C. Berkeley

Domicile; Jurisdiction (including Notice and Opportunity to be Heard, Minimum Contacts, Types of Jurisdiction); Choice of Law (including Vested Rights Approach, Most Significant Relationship Approach, Governmental Interest Analysis); Choice of Law in Specific Substantive Areas; Traditional Defenses Against Application of Foreign Law; Constitutional Limitations and Overriding Federal Law (including Due Process Clause, Full Faith and Credit Clause, Conflict Between State and Federal Law); Recognition and Enforcement of Foreign Judgments.
ISBN: 0-15-900011-4   Pages: 260 $18.95

Constitutional Law

By Professor Jesse H. Choper, U.C. Berkeley

Powers of Federal Government (including Judicial Power, Powers of Congress, Presidential Power, Foreign Affairs Power); Intergovernmental Immunities, Separation of Powers; Regulation of Foreign Commerce; Regulation of Interstate Commerce; Taxation of Interstate and Foreign Commerce; Due Process, Equal Protection; "State Action" Requirements; Freedoms of Speech, Press, and Association; Freedom of Religion.
ISBN: 0-15-900265-6   Pages: 335 $19.95

Contracts

By Professor Melvin A. Eisenberg, U.C. Berkeley

Consideration (including Promissory Estoppel, Moral or Past Consideration); Mutual Assent; Defenses (including Mistake, Fraud, Duress, Unconscionability, Statute of Frauds, Illegality); Third-Party Beneficiaries; Assignment of Rights and Delegation of Duties; Conditions; Substantial Performance; Material vs. Minor Breach; Anticipatory Breach; Impossibility; Discharge; Remedies (including Damages, Specific Performance, Liquidated Damages).
ISBN: 0-15-900014-9   Pages: 326 $19.95

Corporations

By Professor Jesse H. Choper, U.C. Berkeley, and Professor Melvin A. Eisenberg, U.C. Berkeley

Formalities; "De Jure" vs. "De Facto"; Promoters; Corporate Powers; Ultra Vires Transactions; Powers, Duties, and Liabilities of Officers and Directors; Allocation of Power Between Directors and Shareholders; Conflicts of Interest in Corporate Transactions; Close Corporations; Insider Trading; Rule 10b-5 and Section 16(b); Shareholders' Voting Rights; Shareholders' Right to Inspect Records; Shareholders' Suits; Capitalization (including Classes of Shares, Preemptive Rights, Consideration for Shares); Dividends; Redemption of Shares; Fundamental Changes in Corporate Structure; Applicable Conflict of Laws Principles.
ISBN: 0-15-900342-3   Pages: 308 $19.95

Criminal Law

By Professor George E. Dix, University of Texas

Elements of Crimes (including Actus Reus, Mens Rea, Causation); Vicarious Liability; Complicity in Crime; Criminal Liability of Corporations;

Defenses (including Insanity, Diminished Capacity, Intoxication, Ignorance, Self-Defense); Inchoate Crimes; Homicide; Other Crimes Against the Person; Crimes Against Habitation (including Burglary, Arson); Crimes Against Property; Offenses Against Government; Offenses Against Administration of Justice.
ISBN: 0-15-900217-6   Pages: 271 $18.95

Criminal Procedure

By Professor Paul Marcus, College of William and Mary, and Professor Charles H. Whitebread, U.S.C.

Exclusionary Rule; Arrests and Other Detentions; Search and Seizure; Privilege Against Self-Incrimination; Confessions; Preliminary Hearing; Bail; Indictment; Speedy Trial; Competency to Stand Trial; Government's Obligation to Disclose Information; Right to Jury Trial; Right to Counsel; Right to Confront Witnesses; Burden of Proof; Insanity; Entrapment; Guilty Pleas; Sentencing; Death Penalty; Ex Post Facto Issues; Appeal; Habeas Corpus; Juvenile Offenders; Prisoners' Rights; Double Jeopardy.
ISBN: 0-15-900347-4   Pages: 271 $18.95

Dictionary of Legal Terms

Gilbert Staff

Contains Over 3,500 Legal Terms and Phrases; Law School Shorthand; Common Abbreviations; Latin and French Legal Terms; Periodical Abbreviations; Governmental Abbreviations.
ISBN: 0-15-900018-1   Pages: 163 $14.95

Estate and Gift Tax

By Professor John H. McCord, University of Illinois

Gross Estate Allowable Deductions Under Estate Tax (including Expenses, Indebtedness, and Taxes, Deductions for Losses, Charitable Deduction, Marital Deduction); Taxable Gifts; Deductions; Valuation; Computation of Tax; Returns and Payment of Tax; Tax on Generation-Skipping Transfers.
ISBN: 0-15-900019-X   Pages: 283 $18.95

Evidence

By Professor Jon R. Waltz, Northwestern University, and Roger C. Park, University of Minnesota

Direct Evidence; Circumstantial Evidence; Rulings on Admissibility; Relevancy; Materiality; Character Evidence; Hearsay and the Hearsay Exceptions; Privileges; Competency to Testify; Opinion Evidence and Expert Witnesses; Direct Examination; Cross-Examination; Impeachment; Real, Demonstrative, and Scientific Evidence; Judicial Notice; Burdens of Proof; Parol Evidence Rule.
ISBN: 0-15-900020-3   Pages: 359 $19.95

Federal Courts

By Professor William A. Fletcher, U.C. Berkeley

Article III Courts; "Case or Controversy" Requirement; Justiciability; Advisory Opinions; Political Questions; Ripeness; Mootness; Standing; Congressional Power Over Federal Court Jurisdiction; Supreme Court Jurisdiction; District Court Subject Matter Jurisdiction (including Federal Question Jurisdiction, Diversity

Jurisdiction); Pendent and Ancillary Jurisdiction; Removal Jurisdiction; Venue; Forum Non Conveniens; Law Applied in the Federal Courts (including Erie Doctrine); Federal Law in the State Courts; Abstention; Habeas Corpus for State Prisoners; Federal Injunctions Against State Court Proceedings; Eleventh Amendment.
ISBN: 0-15-900232-X   Pages: 310 $19.95

Future Interests & Perpetuities

By Professor Jesse Dukeminier, U.C.L.A.

Reversions; Possibilities of Reverter; Rights of Entry; Remainders; Executory Interest; Rules Restricting Remainders and Executory Interest; Rights of Owners of Future Interests; Construction of Instruments; Powers of Appointment; Rule Against Perpetuities (including Reforms of the Rule).
ISBN: 0-15-900218-4   Pages: 219 $17.95

Income Tax I - Individual

By Professor Michael R. Asimow, U.C.L.A.

Gross Income; Exclusions; Income Splitting by Gifts, Personal Service Income, Income Earned by Children, Income of Husbands and Wives, Below-Market Interest on Loans, Taxation of Trusts; Business and Investment Deductions; Personal Deductions; Tax Rates; Credits; Computation of Basis, Gain, or Loss; Realization; Nonrecognition of Gain or Loss; Capital Gains and Losses; Alternative Minimum Tax; Tax Accounting Problems.
ISBN: 0-15-900266-4   Pages: 312 $19.95

Income Tax II - Partnerships, Corporations, Trusts

By Professor Michael R. Asimow, U.C.L.A.

Taxation of Partnerships (including Current Partnership Income, Contributions of Property to Partnership, Sale of Partnership Interest, Distributions, Liquidations); Corporate Taxation (including Corporate Distributions, Sales of Stock and Assets, Reorganizations); S Corporations; Federal Income Taxation of Trusts.
ISBN: 0-15-900024-6   Pages: 237 $17.95

Labor Law

By Professor James C. Oldham, Georgetown University, and Robert J. Gelhaus

Statutory Foundations of Present Labor Law (including National Labor Relations Act, Taft-Hartley, Norris-LaGuardia Act, Landrum-Griffin Act); Organizing Campaigns, Selection of the Bargaining Representative; Collective Bargaining (including Negotiating the Agreement, Lockouts, Administering the Agreement, Arbitration); Strikes, Boycotts, and Picketing; Concerted Activity Protected Under the NLRA; Civil Rights Legislation; Grievance; Federal Regulation of Compulsory Union Membership Arrangements; State Regulation of Compulsory Membership Agreements; "Right to Work" Laws; Discipline of Union Members; Election of Union Officers; Corruption.
ISBN: 0-15-900340-7   Pages: 243 $17.95

Legal Ethics

By Professor Thomas D. Morgan, George Washington University

Regulating Admission to Practice Law; Preventing Unauthorized Practice of Law; Contract Between Client and Lawyer (including Lawyer's Duties Regarding Accepting Employment, Spheres of Authority of Lawyer and Client, Obligation of Client to Lawyer, Terminating the Lawyer-Client Relationship); Attorney-Client Privilege; Professional Duty of Confidentiality; Conflicts of Interest; Obligations to Third Persons and the Legal System (including Counseling Illegal or Fraudulent Conduct, Threats of Criminal Prosecution); Special Obligations in Litigation (including Limitations on Advancing Money to Client, Duty to Reject Certain Actions, Lawyer as Witness); Solicitation and Advertising; Specialization; Disciplinary Process; Malpractice; Special Responsibilities of Judges.
ISBN: 0-15-900026-2   Pages: 252 $18.95

Legal Research, Writing and Analysis

By Professor Peter J. Honigsberg, University of San Francisco

Court Systems; Precedent; Case Reporting System (including Regional and State Reporters, Headnotes and the West Key Number System, Citations and Case Finding); Statutes, Constitutions, and Legislative History; Secondary Sources (including Treatises, Law Reviews, Digests, Restatements); Administrative Agencies (including Regulations, Looseleaf Services); Shepard's Citations; Computers in Legal Research; Reading and Understanding a Case (including Briefing a Case); Using Legal Sourcebooks; Basic Guidelines for Legal Writing; Organizing Your Research; Writing a Memorandum of Law; Writing a Brief; Writing an Opinion or Client Letter.
ISBN: 0-15-900305-9   Pages: 162 $16.95

Multistate Bar Examination

By Professor Richard J. Conviser, Chicago Kent

Structure of the Exam; Governing Law; Effective Use of Time; Scoring of the Exam; Jurisdictions Using the Exam; Subject Matter Outlines; Practice Tests, Answers, and Subject Matter Keys; Glossary of Legal Terms and Definitions; State Bar Examination Directory; Listing of Reference Materials for Multistate Subjects.
ISBN: 0-15-900246-X   Pages: 210 $19.95

Personal Property

Gilbert Staff

Acquisitions; Ownership Through Possession (including Wild Animals, Abandoned Chattels); Finders of Lost Property; Bailments; Possessory Liens; Pledges; Trover; Gift; Accession; Confusion (Commingling); Fixtures; Crops (Emblements); Adverse Possession; Prescriptive Rights (Acquiring Ownership of Easements or Profits by Adverse Use).
ISBN: 0-15-900360-1   Pages: 69 $14.95

Professional Responsibility

(see Legal Ethics)

gilbert
LAW SUMMARIES

Property
By Professor Jesse Dukeminier, U.C.L.A.

Possession (including Wild Animals, Bailments, Adverse Possession); Gifts and Sales of Personal Property; Freehold Possessory Estates; Future Interests (including Reversion, Possibility of Reverter, Right of Entry, Executory Interests, Rule Against Perpetuities); Tenancy in Common; Joint Tenancy; Tenancy by the Entirety; Condominiums; Cooperatives; Marital Property; Landlord and Tenant; Easements and Covenants; Nuisance; Rights in Airspace and Water; Right to Support; Zoning; Eminent Domain; Sale of Land (including Mortgage, Deed, Warranties of Title); Methods of Title Assurance (including Recording System, Title Registration, Title Insurance).

ISBN: 0-15-900032-7   Pages: 496 $21.95

Remedies
By Professor John A. Bauman, U.C.L.A., and Professor Kenneth H. York, Pepperdine University

Damages; Equitable Remedies (including Injunctions and Specific Performance); Restitution; Injuries to Tangible Property Interests; Injuries to Business and Commercial Interests (including Business Torts, Inducing Breach of Contract, Patent Infringement, Unfair Competition, Trade Defamation); Injuries to Personal Dignity and Related Interests (including Defamation, Privacy, Religious Status, Civil and Political Rights); Personal Injury and Death; Fraud; Duress, Undue Influence, and Unconscionable Conduct; Mistake; Breach of Contract; Unenforceable Contracts (including Statute of Frauds, Impossibility, Lack of Contractual Capacity, Illegality).

ISBN: 0-15-900325-3   Pages: 375 $20.95

Sale and Lease of Goods
By Professor Douglas J. Whaley, Ohio State University

UCC Article 2; Sales Contract (including Offer and Acceptance, Parol Evidence Rule, Statute of Frauds, Assignment and Delegation, Revision of Contract Terms); Types of Sales (including Cash Sale Transactions, Auctions, "Sale or Return" and "Sale on Approval" Transactions); Warranties (including Express and Implied Warranties, Privity, Disclaimer, Consumer Protection Statutes); Passage of Title; Performance of the Contract; Anticipatory Breach; Demand for Assurance of Performance; Unforeseen Circumstances; Risk of Loss; Remedies; Documents of Title; Lease of Goods; International Sale of Goods.

ISBN: 0-15-900219-2   Pages: 222 $17.95

Secured Transactions
By Professor Douglas J. Whaley, Ohio State University

Coverage of Article 9; Creation of a Security Interest (including Attachment, Security Agreement, Value, Debtor's Rights in the Collateral); Perfection; Filing; Priorities; Bankruptcy Proceedings and Article 9; Default Proceedings; Bulk Transfers.

ISBN: 0-15-900231-1   Pages: 213 $17.95

Securities Regulation
By Professor David H. Barber, and Professor Niels B. Schaumann, William Mitchell College of Law

Jurisdiction and Interstate Commerce; Securities Act of 1933 (including Registration Requirements and Exemptions); Securities Exchange Act of 1934 (including Rule 10b-5, Tender Offers, Proxy Solicitations Regulation, Insider Transactions); Regulation of the Securities Markets; Multinational Transactions; State Regulation of Securities Transactions.

ISBN: 0-15-9000326-1   Pages: 415 $20.95

Torts
By Professor Marc A. Franklin, Stanford University

Intentional Torts; Negligence; Strict Liability; Products Liability; Nuisance; Survival of Tort Actions; Wrongful Death; Immunity; Release and Contribution; Indemnity; Workers' Compensation; No-Fault Auto Insurance; Defamation; Invasion of Privacy; Misrepresentation; Injurious Falsehood; Interference With Economic Relations; Unjustifiable Litigation.

ISBN: 0-15-900220-6   Pages: 439 $19.95

Trusts
By Professor Edward C. Halbach, Jr., U.C. Berkeley

Elements of a Trust; Trust Creation; Transfer of Beneficiary's Interest (including Spendthrift Trusts); Charitable Trusts (including Cy Pres Doctrine); Trustee's Responsibilities, Power, Duties, and Liabilities; Duties and Liabilities of Beneficiaries; Accounting for Income and Principal; Power of Settlor to Modify or Revoke; Powers of Trustee Beneficiaries or Courts to Modify or Terminate; Termination of Trusts by Operation of Law; Resulting Trusts; Purchase Money Resulting Trusts; Constructive Trusts.

ISBN: 0-15-900039-4   Pages: 268 $18.95

Wills
By Professor Stanley M. Johanson, University of Texas

Intestate Succession; Simultaneous Death; Advancements; Disclaimer; Killer of Decedent; Elective Share Statutes; Pretermitted Child Statutes; Homestead; Formal Requisites of a Will; Revocation of Wills; Incorporation by Reference; Pour-Over Gift in Inter Vivos Trust; Joint Wills; Contracts Relating to Wills; Lapsed Gifts; Ademption; Exoneration of Liens; Will Contests; Probate and Estate Administration.

ISBN: 0-15-900040-8   Pages: 310 $19.95

Employment Guides

A collection of best selling titles that help you identify and reach your career goals.

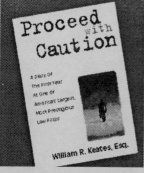

The National Directory Of Legal Employers
National Association for Law Placement

The National Directory of Legal Employers brings you a universe of vital information about 1,000 of the nation's top legal employers— *in one convenient volume!*

It includes:

- Over 22,000 job openings.
- The names, addresses and phone numbers of hiring partners.
- Listings of firms by state, size, kind and practice area.
- What starting salaries are for full time, part time, and summer associates, plus a detailed description of firm benefits.
- The number of employees by gender and race, as well as the number of employees with disabilities.
- A detailed narrative of each firm, plus much more!

The National Directory Of Legal Employers has been the best kept secret of top legal career search professionals for over a decade. Now, for the first time, it is available in a format specifically designed for law students and new graduates. *Pick up your copy of the Directory today!*

ISBN: 0-15-900248-6   **$39.95**

Proceed With Caution: A Diary Of The First Year At One Of America's Largest, Most Prestigious Law Firms
William R. Keates

Prestige. Famous clients. High-profile cases. Not to mention a starting salary approaching six figures.

In *Proceed With Caution*, the author takes you behind the scenes, to show you what it's really like to be a junior associate at a huge law firm. After graduating from an Ivy League law school, he took a job as an associate with one of New York's blue-chip law firms.

He also did something not many people do. He kept a diary, where he spilled out his day-to-day life at the firm in graphic detail.

Proceed With Caution excerpts the diary, from his first day at the firm to the day he quit. From the splashy benefits, to the nitty-gritty on the work junior associates do, to the grind of long and unpredictable hours, to the stress that eventually made him leave the firm — he tells story after story that will make you feel as though you're living the life of a new associate.

Whether you're considering a career with a large firm, or you're just curious about what life at the top firms is all about — *Proceed With Caution* is a must read!

ISBN: 0-15-900181-1   **$17.95**

Guerrilla Tactics for Getting the Legal Job of Your Dreams
Kimm Alayne Walton, J.D.

Whether you're looking for a summer clerkship or your first permanent job after school, this revolutionary book is the key to getting the job of your dreams!

Guerrilla Tactics for Getting the Legal Job of Your Dreams leads you step-by-step through everything you need to do to nail down that perfect job! You'll learn hundreds of simple-to-use strategies that will get you exactly where you want to go. You'll Learn:

- The seven magic opening words in cover letters that ensure you'll get a response.
- The secret to successful interviews every time.
- Killer answers to the toughest interview questions they'll ever ask you.
- Plus Much More!

Guerrilla Tactics features the best strategies from the country's most innovative law school career advisors. The strategies in *Guerrilla Tactics* are so powerful that it even comes with a guarantee: Follow the advice in the book, and within one year of graduation you'll have the job of your dreams… or your money back!

Pick up a copy of *Guerrilla Tactics* today…and you'll be on your way to the job of your dreams!

ISBN: 0-15-900317-2   **$24.95**

Beyond L.A. Law: Inspiring Stories of People Who've Done Fascinating Things With A Law Degree
National Association for Law Placement

Anyone who watches television knows that being a lawyer means working your way up through a law firm — right?

Wrong!

Beyond L.A. Law gives you a fascinating glimpse into the lives of people who've broken the "lawyer" mold. They come from a variety of backgrounds — some had prior careers, others went straight through college and law school, and yet others have overcome poverty and physical handicaps. They got their degrees from all different kinds of law schools, all over the country. But they have one thing in common: they've all pursued their own, unique vision.

As you read their stories, you'll see how they beat the odds to succeed. You'll learn career tips and strategies that work, from people who've put them to the test. And you'll find fascinating insights that you can apply to your own dream — whether it's a career in law, or anything else!

From Representing Baseball In Australia. To International Finance. To Children's Advocacy. To Directing a Nonprofit Organization. To Entrepreneur.

If You Think Getting A Law Degree Means Joining A Traditional Law Firm — Think Again!.

ISBN: 0-15-900182-X   **$17.95**

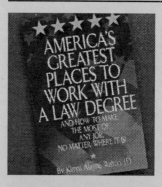

America's Greatest Places To Work With A Law Degree
Kimm Alayne Walton, J.D.

"Where do your happiest graduates work?" That's the question that author Kimm Alayne Walton asked of law school administrators around the country. Their responses revealed the hundreds of wonderful employers profiled in *America's Greatest Places To Work With A Law Degree.*

In this remarkable book, you'll get to know an incredible variety of great places to work, including:

- Glamorous sports and entertainment employers – the jobs that sound as though they would be great, and they are!
- The 250 best law firms to work for between 20 and 600 attorneys.
- Companies where law school graduates love to work and not just as in-house counsel.
- Wonderful public interest employers – the "white knight" jobs that are so incredibly satisfying.
- Court-related positions, where lawyers entertain fascinating issues, tremendous variety, and an enjoyable lifestyle.
- Outstanding government jobs, at the federal, state, and local level.

Beyond learning about incredible employers, you'll discover:

- The ten traits that define a wonderful place to work…the sometimes surprising qualities that outstanding employers share.
- How to handle law school debt, when your dream job pays less than you think you need to make.
- How to find – and get! – great jobs at firms with fewer than 20 attorneys.

And no matter where you work, you'll learn expert tips for making the most of your job. You'll learn the specific strategies that distinguish people headed for the top…how to position yourself for the most interesting, high-profile work…how to handle difficult personalities… how to negotiate for more money…and what to do now to help you get your next great job!

ISBN: 0-15-900180-3   **$24.95**

Presented by The National Law Journal

The Job Goddess column is a weekly feature of the *National Law Journal's Law Journal Extra*, and is written by Kimm Alayne Walton, author of the national best seller *Guerrilla Tactics For Getting The Legal Job Of Your Dreams.* View recent columns or e-mail the Job Goddess with your job search questions on the Internet at www.gilbertlaw.com

---

Call 1-800-787-8717 or visit our web site at http://www.gilbertlaw.com for more information.